DR

Aspirations, Education and Social Justice

Also available from Bloomsbury

Children's Lives, Children's Futures: A Study of Children Starting Secondary School, Paul Croll, Gaynor Attwood and Carol Fuller

Educating the Postmodern Child: The Struggle for Learning in a World of Virtual Realities, Fiachra Long

Justice and Equality in Education: A Capability Perspective on Disability and Special Educational Needs, Lorella Terzi

Sociology, Gender and Educational Aspirations: Girls and their Ambitions, Carol Fuller

Aspirations, Education and Social Justice

Applying Sen and Bourdieu

Caroline Sarojini Hart

B L O O M S B U R Y
LONDON · NEW DELHI · NEW YORK · SYDNEY

Continuum International Publishing Group
A Bloomsbury company

50 Bedford Square	80 Maiden Lane
London	New York
WC1B 3DP	NY 10038

www.continuumbooks.com

British Library Cataloguing-in-Publication Data
A catalogue record for this book is available from the British Library.

ISBN: 978-1-4411-8574-7 (hardcover)
978-1-4411-2332-9 (PDF)

Library of Congress Cataloging-in-Publication Data
A catalog record for this book is available from the Library of Congress.

Typeset by Newgen Imaging Systems Pvt Ltd, Chennai, India
Printed and bound in Great Britain

In memory of Sarojini Rowntree (1931–2011)

The author will be donating all royalties from the sale of this book to the charity Action Duchenne. Action Duchenne is a parent-led organization that primarily focuses on Duchenne and Becker Muscular Dystrophy; pledging more money into research and educational projects for these conditions than any other charity in the UK. For further information see www.actionduchenne.org.

Contents

List of Figures

List of Tables

Acknowledgements

I would not have been able to produce this book without the support of Continuum publishers and I thank Alison Baker and Rosie Pattinson for their personal support and interest along the way.

I am extremely thankful to all the young people who took part in my research, and for their generosity in allowing me to share their voices with others, in the pursuit of greater social justice for future generations. I am also indebted to the many teaching professionals and government representatives who have helped to inform my thinking. I would like to thank all my colleagues in the Human Development and Capability Association.[1] I have found the annual international conferences to be enormously fruitful as well as sociable and recommend them to others interested in delving into the world of capabilities. I am also grateful to colleagues at the University of Cambridge for encouraging me in my endeavours and particularly thank Lesley Dee, Diane Reay, Madeleine Arnot, John Gray, David Bridges and the late Jean Rudduck. Over the last two years I have had the pleasure of working with many students in the Faculty of Education at Cambridge. I have found their insights on matters of social justice, education and human development to be stimulating and challenging and I have benefited from their enthusiasm and scholarship. Special thanks go to Richard Wilkinson, former Director of Bradford Aimhigher, for supporting my research in the early days, and for giving me the freedom to try new ways of working with young people in Bradford.

I have had many teachers over the years and I would personally like to take this opportunity to thank Zygmunt Bauman, John Martin, Ollie Smith, Richard Merryfield, Ian Redwood, Meg Jepson, Hugh O'Neill, Will Patterson, Robin Klymow, Richard Wilkinson, Lesley Dee and Diane Reay. I have also been fortunate to gain powerful insights into human development through my association with a number of organizations outside of formal education including the Yorkshire Schools Exploring Society, The Tall Ships Youth Trust, Raleigh International and Outward Bound. I name them here both to acknowledge my thanks but also because others may gain from their practices.[2]

Writing this book has been something of an endurance test, not only for me but also my family and friends. I would like to acknowledge their continued support as without them I would not have made the finish line. In particular, I thank Helen Williams, Michelle Maycock and Zeba Shoaib for being excellent friends and confidentes.

I would like to thank all the members of my family who have supported my endeavours. In particular, I thank my husband Ollie, who has stayed stoically by my side throughout this project, and passionately debated with me the pursuit of social justice in education, health and further afield. I could not have asked for more. My daughters, Jasmine and Martha have also been very patient with me and I hope that, one day, they will understand why this project was important to me. I deeply appreciate the eternal inspiration of my late mother, Sarojini Rowntree. Words cannot express my gratitude.

Finally, I am very grateful to Amartya Sen for taking the time to discuss many of the issues raised in this book, and for his capacity to take my mind to new galaxies in his intellectual 'TARDIS'.[3] It continues to be a remarkable adventure.

Caroline Hart,
University of Cambridge, UK

List of Abbreviations

A/S	Advanced subsidiary qualification
AVCE	Advanced vocational certificate of education
BIS	Department of Business Innovation and Skills
CA	Capability approach
CEP	Coalition education policy
CHC	Central Human Capabilities
CTA	'capability to aspire'
CTR	'capability to realise' [aspiration]
DFE	Department for Education
DfES	Department for Education and Science
DfID	Department for International Development
DIUS	Department of Innovation Universities and Skills
Eastside	the two sixth form colleges in the S2 Sheffield study
EMA	Educational Maintenance Allowance (means-tested grant)
FSM	free school meal/eligible for free school meal
FTR	'failure to realise' [aspiration]
G and T	'gifted and talented' programme in schools/colleges for top achieving 5–10% of pupils
GCSE	General Certificate of School Education
HE	higher education
HEFCE	Higher Education Funding Council for England
HEI	higher education institution
NEET	Not in education, employment or training
OECD	Organization for Economic Co-operation and Development
PFAP	Panel on Fair Access to the Professions
S1	Study S1 (Bradford)
S2	Study S2 (Sheffield)
SBAF	Sen-Bourdieu analytical framework
SHS	Students at the Heart of the System White Paper (2011)
UCAS	universities and colleges admissions service
UNCRC	United Nations Convention on the Rights of the Child
UNICEF	United Nations Children's Fund
Westside	the two school sixth forms in the S2 Sheffield study
WHO	World Health Organization
WP	widening participation
YPR	Young participation rate

Introduction

Education continues to be a priority for human development in countries worldwide. However, the challenges are significant, ranging from unpredictable environmental disaster, to self-destruction and wanton violence. One of the greatest issues confronting education policy and practice is finding an approach that offers ethical principles for the pursuit of human flourishing and social justice in the face of environmental, socio-economic, technological and political constraints.

Just over 20 years ago, in a small village in Zimbabwe, I toiled alongside local bare-foot children and their parents to build a school. To make the building bricks we had to dig sand from the hot parched earth, and pump water from a well over 2 kilometers away. It took a great deal of hard work, time, money and belief to complete the project. In 2008, in a brief moment in time, the school was destroyed by floods.

Twelve years ago I lived and taught in Florence, Italy. I found it to be one of the most beautiful places I have ever visited. A walk around the city was an education in itself, with wonderful architecture and sculptures freely accessible. The visible history was a constant reminder of the influence of the Medici Dynasty and its support for the European Renaissance in art, literature and architecture, dating back to the fifteenth century. The term *Renaissance Man* became used to describe someone educated in many different fields. It embraced the idea that individuals had the potential to pursue universal aspects of human development and understanding. Yet at that time only a few were able to benefit from such opportunities to learn.

I left Florence to return to England where, in 2001, I worked in a large state comprehensive school in Bradford in Yorkshire, England. I was responsible for working with half a dozen secondary schools, local further education colleges and higher education institutions on the British government's programme to widen participation in higher education. The strategy was aimed at 'raising aspirations' in order to improve examination results, staying on rates and participation in higher education. However, before long I began to question the government interpretation of the nature of aspiration and the (mis)appropriation of this concept in both policy and practice. It quickly became apparent that the policy vision of raising achievement and raising aspirations would not come close to solving the deep-rooted issues that created stark socio-economic deprivation across large swathes of the multi-ethnic Bradford community, and indeed elsewhere. Violence and criminal behaviour were common occurrences at the school where I was based, with the police and teachers on first-name terms. Several pupils at the school had criminal records and some received custodial sentences for their roles in the Bradford riots that occurred in July 2001. The riots had originally been fuelled by the threat of a National Front demonstration, but developed into large-scale conflict between the police and local communities reflecting other long-standing tensions. As the new academic year began in Autumn 2001, school staff turnover increased dramatically with two-thirds of the staff leaving in less than 12 months. Burnt-out cars were regularly found on the school fields and an arson attack destroyed the science block shortly before the school received an inspection from Ofsted.[1] The school inspectors found 'serious weaknesses' at the school, leading to the resignation of the head teacher.

Then on the last day of term, the head teacher's top-of-the-range Audi was blown up by a petrol-bomb in the school car park, just a few feet from the glass foyer of the school. Cars on both sides of the blazing Audi quickly became engulfed in flames. Over a thousand students were evacuated onto the playing fields, with the place descending into chaos as the fire brigade and police arrived on the scene. One of the students looked at me and said, 'none of the teachers want to be here Miss, why should we?' It was a turning point for me. I responded in the best way that I could, but I knew the answer was inadequate. I knew that the school policy of locking students out of the school at lunch times and breaks, because the school management did not trust the students to be inside, created a negative and hostile atmosphere. I knew the policy of raising aspirations to increase higher education participation failed to respond to the real needs of those young people. These events in Bradford were the catalysts for the research that I am sharing in this book.

My interest in the nature of aspirations and capabilities is also influenced by my own experience of growing up and the people I encountered along the way.

I have been lucky enough to have some brilliant teachers in my life. I have also had a fair share of teachers, who frankly, were not fit for the job. But then, having been a teacher myself, for over a decade, I know that the job is never easy. I still vividly remember the day my physics teacher threw my pen across the floor after scrawling 'mediocre' on my work. I also remember the biology teacher who told me my knowledge of biology was 'superficial'. I had actually enjoyed science up until that point but, perhaps not surprisingly, my career trajectory changed around the time of these comments. In fact at that time, there was a lot going on in my life that might have accounted for less than perfect performance, but nobody took the time to ask.

By contrast, I will be eternally grateful to the small handful of fantastic teachers, who exuded enthusiasm and interest in their students, as well as their subjects, and were able to help me to find the best in myself. This is true to say of my teachers both when I was a child and later as an adult. I still remember the teachers who took the time to talk with me and who helped me to grow. I met some of those teachers in schools and university but others I have met in less conventional places, climbing mountains, kayaking whitewater and jumping out of aeroplanes. They all had one thing in common. They believed in me. At least they made me think they did. I have a hunch that many of the young people in schools today want someone to believe in them. To believe that they are worthy of having the freedom to aspire and that they are worthy of having the support of significant others in their endeavours.

When I was in my twenties two opportunities presented themselves to me. One was to lead an expedition of teenagers to the Indian Himalayas and the other was to be one of a four strong sailing crew on a transatlantic yacht adventure. The timing of the events meant I could only choose one of them even though I would have loved to do both. I went to talk things over with my former university careers advisor to help my decision-making process. After a while, he suggested that I toss a coin three times, heads for the hills and tails for the ocean. He said the outcome of tossing the coin would tell me what to do. I went away and tossed the coin, and the first time it came down tails. I threw the coin twice more, it came down heads and then finally tails. So the ocean it was then, I said to myself. But in that moment I knew that I was bound for the hills. I am not sure what this tells us about careers advice, but maybe it does show that human beings can be unpredictable, contradictory and even impulsive. Maybe also that our feelings and inner thoughts can be hard to find. Decision-making, as this book reveals, is a complicated process.

There is a Yorkshire saying that my father used to say 'if it's for you, it won't go by you'. He used to say it if either myself, or one of my three siblings, was trying for something we really wanted to do, but where we were not sure if we would succeed. It was a way of saying do your best, but if your best is not enough, then do not fret because it (whatever it was) was never for you in the first place. Another phrase my father liked to use was 'if you see a window of opportunity, then shoot for the moon'. I think by this he meant, if you see a chance, then take it and believe that you can get there. At the same time there was an acknowledgement that, if you shot an arrow through a window at the moon, it was probably very unlikely you would hit the lunar target. I have always been a bit confused about the advice my father gave me. Was he encouraging me? Was he trying to cushion my possible failures?

My mother took a similar, but slightly more direct approach with her gems of advice. Somehow she had a way of instilling a calmness and inner confidence in me that has been invaluable. My mother told me to 'go forward bravely' and to 'tie your head on child'. Somehow the two pieces of advice go hand in hand. I would probably feel less brave without my head. On the other hand, I might be braver in some scenarios than in others without my head. Now there is a thought. I think the point here is that there are both big and small things that parents can do that have a huge impact on children and how they are able to live their lives.

Neither of my parents studied for an undergraduate degree at university. My mother trained as a nurse, midwife and health visitor. My father was excluded from three schools and tried to join the navy at 14, unsuccessfully. He went back to studies as a mature student after a stint in the armed forces. He went on to achieve a masters degree in medical science and was later awarded an OBE for his work in public health. Funnily enough, looking back it is not the educational or career achievements of my parents that matters most to me. It is much more about the way they were as humans, for better or worse. Undoubtedly, some of that has rubbed off on me as I grew up in their company, yet I know that I am different in significant ways from my three siblings, who also grew up in the same household.

These autobiographic snapshots of my teachers' comments, careers advice, parental wisdom and my own teaching practice, bring me to the introduction of the research in this book. It draws on the works of Amartya Sen and Pierre Bourdieu who have both contributed greatly to our understandings of the nature of social arrangements and the factors that help and hinder human development in different spheres of life.

The book sets out to examine three distinct but related ideas encompassed in the title, Aspirations, Education and Social Justice. The term, 'idea' is used deliberately to highlight that the phenomena in question are to a large degree constructed by the way we think about them. There are diverse ways in which aspirations, education and social justice are conceived and understanding how education policy has charted a course through these waves of diversity is a key concern in Chapter 1. This is followed by the introduction of Amartya Sen's capability approach, and its location with regard to matters of education in Chapter 2 (Sen, 1992). The conceptual framework guiding the examination of aspirations, education and social justice is strengthened in Chapter 3 by synthesizing Sen's work with Pierre Bourdieu's conceptions of *habitus, field* and different forms of *capital* (Bourdieu, 1986). The theoretical framework illuminates the nature of aspirations and their relationship to capabilities. In particular, connections are made between Sen's concept of capability and Bourdieu's conceptualization of 'capital'. In Chapter 4 the discussion goes on to address issues of methodology, particularly in relation to the application of the capability approach. This provides a basis for the presentation of the research strategy used for the research drawn upon in the book. The findings that I discuss here are based on two research studies. The first study (S1) took place in Bradford from 2003–4 and the second (S2) was undertaken in Sheffield, another city in Yorkshire, from 2006–8. Chapter 5 presents findings from S1 and S2 on the dynamic nature of aspirations. Then Chapter 6 continues with an examination of the factors influencing the conversion of aspirations into capabilities (as construed by Sen). The influences on decision-making emerged as a crucial factor in the transformation of aspirations and thus Chapter 7 takes up this matter in detail. Chapter 8, leads onto a critical reflection on what I refer to as the 'promise' of higher education. Finally, the conceptual discussion and empirical analyses are used to inform the closing chapter, dedicated to proposing the direction for a new pursuit of social justice in education and beyond.

Undertaking the research I am presenting in *Aspirations, Education and Social Justice* offered me the opportunity for both personal and professional reflection. I hope readers will find some value in my contribution to the literature in both of these respects. In this small volume it was not possible to say everything I would have liked to say on the matters raised and nor is it intended to be the final word on the relationships and dynamics of aspirations, capabilities, education and the pursuit of social justice. It is intended to contribute to a vibrant ongoing conversation and to stimulate much needed further debate. The critique of

English education policy, past and present, is aimed at improvement rather than repudiation and I hope it will be received in that spirit. Michael Gove, in his role as Secretary of State for Education, voiced his support of 'rambunctious' debate on education reform and I hope this text will act as a catalyst for exactly that (Gove, 2012). In equal measure, I urge readers to take time for reflection and less boisterous, more open discussion on the matters raised here.

Education Policy Issues

Introduction

There is a current global trend to expand participation in education by people from diverse backgrounds. Expansion has involved extending provision from preschool to tertiary education and increased attention to addressing social inequalities. This is taking place against a backdrop of globalization manifested in the development of global systems of communication, governance, finance, transportation and markets.

In this book, the nature of young people's participation in formal education settings comes under scrutiny, with a particular focus on secondary education and transitions to life beyond school and sixth form college.[1] In seeking to contextualize the discussion this chapter considers different ideas about the role of education in society and some key issues in education policy in England.

The role of education

In different times and places, the role of education in society has been interpreted in diverse ways reflecting competing ontologies. Within sociology there are competing ideas about the role of education. For example, consensus theorists such as functionalists may argue that the role of schools is primarily to sort and prepare young people to support society by taking on roles commensurate with their ability and skills. Conflict theorists on the other hand, such as Marxists or feminists, may argue that the filtering and sifting that takes place during schooling processes work to oppress and disadvantage some individuals (e.g. working classes, females) whilet unfairly advantaging others (Freire, 1972; Willis,

1977; Gillbourn and Youdell, 2000). Some governments aim to use educational institutions to maintain the *status quo*, others to promote social mobility or to reinforce oppressive regimes. The perceived goals of education are wide-ranging from social control and serving the needs of industry to knowledge transmission and human flourishing.

Current trends in British education policy are fuelled by the government's economic instrumental goals. The government commissioned report, Unleashing Aspirations, has estimated that in the United Kingdom, 'we will need up to seven million new professionals in employment by 2020' and this has driven officials to consider ways of encouraging talented non-traditional students into the professions (Milburn, 2009: 5). The report, focused on building aspirations towards the professions but this neglects those who do not aspire to join the professions. It aimed to broaden representation of different social groups across a range of professions but this was to pursue economic growth rather than human development. The Chair of the Panel on Fair Access to the Professions, Alan Milburn, claimed, 'in a globally competitive economy, the key to success depends on unlocking the talents of all our people' (Milburn, 2009: 27). The report was strongly driven by the economic motive of preparing individuals to work in the imagined global economy of the future envisaged by the British government (Panel on Fair Access to the Professions, 2009).

The 2010 general election in the United Kingdom led to the formation of a Coalition government led by the Conservative and Liberal Democrat parties (henceforth, 'the Coalition'). A wave of new CEP signalled a renewed claim for the importance of the role of education in building a globally competitive and socially just society. CEP is characterized by a neo-liberal outlook, supportive of the marketization of education, devolvement of responsibility away from local authorities, and central government, and towards schools. This appears to signal a shift in the locus of control away from the state. However, a raft of accountability measures, inspections and upgraded surveillance of teaching professionals, together with an open invitation to the private sector to step in where government has stepped out, ensures that the autonomy of schools will remain limited (Department for Education, 2010; BIS, 2011a, 2011d).

The Coalition government has clearly stated that the number one priority on forming the government was to address and reduce the fiscal debt. Thus Coalition education policy (CEP) exists in a web of tensions between the state, institutions and individuals, between rich and poor, social and economic needs and among other policy priorities jostling for centre stage. The Coalition government has been challenged on a number of fronts, on welfare, health and education reform, regulation of the press and the implementation of the 2010 Spending Review (HM Treasury, 2010).

In 2012, opposition to the Coalition plans for health reform, alongside debate over the proposed Bill of Rights, sidelined some controversial educational policy issues regarding a new education bill. So the physical timing of education policy debates in relation to other policy debates is significant. Similarly, the wider austerity climate plays a hand in the shaping of specific reforms that may have very long-term effects. Coupled with this complex arena of policy debates is the challenge of the implementation of policy in the context of diverse cultures of different stakeholders. Such dilemmas can reduce the focus of policy to narrow issues of 'getting the job done' and overcoming or managing resistance.

In order to expand the sphere of thought on the diverse roles education might play in society I have drawn on the perspectives of two pioneers in education and human flourishing, namely Rabindranath Tagore and Alexander Sutherland Neill.

In 1901, Nobel laureate, Rabindranath Tagore (1861–1941) founded a school in Shantiniketan in India. He proposed that the object of education was to give man the unity of truth comprised of spiritual, intellectual and physical elements. The emphasis was on harmony, sympathy and the educational experience of body and soul.

Tagore argued that, 'We devote our sole attention to giving children information, not knowing that by this emphasis we are accentuating the breach between the intellectual, physical and spiritual life' (Tagore, 1999: 399). Tagore was resistant to education which failed to acknowledge the importance of play and freedom in human development. Indeed, as a parent I have experienced school consultation evenings where my child is reduced to a basic set of mechanical operations related to reading, writing and numeracy skills. There is no mention of her social, emotional, spiritual or physical well-being. Progress is relayed in numerical ranked sequences according to national and school averages and my child's place in relation to these norms. I am expected to be pleased if she is on the high achieving side of these averages but actually I am left with a silent antagony towards a system that reduces a beautifully vivacious lively child into a set of assessment indicators devoid of any meaningful form of life. This stripped down, mechanized version of human being is far removed from Tagore's ideas of childhood which he regarded as, 'the period when we have or ought to have more freedom – freedom from the necessity of specialisation into the narrow bounds of professional conventionalism' (Tagore, 1999: 399).

A. S. Neill provides us with another interesting perspective on the role of education which he put into practice by opening Summerhill school in England, in 1921. At Summerhill, 'pupils are free to choose whether or not they attend lessons. When not in lessons, pupils can be involved in whatever activity that captures their interest. These include making films, organising and performing in musical or dramatic events, and learning different languages. Physical activities include trampolining, skateboarding, riding bikes and climbing trees' (Ofsted, 2011: 4).

This outlook contrasts with the thinking behind much CEP which assumes individuals make rational decisions based on the pursuit of long-term economic rewards for labour market participation. In this sense the policy rhetoric is both decontextualized and dehumanized, failing to recognize the multi-faceted nature of human being.

Summerhill was subject to an Ofsted inspection in Autumn 2011 and judged to be outstanding on a number of measures including, 'helping to achieve well-being and enjoy what they do' and, 'spiritual, moral, social and cultural development' (Ofsted, 2011). Interesting, Summerhill's school aims include, 'allowing children to be free from compulsory or imposed assessment, allowing them to develop their own goals and sense of achievement' and, 'allowing children to be completely free to play as much as they like' (Ofsted, 2011: 1). Exploring alternative approaches to the holistic develop of children may help to balance the slim-lined view of humanity inherent in CEP.

Interestingly, Andrew Pollard and Mary James (expert panel members responsible for reviewing the English National Curriculum in 2011), in a personal comment on the review, noted that it was disappointing that the terms of reference for the National Curriculum review omitted the subject area of personal, social and health education. This is indicative of the focus on traditional academic subjects and the exclusion of scope for personal reflection and holistic development. They also remarked that the focus of the curriculum strategy on levels, 'diverts attention away from what is being taught' (2011: 2).

Overall the Coalition policy strategy on education is hard to define, partly due to what Michael Gove, Secretary of State for Education (henceforth, 'Gove'), describes as his 'magpie' approach to policy development (Gove, 2011b). He looked at other countries and took the ideas that seemed to him to work. Unfortunately divorcing policy from social context may be a mistake and this pick 'n' mix strategy is potentially high-risk and lacks a clear ideology. Examination of Gove's policy rhetoric gives more insight into his position on education as he identified the English education system as a 'cure for unemployment and welfare dependency' (Gove, September, 2011b).

The last two years have seen an overhaul of the National Curriculum, with a return to an emphasis on traditional subjects. Gove, has vociferously outlined his belief that examination results are the best way to judge an individual's ability, stripping away the social contextualization of differential achievement. In 2011, Gove argued that, 'A-levels should help universities select the students best equipped to succeed, by the simple and old-fashioned expedient of giving the most able students the highest grade' (Gove, 2011c). The perceived economic and social needs of society are privileged above individual freedom to pursue well-being.

It is important to question whether the assessment measures are measuring what we think they are measuring, in other words their validity, and whether the measures are equitable, whether different kinds of assessment would allow different individuals to demonstrate learning, for example in an applied situation. Gove adopts a confrontational approach to a suggestion that social context should be taken into account alongside examination grades when considering university admissions. He remarks on, 'the deluded notion that background matters more than ability . . .'. However, there is an interesting comment in the Students at the Heart of the System White Paper (SHS) which accepts 'exam grades alone are not the best predictor of potential to succeed at university' (BIS, 2011a: 58). The question is whether it is the most able students who achieve the highest grades. Do student–teacher ratios, class discipline, study facilities, caring responsibilities at home make a difference to the capability of an individual to secure top examination grades? If these conversion factors do impede the achievement of the highest grades does this mean that the B grade comprehensive student is less able than their A* privately educated peer?[2]

Gove has also instigated a review of the school examination system, deriding the present provision and standards. He argues, 'what is taught is determined as much if not more by examinations as by the National Curriculum. This means we need to consider GCSE reform alongside the development of the new curriculum' (Gove, 2011b). The attention to detail of how we measure students' 'intellectual effort' and the assimilation of the class-based, 'treasure house of wonder' Gove endorses, ambushes attempts to question how we address the deep social inequalities that disadvantage young people before, during and beyond their formal schooling (ibid.). It also underlines the fact that while the new free schools, advocated by the Coalition, may appear to have more freedom in the design of their school curriculum, in fact Westminster will effectively retain control via the examination system.

One of the key aims of this book is to vividly portray the social context that is silenced in a policy discourse focused on promoting examination achievement by raising aspirations, ambitions and standards of teaching. Specific attention is given to youth transitions from school and college to higher education along with related decision-making processes. The arguments put forward in the SHS White Paper (2011a) suggest that increased competition will both improve the quality and value of higher education and that increasing participation in HE will promote social mobility. The policy discourse of pairing competition with quality diverts attention from the crucial issues of the differential experiences, risks, benefits and outcomes in relation to education. Social mobility is a complex matter that requires more than widening participation in education to generate long-term change. Each of these issues is explored in the ensuing chapters.

Policy theory

The dominant focus on the *generation* and *implementation* of policy has tended to reinforce the ideologically powerful construction of policy as a linear process. It suggests policy is initiated by government and implemented by practitioners where the former is privileged (Bowe et al., 1992; Fitz et al., 1994). Ball (1990, 1997) has suggested that a more accurate view would be to consider policy as cyclical, rather than linear, where policy is created and recreated throughout its journeys between policy authors, practitioners and recipients. Thus Bowe et al argue, 'policy is not done and finished at the legislative moment, it evolves in and through the texts that represent it . . . texts have to be read with and against one another – intertextuality is important' (Bowe et al., 1992: 21). They argue that through interpretations the policy is recreated and in this sense policy can be seen as constantly in motion. In relation to this the intended and actual goals and outcomes of policy are also in flux; while an initial policy aim may be one thing the actual processes and outcomes which occur may be something quite different. Thus policies which aim to give greater access to education, qualifications and job opportunities may in fact act to legitimize an unequal system where the power and agency of dominant groups are reproduced and strengthened.

In summary, the traditional linear model of policy encourages an emphasis on outcome-based evaluations whereas the cyclical model favours an emphasis on evaluating the processes of policy. Hence our understandings of how policy works both informs and shapes the development of policy and its evaluation. Ball's cyclical model seems to work well within a capability paradigm that focuses on processes as well as outcomes. Understanding education policy is crucial because policies give voice to government interpretations of the way educational institutions may be used as instruments of the state.

Policy encounters resistance and acceptance. It is used in different ways with intended and unintended consequences. The creation of policy may in practice be left very much up to educational practitioners in schools and colleges and thus Weatherley et al argue that 'street-level bureaucrats are the policy-makers' (1977: 172). The term, 'policy', has been variously described as text, as discourse, as an intervention in practice or as something which leads to practice (Ball, 1994). Policy documents certainly do not exist in isolation and there are conflicts within and between documents. Policy is commonly understood as something which is 'put into practice'. Although this conceptualization is somewhat limited it does suggest that there are certain changes or transitions that must occur in order for a 'policy' to have meaning in the world. In this sense, it is useful to think of policy as something which is dynamic and changing.

Different local education authorities under diverse policy regimes may be better or less able to negotiate local policy; central government may be able to achieve objectives more easily in some areas rather than others. It has been argued that although school practitioners may tend to implement policies in ways which meet the needs of students, the extent to which this might be achieved depends to some extent on institutional needs and the mode of management of a given school (Foskett et al., 2004). In addition, individual students have diverse needs. Individual teachers in different institutions at different levels of management may feel more or less powerful or able to exert influence. Therefore power differentials may still exist both within and between institutions (Weatherley and Lipsky, 1977: 172).

International policy context

International policy directives relating to education such as the United Nations Convention on the Rights of the Child (UNCRC) and the Millennium Development Goals have strived to provide better access to all for education at primary, secondary and tertiary levels (United Nations (UN), 1990; Department for International Development (DfID), 2006). In terms of education, the UNCRC recognizes, 'the right of the child to education' (Article 28) and directs that this right should include access to, 'Different forms of secondary education (general and vocational)' and higher education accessible, 'on the basis of capacity by every appropriate means' (United Nations Children's Fund (UNICEF), 2007). However, access and participation in a formal educational setting does not indicate the quality or meaning of the experience for a given individual. The UNCRC states, '. . . the education of the child shall be directed to . . . the development of a child's personality, talents and mental and physical abilities to their fullest potential' (UN, 1990: 9). This can only be carried out with the active and willing participation of children. There are numerous examples of students recounting negative experiences of schooling and higher education, particularly relating to class but also other aspects of individual identity (Archer et al., 2003; Power et al., 2003; Unterhalter, 2003; Reay et al., 2005). This evidence suggests that the nature of children's participation and well-being in education needs to be scrutinized more closely if we are to pursue an education agenda in the interests of social justice.

Over the last 25 years there has been a growing interest in the study of well-being and this has gathered momentum over the last few years. Ben-Arieh reports that, 'some 200 experts from more than 30 countries have been trying in the last ten years to re-define the concept of children's well-being and to find more appropriate indicators' (Ben-Arieh in Medchild, 2006: 77). Key contributors have included international organizations such as the United Nations Children's Fund (Unicef), the World Health Organisation (WHO), Save the Children and the European Union (EU) as well as policymakers and researchers worldwide (Bradshaw et al., 2005; Unicef, 2005; Organisation for Economic Co-operation and Development (OECD), 2006). There seems to be greater recognition that, 'we must look at how well children are living as children and not only how well we are preparing them to be better adults in the future' (Ben-Arieh in Medchild, 80: 2006). This chimes well with the perspective of Amartya Sen's capability approach and the pursuit of new avenues for understanding the well-being of young learners in their present and future lives.

However, international policies and directives on education have tended to be assessed and evaluated using quantitative measures and this is reflected in national-level evaluations. For example, the indicators used in the Unicef report on 'Child Well-being in Rich Countries' to assess educational well-being were based on average literacy in mathematics, science and reading achieved by age 15 (Unicef, 2007). They also include statistics on the percentage of 15–19-years-olds remaining in education and the percentages of 15–19-year-olds not in employment education or training (NEET). Finally the education section of the study considered data on the percentage of 15–19-year-olds expecting to find 'low-skilled work' (Unicef, 2007: 18). In the United Kingdom there has been a similar approach to assessing the success of initiatives to engage learners in education and to reduce the national statistics of youths who are NEET. While these kinds of data provide an overview of certain aspects of educational achievement tell us little about the quality of education received or the impact on learners' overall well-being.

Government statistics on enrolment in HE, as a policy outcome measure, reinforce the tendency to view participation from a binary perspective with individuals either inside or outside of formal education, that is participation or non-participation. Efforts have been principally directed at continuing to engage young people in education as they reach the end of each stage of schooling and to raise their attainment in terms of examination success. The Coalition proposes to raise the participation age to 18 by 2015 (DfE, 2011).[3] This renews concern over the nature and terms of young people's future participation in education. A sufficient account of social justice cannot be generated by considering only increases in numbers staying in school and going onto HE. It is also necessary to evaluate the way in which these targets are achieved and the impact of policy on the destinies of young people both inside and outside of HE. The discussion turns now to a more specific focus on HE policy developments in England.

The development of higher education in England

UK policy to widen participation in HE has a history stretching back to the formation of the University Grants Committee in 1919 (David et al., 2008). Prior to the current wave of expansion in HE there were two previous significant waves of expansion from 1963–70 and from 1988–93 (Archer, Hutchings and Ross, 2003: 75). Trow identifies the 1980s as a period of rapid growth and what he termed 'mass' participation stemming from a succession of policy developments (Trow, 1972). Scott describes how Trow, 'defines elite systems of HE as those which enrol up to 15 per cent of the age group [school leavers]; mass systems as those enrolling between 15 and 40 per cent; and universal as those which enrol more than 40 per cent' (Scott, 1995: 2). Scott notes that, 'between 1987 and 1992 participation almost doubled from 14.6 to 27.8 per cent' (Scott, 1995: 5).

In Trow's terms, the shift to a mass system of HE in England is therefore fairly recent. David et al. (2008) note that after a sustained period of HE predominantly for the elite in society in the 1960s the growth of new polytechnics offering a different range of courses led to significant growth and diversification of the HE sector. In 1992 the Further and Higher Education Act attempted to homogenize the HE sector by allowing polytechnics to be rebranded as universities.

In 2001, the 'Excellence Challenge' policy initiative was launched in England with the aim of, 'improving access to higher education for able young people from poorer backgrounds' (DfES, 2005: 1). In 2003, following the recommendations of the White Paper, The Future of Higher Education, the programme was broadened and became known as Aimhigher (DfES, 2003). In total 42 Aimhigher Partnerships worked across England to deliver the programme. In the 2009–10 academic year Aimhigher partnerships worked with 2,700 schools (including 188 Academies and 413 primary schools), 108 higher education institutions, 368 FE Colleges and 114 Local Authorities (HEFCE, 2012a). Funding for the Aimhigher programme ceased in July 2011 and the success of the initiative had mixed reviews. Undoubtedly, many young people benefited from the many activities and opportunities funded through Aimhigher, such as university open days, master classes, theatre events, undergraduate visits in schools and higher education summer schools. However, the issues that the initiative aimed to address in terms of long-standing social inequalities in access and participation in HE endure. Furthermore, the Aimhigher scheme, largely aimed at 14–19 year-olds, but also including some younger students, was a targeted initiative. The policy directives were implemented in different ways in different institutions but essentially, some students were seen as part of an Aimhigher widening participation cohort and other students were excluded. Therefore, although many young people benefited from the Aimhigher programme it was not open to all.

The key stakeholders were the Higher Education Funding Council for England (HEFCE), the Learning and Skills Council (LSC) and the Department for Education and Skills (DfES). The overall aim was to increase participation of 18–30-year-olds in HE to 50% by 2010.[4] A goal of participation by 50% of those aged 18 to 30 by 2010 was set although the participation rates for young people aged 18 or 19 have consistently remained well below this target (HEFCE, 2005, 2010; Chitty, 2009).[5] The HEFCE strategy emphasized, 'reaching out to those for whom higher education seems beyond reach, not for lack of ability, but often simply for reasons of background or family tradition' (HEFCE, 2003). The ultimate aim of increasing the number of young people in higher education was to be brought about by increasing staying on rates and widening access to higher education institutions. The key aim of increasing numbers in HE was to be supported through outreach work, fair access policies and efforts to retain students through to successful course completion. Government Aimhigher WP policy suggested that raising students' aspirations would lead to greater participation in higher education which in turn would raise the nation's ability to compete in a global knowledge economy (Action on Access, 2003; DfES, 2006). Again, the focus on an economic instrumental agenda is implied in the language of policy.

Higher education under the Coalition government

The Coalition government's White Paper, SHS proposed a new regulatory framework to cover all institutions that are part of the English HE system (BIS, 2011a). The SHS identified three key challenges, to create a sustainable HE system, to improve students' HE experience (by focusing on improving teaching, assessment, feedback and preparation for work) and greater responsibility of HEIs for improving social mobility.

Sustainability

The Browne Review of HE funding recommended to the government that substantial increases in student fees were necessary to secure a sustainable future for the HE sector. University tuition fees, payable by students were originally introduced, in England, in 1998 under the former Labour government (DfE, 2003). Fees have increased from £1,100 per year then, to up to £9,000 per year from 2012 under the new system of variable fees endorsed by the Coalition government. The recommendation for raising the cap on variable fees was made in the report from the Browne Review. Although there has been a shift from upfront fees to tiered repayment of fees based on future salary, the interest rates are higher than previously and clearly the amount to be repaid is substantially greater. The government policy on fee increases can be seen as incongruent with a policy to widen participation in HE and this has led to substantial debate on the matter.

There was some tension within the Coalition government over the introduction of higher fees for HE. The Liberal Democrat Party's website stated that, 'Liberal Democrat party policy remains to phase out tuition fees, but in the circumstances of the Coalition that was a policy we could not deliver' (Liberal Democrat Party, 2012). The open opposition to the idea of tuition fees is illustrative of the difficulties of generating policy to reflect two divergent political party perspectives. This has led to what I term a 'hybrid' policy approach where compromises are constantly being made.

Early figures on the impact of the fee rises on student applications to university show that there has been a significant drop in applications to some subjects, such as European languages (down 11%) and non-European languages (down over 21%). There have also been significant drops in applications to some universities including Warwick (down 10%), Birmingham (down 11%) and Hull (down 17%) (Vasagar, 2012: 4). There has been a sharper drop in male applicants, down 8.5% compared with 6.7% females, compared to last year's applications for higher education (ibid., p. 4).

Social mobility

The SHS White paper noted that, 'the most advantaged 20% of the young population were around six times more likely to attend a selective university in the mid-1990s but seven times more likely to by the mid-2000s' (BIS, 2011a: 56) and that, 'Currently fewer than one in five young people from the most disadvantaged areas enter higher education compared to more than one in two for the most advantaged areas. The participation rate of disadvantaged young people at institutions requiring higher entry tariffs has remained almost flat over recent years at under three per cent' (ibid., p. 55).

HEFCE (2010: 2) reported that, 'young participation has increased from 30 per cent in the mid-1990s to 36 per cent at the end of the 2000s'. However, the figures are for young 'entrants' to HE and therefore do not take account of students who do fail to complete their studies. The Department for Business Innovation and Skills (BIS) reported that, 'Full-time young participation for 18 year olds from the bottom four socioeconomic classes has increased from 10.5% to 13.7%' (BIS, 2010: 1). This compares with 28.4% and 27.8% for the same periods for the top three socio-economic classes. Although the figures suggest the gap has reduced it does not take account of gap year students from higher social classes starting university aged 19. Due to changes in data collection techniques BIS have stated that data are not comparable across years. The Higher Education Funding Council for England divides geographical areas up into five divisions based on HE participation levels and the education, occupation and income levels of parents. In 2008/9 it was found that 58% of 18-year-olds in the highest band went onto higher education compared to just 18% of the lowest band (BIS, 2010: 10). There is a significant difference in participation rates based on gender with more females in all social classes participating in HE. In 2010, participation rates in the lowest four socio-economic groups (SEGs) stood at 11.1% and 16.4%

for males and females respectively, compared to 24.5% and 31.3% for males and females in SEGs 1, 2 and 3 (BIS, 2010). The government figures illustrate that, first only around one in three 18-year-olds goes onto higher education and secondly, that more that the vast majority of lower social class pupils will not go on to higher education. If social justice is to be pursued by supporting all young people to flourish beyond school and college, then this is an issue that deserves specific, concentrated policy attention.

Student experience

Coalition policy has positioned the students as customer with an onus on HEIs to provided comparable information to prospective applicants. Those planning to apply to HE now have access to a website where they can compare 'Key Information Sets' on different courses at different institutions. They can also view current student feedback on undergraduate experiences along with graduate employment data and salaries. In Chapter 7, the information and guidance available to prospective HE applicants is discussed further in the context of the 'promises' of HE implicit in this information.

WP policy evaluation

The discourse of raising aspirations, a mainstay of the Aimhigher initative, founded under a Labour government, is still prevalent in the Coalition policy. Regarding the ceasing of Aimhigher funding, Sir Alan Langlands, Chief Executive of HEFCE, said,

> *Raising aspirations and delivering effective information, advice and guidance about higher education remain critical if we are to maintain the progress made in widening participation. Aimhigher innovative outreach activity ... has encouraged young people to aspire to higher education. Widening participation in HE remains a core element of the Coalition education policy strategy.* (HEFCE, 2012b)

HEFCE have a key role in overseeing the implementation of the government's widening participation directives commenting,

> *widening access and improving participation in higher education are a crucial part of our mission. Our aim is to promote and provide the opportunity of successful participation in higher education to everyone who can benefit from it. This is vital for social justice and economic competitiveness.* (HEFCE, 2012b)

Widening participation policy is grounded in a deficit model where strategies focus on the deficit of individuals who lack aspiration. There is an assumption that there is a problem and that it lies with individual students rather than institutions and this had been echoed by others (Burke, 2002).

There is an implication that if similar percentages of young people from diverse socio-economic groups go onto experience higher education then a greater degree of equality will have been reached. However, the way the policy has been implemented has led some students with non-university aspirations to feel excluded. A multi-faceted concept of 'disadvantage' is needed to highlight within group differences and to go beyond the traditional structural notions of inequalities based on class, gender and ethnicity. A closer examination of the nature of participation in education helps to re-orientate understandings of disadvantage in education and through education.

Government evaluation of the Aimhigher initiative was strongly outcome oriented and assumed that the policy was promoting equal opportunity. In 2003, the HEFCE strategy stated, 'the new Aimhigher will be outcome-focused, and will seek to identify and spread approaches which evidence shows to be most effective and which offer best value for money' (HEFCE, 2003: 5). Increased participation in HE was used as the key outcome measure at national level and in the medium term HE application rates, staying on rates and attainment rates were used as success indicators (HEFCE, 2003: 7). The evaluation strategy for WP in HE has remained static over the last decade. However, retention rates for different courses and universities still vary widely with recent figures showing that 9% of, 'students (a total of 28,785) who started full-time first degrees in 2006–07 did not complete their first year' (THE, 2009: 12). This figure is remarkably consistent with the previous year's figure at 28,825 (Higher Education Statistics Agency (2009).[6] Students with lower entry grades, and without a family history of HE, are more likely to drop-out (HESA, 2009). David Curry, a member of the House of Commons Public Accounts Committee reported that, 'institutions with the higher proportions of students from deprived backgrounds have higher drop-out rates' (Curry, 2008: 20). It is of concern that the key outcome of WP policy is stated as, 'increased admission rates to HE from those under-represented groups' (HEFCE, 2003: 22). This does not take account of the diversity of institutions and courses students enrol on and the percentage of young entrants to HE from NS-SEC classes 4, 5, 6 and 7 varies widely across different sites (HESA, 2009). These statistics indicate that enrolment figures alone are insufficient to understand the full picture of participation in HE and a review of evaluation measures is overdue. This matter is taken up in the light of the S1 and S2 study findings in later chapters.

Sen's Capability Approach

Introduction

Amartya Sen comments that, 'my work on the capability approach was initiated by my search for a better perspective on individual advantages than can be found in the Rawlsian focus on primary goods' (2009: 231). Hence, the capability approach (CA) developed as an alternative to resourced-based approaches to the evaluation of advantage and has been used to respond to the challenges of evaluating the kinds of lives we are living, the forms of justice we are seeking and assumptions which inform the kinds of equalities and freedoms towards which societies are striving (Sen, 1999b; Walker, 2006b). The CA has been widely applied in the arena of human development and in more recent years applications have broadened across disciplines as the potential of Sen's CA has become more widely understood. The capability space offers a range of new metrics for comparison and evaluation of human development, while highlighting the problematic nature of existing measures (Sen, 1992; Pogge, 2002; Terzi, 2005).

The capability approach

Sen has observed, 'Different aspects of the CA have been discussed, extended, used, or criticized by several authors, and as a result the advantages and difficulties of the approach have become more transparent' (Sen, 2006b: 31). In Sen's writings on the CA there have been subtle changes in the terminology used and greater emphasis at different points in time given to certain key concepts such as inequality (1992), freedom (1999b), rationality (2002), identity (2006a) and justice (2009). Martha Nussbaum and others interested in the CA have also offered their own insights and contributions which have converged as well as diverged from the main flow of Sen's work (see for example, Agarwal et al., 2005; Nussbaum, 2005a; Comim et al., 2008). It is for clarity, therefore, that I occasionally refer to 'Sen's CA' or 'Nussbaum's CA' in order to specify to which version of the CA is being considered.

The CA draws attention to myriad complex factors which affect what a person is able to (and chooses to) do and be (Alkire, 2005). The approach does so by redefining a number of overarching ideas and using them to inform the language of capabilities. Sen has adopted a range of commonly used terms but each is given specific meaning in the context of the CA. It is necessary to have a basic understanding of these meanings before fuller discussion of the CA is possible. Sen's key concepts are best understood in relation to one another rather than in isolation and indeed some of the critiques of Sen's work stem from a weak understanding of the connections between concepts.

The capability space and the pursuit of well-being

When considering how well off a nation is, the tendency has been to look at resource indicators such as gross national product (GNP) and the accumulation of financial assets and possessions (Nussbaum, 2010). Nussbaum points out that, 'It has by now become obvious that this [resource-based] approach is not very illuminating, because it does not even ask about the distribution of wealth and income, and countries with similar aggregate figures can exhibit great distributional variations' (Nussbaum, 2005a: 60). Sen argues, 'commodity command is a means to the end of well-being, but can scarcely be the end in itself . . . A person's well-being is not really a matter of how rich he or she is . . .' (Sen, 1999a: 19). Sen's claim for the strength of considering *capability* in relation to well-being, 'builds on the straightforward fact that how well a person is must be a matter of what kind of life he or she is living, and what the person is succeeding in "doing" or "being"' (Sen, 1999a: 19). For example, being healthy, being sheltered, (doing) working, as compared to having money, possessions and so on. The CA is not opposed to having, nor is it proposing being and doing instead of having. Each has a role to contribute.

Berges (2007) uses the example of an Eastern Turkish girl's right to education to show the advantage of the CA over a resource-based approach to social justice in taking account of personal heterogeneities. She argues that irrespective of 'compensation' from a resourcist approach, in terms of the educational provision through local schools, this will not necessarily change the girl's parents' view of whether she should have an education. Even if the resourcists take account of 'institutional structures' as part of their resources this still does not adequately address the problem. According to Berges, studies have shown that additional educational resources have not necessarily led to increased participation in education by Eastern Turkish girls. The same argument could be made by looking at the resources put towards increasing the participation of 'non-traditional students' in HE in the United Kingdom. That is to say, the provision of more university places or funding initiatives to increase applications will not in itself ensure the capability of all young people to enter HE. Berges concludes, 'in order to institute access to resources as an indicator of social justice, it seems we need to enter the capabilities discourse' (ibid., 19). The example of Eastern Turkish girl's education shows that additional resources will make no difference if the main reason they do not attend, 'is that their parents do not encourage them (or in some cases allow them) to do so' (ibid., 22).

Critique of utilitarianism

Both Sen and Nussbaum discuss the weakness of preference or desire satisfaction as an adequate means of assessing advantage and well-being (Sen, 1999a; Nussbaum, 2005a). Their discussions bear comparison with the earlier work of Jon Elster (1983) who developed a detailed conceptualization of 'adaptive preference' in contrast to autonomous preference. He argued for the freedom to do otherwise as instrinsically important. Nussbaum contrasts somewhat with Elster, arguing for the positive value of some adaptive preferences. She comments, 'we probably shouldn't encourage people to persist in unrealistic aspirations' (Nussbaum, 2005a: 138). In this sense, Nussbaum is arguing that adapting unrealistic preferences, in the form of aspirations, is probably a good thing. Now the question of assessing the feasibility of aspirations is a crucial question, to which Sen himself helpfully focussed my attention. Feasibility hinges on making judgements about what is possible and yet it depends on knowing about the future as well as the present. What is not possible today might become possible in the future with adequate support, effort and possibly even a little luck. Often when decisions are made in the name of feasibility they are actually considering probability, and even then, from a conservative perspective. I will return to this crucial question of feasibility in more detail in Chapter 9.

The term, 'adaptive preference', has been used to describe the way choices emerge from the interaction of social, psychological and environmental constraints on individuals (despite their apparent agency and well-being freedoms).[1] Therefore, preferences are shaped to a greater or lesser extent contingent on variable constraints and thus choices do not necessarily reflect 'pure' preferences but possibly adapted preferences. Bridges summarizes that, adaptive preference,

> *at its simplest, reflects the observation that in choosing what they will do, how they will spend their time or resources or what kind of life they will lead people are affected by or take into account, for example, what they can afford, the likely responses of others to their choice and the values and practices which shape them and the communities in which they live.* (Bridges, 2006: 1)

Sen and Nussbaum use different terminology to describe this process of adapted preference and the importance of individual choice is crucial to both Sen and Nussbaum (Nussbaum, 2005a). For example, Sen argues,

> *the problem is particularly acute in the context of entrenched inequalities and deprivations. A thoroughly deprived person, leading a very reduced life, might not appear to be badly off in terms of the mental metric of desire-fulfilment, if the hardship is accepted with non-grumbling resignation. In situations of longstanding deprivation, the victims do not go on grieving and lamenting all the time, and very often make great efforts to take pleasure in small mercies and to cut down personal desires to modest – 'realistic' proportions.* (Sen, 1992: 55)

This example shows how an individual may change their preferences in order to make it easier to live in the extremely deprived circumstances in which they find themselves. Nussbaum argues that, 'habit, fear, low expectations and unjust background conditions deform people's choices and even their wishes for their own lives' (Nussbaum, 2005a: 114). She has focused much of her attention on the way individuals adapt their preferences because they see the world in a restricted way. She argues this is due to the sub-ordination of individuals due to enduring inequalities in society relating, for example, to gender and disability (Nussbaum, 2005a, 2006a).

The understanding generated by the concept of *adaptive preferences* is very useful in critiquing the utilitarian view of human development, originally developed by Jeremy Bentham.[2] It highlights the fact that although an individual may say they are satisfied with their lot in life this is not to say that they are more advantaged than someone else who does not feel they enjoy a similar level of satisfaction. This is because a person may adapt their preferences in response to the social constraints they experience, consciously or unconsciously. These ideas build on the work of Berlin who argued, 'The doctrine that maintains that what I cannot have I must teach myself not to desire; that a desire eliminated, or successfully resisted, is as good as a desire satisfied, is a sublime, but, it seems to me, unmistakable, form of the doctrine of sour grapes: what I cannot be sure of, I cannot truly want' (Berlin, 1979: 139). In summary, advantage and preference satisfaction do not necessarily go hand in hand. In Chapter 7, further attention is given to the theorization of preference, and adapted preference as distinct from free choice, in the evaluation of widening participation strategies.

Equality, advantage and disadvantage

In discussing equality, Sen observes that from a utilitarian perspective, 'there is an insistence on equal weights on everyone's utility gains in the utilitarian objective function' (1992, 13). There are two key problems with this utilitarian perspective. First, from a capability perspective it could be argued that not all individuals can achieve the same utility gain from the same set of circumstances and hence the emphasis on equal weighting of (presumed) utility is limited. As Sen puts it, 'the idea of equality is confronted by two different types of diversities: (1) the basic heterogeneity of human beings, and (2) the multiplicity of variables in terms of which equality can be judged' (ibid., 1). As discussed above, Elster (1983) has drawn attention to the way utility may be derived through adaptation of preferences and the manner and likelihood of adapting preferences is likely to vary across diverse individuals. In any case the utility derived in terms of happiness is not correlated with fairness in a Rawlsian sense.[3] For example, one individual may be privileged in a society while another is treated very poorly, although not on the basis of merit. The latter individual adapts his or her preferences such that they are satisfied with their position in life. Utility is derived through adaptation of preferences rather than through fair treatment. Hence it becomes tenuous, at best, to use utility as a measure of human development and justice. The second type of diversity Sen describes highlights differences of opinion in terms of how equality should be judged, in terms of the choice of variables which might be said to measure some form of equality. Sen argues that what becomes crucial then, is not that a particular school of thought purports to be egalitarian, but that in doing so it defines equality with respect to a particular 'space' of evaluation (ibid., 14).

Hence, while there may be general agreement that equality is a noble cause, being an egalitarian is not a uniting feature as there is disagreement about the form and metric of equality (Sen, 1992). There is a flipside to this point which is that greater equality in one aspect of life may lead to greater inequality in another. Sen invites us to reconsider what kind of equality is worth pursuing and whether it can justify potentially greater inequality accruing in other areas of life. Sen queries why theorists and policymakers alike are entranced with the consideration of equality, remarking, 'equal consideration at some level . . . is seen as a demand that cannot be easily escaped in presenting a political or ethical theory of social arrangements' (1992: 18). He asks not only why we should consider equality, but also, equality of what? (Sen, 1992). In other words, it is necessary to justify why one space is more important than another in evaluating equality.

> *The relative advantages and disadvantages that people have, compared with each other, can be judged in terms of many different variables, e.g. their respective incomes, wealths, utilities, resources, liberties, rights, quality of life and so on. The plurality of variables on which we can possibly focus (the focal variables) to evaluate interpersonal inequality makes it necessary to face, at a very elementary level, a hard decision regarding the perspective to be adopted. This problem of the 'evaluative space' (that is the selection of the relevant focal variables) is crucial to analysing inequality.* (Sen, 1992: 20)

Sen has questioned whether a social justice agenda necessarily needs to pursue equality and if so what kind of equalities might be sought. For example, two individuals might need different resources to arrive at a similar level of 'well-being achievement' (Sen, 1985). The evaluative space of the CA offers the opportunity to consider the benefits of expanding an individual's capabilities so that she or he is able to choose between a range of ways of being and doing they have reason to value in order that they might live a flourishing life. The CA places a spotlight on the nature of inequalities and this provides a helpful anchor point for critically evaluating education policies which purport to promote equality. The term equality is often associated with ideas of justice yet views of justice vary geographically, culturally and temporally. Any given government may decide certain freedoms or equalities are fundamental to justice within a society while others are not. Depending on the formulae used different priorities are derived. In some sense this may relate to cultural views of what constitutes a 'good life' and the nature of well-being and human flourishing. White points out, 'there is no community of experts on what constitutes a flourishing life' (White, 2007: 23). In turn, views of justice, the 'good life' and what constitutes well-being inevitably influence social policy and pedagogical practices. Sen argues that rather than devoting all our attention to devising a structure of society that might theoretically provide perfect justice, but may at the same time be unattainable, perhaps it is more realistic to focus on reducing the unnecessary injustices that exist. In this way constant progress can be made towards the project of perfect justice (Sen, 2009). Moreover, we need to be specific about how we interpret justice in terms of access, entitlement and rights. This perspective informs the policy reflections in Chapter 9.

Freedom and five instrumental freedoms

The value of human freedom forms a central focus of Sen's work, who argues, 'the success of a society is to be evaluated . . . primarily by the substantive freedoms that the members of that society enjoy. This evaluative position differs from the informational focus of more traditional normative approaches, which focus on other variables, such as utility, or procedural liberty or real income' (Sen, 1999b: 18).

Sen has further expanded the role of freedom in human development by identifying five instrumental and connected freedoms which he sees as central to, 'the overall freedom people have to live the way they would like to live' (Sen, 1999b: 38). These include political freedoms, economic freedoms and social freedoms (including the freedom to be educated) as well as transparency guarantees and protective securities (Sen, 1999b: 38–40; Alkire, 2008: 32–3). Transparency guarantees are particularly important in the context of widening participation in HE since they relate to being able to trust others and know that information provided is both reliable and honest. Students are provided with certain kinds of information, often biased towards higher education and the information from institutions themselves aims to presents particular images of the experience and outcomes of higher education.

Sen argues that these five instrumental freedoms (which are not exhaustive) enable further capabilities (freedoms) to be developed and, hence, that freedom is both the ends and the means of development (ibid., 38). Sen acknowledges that the work of Rawls and Dworkin both move in the direction of including the freedom to achieve as well as actual achievements in the evaluation of a person's situation (Rawls, 1971; Dworkin, 1981). Rawls focused on the distribution of primary goods and Dworkin on resources but both perspectives are also concerned with how resources and primary goods facilitate an individual's achievements. The part that is missing though is the means by which goods and resources are converted into achievement and this is where Sen's notion of capability offers further insight into understanding individual freedom (Sen, 1992: 33). In other words, the CA argues that freedom cannot be fully understood only with reference to achievement and that this needs to be supplemented with greater understanding of the *real* freedom an individual has to achieve ways of being and doing they have reason to value. For example, this is critical to appraising Secretary of State for Education, Michael Gove's perspective on examination achievement as an accurate barometer of student ability. Examination results say little of the real freedom an individual has to demonstrate their full potential and the context of multifarious constraints. Indeed, as an undergraduate I sat my Part I final examinations shortly after learning that someone close to me had been diagnosed with cancer. I saw their health rapidly deteriorate over the following months and as I prepared for my Part II finals they tragically died. The situation was overwhelming to me as a young person but not one I was able to convey to my tutors at university and therefore my personal situation was not taken into account when I sat my examinations. Young people face all kinds of difficulties and challenges and thus the face value of examination results is limited in both assessing achievement and predicting potential.

Capabilities

Sen argues that in evaluating an individual's well-being it is important to look at the *capabilities* or real opportunities an individual has to lead a valued life (Sen, 1985). According to Sen, 'the CA to a person's advantage is concerned with evaluating it in terms of his or her actual ability to achieve various valuable functionings as a part of living' (Sen, 2001: 30). He observes that, '. . . the relationship between primary goods (including incomes), on the one hand, and well-being, on the other, may vary because of personal diversities in the possibility of converting primary goods (including incomes) into the achievements of well-being' (Sen, 1992: 27). A similar argument can be made about the variable ability of individuals to convert an educational qualification, which may be deemed to be a 'good', into well-being achievement. This is a crucial point and one that will be returned to throughout this book in the context of policies to widen participation in HE in England. Sen criticizes approaches to inequality measurement which used solely income as the focal variable as this overlooks the ability of an individual to convert income into well-being achievement (ibid., 29). Sen argues, 'differences in age, gender, special talents, disability, proneness to illness, and so on can make two different persons have quite divergent opportunities of quality of life even when they share exactly the same commodity bundle' (Sen, 1999b: 69).

Capabilities represent the freedoms an individual has to achieve beings and doings they have reason to value although only some of them will become realized as functionings. Sen argues, 'once we shift attention from the commodity space to the space of what a person can, in fact, do or be (or what kind of life they can lead), the sources of interpersonal variations in conversion can be numerous and powerful' (Sen, 1992: 37). Applying Sen's argument to the commodity of HE, for example, leads to questioning the value of HE commodity acquired by different individuals in diverse HE contexts. It cannot be assumed, that even with the same amount and quality of the commodity of HE, two different individuals will be able to convert this resource in the same way (Bourdieu, 1986; Sen, 1999a).

A number of different kinds of capabilities have been distinguished within the approach by others and they are summarized in Table 2.1 below. Sen has identified 'basic' freedoms which have been interpreted as capabilities by others. These do not constitute a list of capabilities but include, being well-nourished, well-sheltered, avoiding escapable morbidity and premature mortality, being educated, having good health and being able to participate in social interactions without shame. Nussbaum's version of the capability approach, on the other hand, distinguishes basic, internal and combined capabilities. Nussbaum (2005a: 85)

Table 2.1 To show the definitions of different kinds of capabilities distinguished by Sen and Nussbaum

Capability	Definitions
Sen 'Basic'	Sen has identified 'basic' freedoms which have been interpreted as capabilities by others. These do not constitute a list of capabilities but include, being well-nourished, well-sheltered, avoiding escapable morbidity and premature mortality, being educated, having good health and being able to participate in social interactions without shame.
Nussbaum 'Basic'	'the innate equipment of individuals that is the necessary basis for developing the more advanced capabilities, and a ground of moral concern' (p. 84).
Nussbaum 'Internal'	'mature conditions of readiness' such as 'bodily maturity'. Being able to 'speak a native language'.
Nussbaum 'Combined'	'internal capabilities combined with suitable external conditions for the exercise of the function' (p. 85).

Source: Nussbaum (2005a: 84–5).

accepts that, 'the distinction between internal and combined capabilities is not a sharp one' but argues that it is useful to distinguish the internal readiness of an individual to function and the social circumstances that will support the functioning. For example, an individual may be articulate (internal capability) but may not be given freedom to express themselves in a particular society. Hence, Nussbaum describes the capabilities on her list of 'central human functional capabilities' as combined capabilities (ibid.).

Functionings

Sen uses the concept of *functionings* to denote the beings and doings individuals actually achieve that they have reason to value (Sen, 1985). The range of capabilities an individual has is reflected by their *capability set* and this in turn is an indicator of their *well-being freedom*. Sen is concerned with 'combinations of functionings' that individuals are able to achieve.

Well-being freedom and well-being achievement

Sen states that, 'the capability approach is concerned with showing the cogency of a particular space for the evaluation of individual opportunities and successes' (Sen, 2006b: 50). Hence the CA is often employed as an 'evaluative framework' (Hart, 2007). Table 2.2 summarizes four central concepts used by Sen in developing this evaluative space. By introducing these concepts around agency and well-being Sen is able to question prevailing strategies and philosophies for human development (and hence education policy). He offers alternatives to the dominant resource-based approach of looking at achieved outcomes (such as accumulation of economic capital or educational qualifications) as indicators of progress and development. Sen provides the four concepts of *well-being freedom, well-being achievement, agency freedom* and *agency achievement* as potential foci for the evaluation of human development. In this book it is argued that these concepts may be useful in both evaluating and developing education policy (although this is not an area pursued extensively by Sen).

Table 2.2 Four principal concepts in Sen's capability approach

	Freedom	Achievement
Well-being	*Well-being freedom*	*Well-being achievement*
Agency	*Agency freedom*	*Agency achievement*

It is because Sen foregrounds the importance of agency that his approach seems apt for the evaluation of education policies such as England's agenda to widen participation in HE since in this policy context individual agency is subject to very limited interpretation. Sen's views on the role of agency contrast somewhat with those of Martha Nussbaum. In particular, Nussbaum avoids placing an emphasis on the agency and freedom concepts to which Sen gives a key role stating, 'I believe that all the important distinctions can be captured as aspects of the capability/function distinction' (Nussbaum, 2005a: 14).[4]

Sen is interested in 'one's freedom to achieve those things that are constitutive of one's well-being' and this concept is termed 'well-being freedom' (Sen, 1992: 57). Sen separates the notion of well-being freedom from well-being achievement arguing that individuals may choose to pursue valued goals other than those based purely on self-interest. Well-being freedom represents the freedom an individual has to pursue their own well-being, based on their capabilities, whereas well-being achievement represents the well-being actually derived (Sen, 1992). Sen argues, 'the quality of life a person enjoys is not merely a matter of what he or she achieves, but also of what options the person has had the opportunity to choose from. In this view, the "good life" is partly a life of genuine choice, and not one in which the person is forced into a particular life – however rich it might be in other respects' (Sen, 1999a: 45).

Sen argues that a significant aspect of well-being is related to an individual's freedom to choose in what way to promote their sense of well-being from a set of 'capabilities'. The individual's freedom is associated with the range and nature of the capabilities available. Sen describes what might be understood as an individual's best option as the 'maximal element' in their capability set (Sen,1999a: 44). However, he also points out that although an individual is free to choose that option they may choose some other possibility from within their capability set. Therefore two individual's well-being achievements may vary even where their well-being freedoms are similar.

The idea of a 'maximal element' can be applied to the example of a student with a strong academic record deciding whether or not to apply for a university place. The individual may decline the opportunity to go to university which might subjectively be considered by others as the 'maximal element' in their capability set. The individual would still be seen by Sen as 'advantaged' in the sense that this individual has had a 'real opportunity, especially compared with others' (Sen,1999a: 3). Sen concludes that, 'the freedom to achieve well-being is closer to the notion of advantage than well-being itself' (Sen,1999a: 3). In other words it is not enough to consider only the achievements and actual life choices of an individual as this does not fully represent the capability set from which they are choosing.

Agency freedom and agency achievement

When discussing agency, Sen separates the terms '*agency freedom*' and '*agency achievement*'. Agency freedom refers partly to the freedom an individual has to turn any of a range of capabilities (potential functionings) into (achieved) functionings. Sen describes 'agency freedom' as 'one's freedom to bring about the achievements one values and attempts to produce' (Sen, 1992: 57). He describes 'agency achievement' as the 'realization of goals one has reason to pursue which need not be guided by her own well-being' (Sen, 1992: 56–7). Hence the notion of agency is more wide-ranging than personal well-being. The agency of an individual affects others in ways that may either enhance or diminish their own well-being achievement (see for example, Sen, 1985: 205). For example a mother may use her agency freedom to promote her child's survival, and hence their well-being achievement, but in doing so this may compromise her own well-being achievement (Sen, 1999b: 202). Therefore potentially an individual's agency freedom may be used to achieve goals (agency achievement) that could either enhance or diminish the same individual's well-being achievement.[5]

Capabilities and rights

Nussbaum considers rights and capabilities seeing the CA as a species of the rights-based approach to justice (Nussbaum, 2006a). However, it is probably more accurate to see the CA as an extension to rights-based approaches as capabilities are qualitatively different from rights. Nussbaum also identifies primary and secondary rights and notes that, for example, the American constitution denotes rights by absence of state interference whereas the American Indian constitution goes further and promotes affirmative action, also recognizing it is not only state abstinence but also actions of others that make a difference to the securing of rights (Nussbaum, 2006a). The CA stems from the latter in the sense that rights are seen as a tool for developing capabilities but it is not assumed that a declaration of rights will result in everyone in a society being fully able to exercise the freedoms implied by those rights. For example, everyone may have the right to free speech but many may not exercise this right for fear of repercussions. Hence, from a capability perspective it is argued that the state has an active role to play in securing rights as well as in legislating about them.

The distinction between rights and capabilities highlights the limitations of a rights-based approach to social justice and helps to illustrate the potential of the CA to contribute to this area.[6] This is not to say that rights are not seen as significant to the achievement of justice but rather that the obligations of the state need to go further than simply endorsing a set of rights to which people are entitled. Capabilities differ from rights in a number of ways some of which are beneficial and others which are not. Individual capabilities do not currently have the public recognition that rights do and therefore they cannot be protected in the same way. Beyond basic human rights there is a tendency in policy and legislation to protect the rights of individuals on the basis of group characteristics such as age, gender, neighbourhood and so on. This reflects the way in which rights have tended to be secured through group action and struggle such as civil rights and feminist movements. There is still much work to be done within the CA to consider the practical implications of developing policies which are driven by a capability ethos based on individual rather than group values.

Robeyns (2006) sees rights as a strategic tool to achieve capability. A closer inspection of rights reveals an overlap between rights and capabilities where ways of being and doing that are valued by individuals are also recognized as rights (e.g. the right to work in a smoke-free environment). Rights however, may reflect ways of being, doing and having that are valued by society but *not* by the individual, for example, the right to vote. Furthermore, Sen notes that, 'human rights to important process freedoms cannot be adequately analysed within the capability framework' (Sen, 1995: 151). On the other hand, individuals will have ways of being and doing they have reason to value that are not formally recognized as rights (though that is not to say that they would necessarily be seen as socially unacceptable). For example, an individual may value listening to music while working. This is illustrated further in Figure 2.1. The degree of

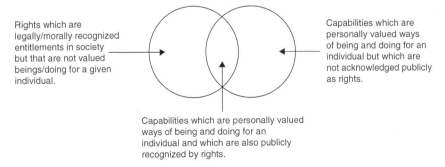

Rights which are legally/morally recognized entitlements in society but that are not valued beings/doing for a given individual.

Capabilities which are personally valued ways of being and doing for an individual but which are not acknowledged publicly as rights.

Capabilities which are personally valued ways of being and doing for an individual and which are also publicly recognized by rights.

Figure 2.1 The relationship between rights and capabilities

overlap between rights and capabilities will vary over time and from one society and one individual to another. Similarly, the balance of rights to capabilities will vary between individuals and societies and Figure 2.1 is therefore presented as a conceptual tool rather than an accurate depiction of the overlap of rights and capabilities.

Sen comments that, 'The two concepts – human rights and capabilities – go well with each other, so long as we do not try to subsume either category within the territory of the other' (Sen, 2005: 151). Capabilities seem to move in a different direction from rights. The latter can be seen to focus on legally or morally predetermined entitlements for life which an individual then chooses to take advantage of or not. In contrast, capabilities are valued ways of being and doing that emerge from the individual and they do not necessarily have a moral or legal basis. However, what an individual chooses to value may be influenced by moral and legal norms which they have been socialized to accept. Future policy initiatives could benefit from further analysis of the role of rights in expanding and protecting the capabilities of different individuals in a given society.

Challenges to the capability approach

In offering an overview of the CA it seems appropriate to give some air time to critiques, challenges and dilemmas related to the development of this perspective. Key criticisms of the CA are briefly described in the following section and the reader is directed to other works which have dealt with the various criticisms of the CA more thoroughly. These criticisms have been responded to both by Sen and others working in the field and there are clearly vibrant and ongoing discussions relating to the points of contention.[7] Indeed, Sen acknowledges, 'I have often been left with residual gain from the dialectic encounter' (Sen, 1992: xiv). The criticisms have been arranged under six main headings in relation to language and concepts; listing capabilities, the individual and social structures, the individual and social relations, the under-theorizing of education within the CA and finally, operationalizing concepts in the CA. The challenge of operationalizing the CA will be addressed in depth in Chapter 4 on methodological issues.

Key divergences in the capability approach

Table 2.3 offers a simplified summary of some of the principal divergences between Sen's CA and Nussbaum's CA. It is not comprehensive but indicative of

Table 2.3 Key points of divergence within the capability approach

Criteria	Amartya Sen	Martha Nussbaum
Use of the evaluative space	No specific list, capabilities must be context-specific	List of Central Human Capabilities
Concept of freedom	Comfortable with the term 'freedom'	Not so comfortable
Concept of capability	Basic capabilities can be identified in extreme situations for example famine situations. Personal, social and environmental factors influence the conversion of commodities into capabilities and functionings	Distinguishes three kinds of capabilities: (a) Basic (essential to human life), (b) internal (individual has the ability to achieve a particular functioning), (c) combined (external factors allow individual opportunity to use their ability)
Threshold	Not specified	Threshold level of each capability (below this human functioning not possible)
Concept of agency	Agency is more wide-ranging than personal well-being for example a mother's agency may promote child survival (Sen, 1999b: 202)	Not necessary to use this concept as capability and functionings cover this area

key contested spaces within the CA addressed in different ways by those working with this perspective on human development.

The language and concepts of capabilities

'Sen by now has given many different versions of his CA' (Qizilbash, 1996: 145). Sen has been criticized for both a lack of clarity in some of his central concepts as well as for using multiple definitions (Qizilbash, 1996; Gasper and Staveren, 2003; Clark, 2005). For example, Gasper and Staveren argue that the language Sen uses to describe key concepts within the CA can be confusing as Sen uses language such as 'freedom' and 'capability' in a, 'specific and distinct way, diverging from most of its common usage' (Gasper and Staveren, 2003: 144). However, it cannot be assumed that there is shared understanding of many commonly used concepts, for example, class, power or poverty. Indeed, many disciplines have developed specific languages to describe important concepts and at times the words employed have quite different meanings from their so-called common usage. While it is important for Sen to be clear in explaining the distinctive qualities of the kinds of freedom to which he refers, it is not necessary to choose a different language. The latter suggests that others have some kind of historical hold over particular concepts and this is unhelpful. Sen gives a very crucial position to the role of freedom in enabling an individual to pursue a life they have reason to value (Sen, 1992, 1999b). Pettit's (2001) criticism of Sen's CA centres on whether an individual's capability is context-dependent. He draws on examples where an individual's capability depends on the grace and favour of others, in this sense the 'context' relates to 'favour-dependence'. He argues that Sen does not take account of how a capability is secured and whether it does or does not depend on the goodwill of others. Sen accepts this is the case, however, he argues against revising the CA as he argues that Pettit is drawing attention to a different form of freedom not addressed by the CA. Sen argues that the Republican approach which Pettit puts forward would see an individual as unfree if their capability is favour-dependent. Thus, a Republican approach, according to Pettit, would not acknowledge the capability this individual has for the favour-dependent functioning. By contrast, the latter would be recognized by the CA and Sen argues it is important to maintain this distinction between the two kinds of freedom. In this sense, Sen acknowledges that the CA does not address the issue Pettit raises but argues there is a sound reason for this difference (Sen, 2001: 54). That is to say, the freedom to choose a future an individual has reason to value rather than necessarily being free of dependence on others as Pettit suggests. Notwithstanding this point, Sen (2001: 56) does accept that freedom has, 'many distinct aspects'. This view underpins a version of freedom whereby students choose freely among a range of ways and beings they have reason to value albeit with the acknowledgement that other social beings may be a part of the realization of that freedom. As Sen observes, 'we live in a world in which being completely independent of the help and goodwill of others may be particularly difficult to achieve, and sometimes may not be the most important thing to achieve' (Sen, 2001: 56).

Capabilities and the capability space

Clark notes that, 'several attempts have been made to clarify the concept of capability' (Clark, 2005: 9). Cohen argues that the term 'capability' is ambiguous in Sen's work and refers to the, 'unfortunate and ambiguous nomenclature' of the CA (Cohen, 2006: 19). In Sen's earlier writings the term 'capability' was synonymous with capability set whereas more recently it has been used to describe elements in the capability set (Robeyns, 2005a: 100). In part, this has led to divergences within the CA with others, such as distinguishing different kinds of capabilities.[8] Sen has been criticized for lack of, 'distinction between internal powers and skills and actual opportunities or outcomes' (Clark, 2005: 9). Indeed, Gasper (2002: 447) has argued that Sen should modify terminology in line with Nussbaum's basic, internal, combined capabilities. Certainly, the proliferation of definitions of capability within the CA as a whole may impede clear understanding in this respect, particularly to scholars new to the field.

Cohen (2006) explains that while resourcists focus on goods and welfarists focus on utilities, Sen is looking at the space in between. However, the term capabilities is used to describe the opportunities an individual has to choose to live in different kinds of valued ways. Cohen's criticism is that the space between commodities and utilities, which he describes as 'midfare' is not only related to what an individual can do with the commodities he or she has. Cohen argues that, 'goods cause further desirable states directly, without any exercise of capability on the part of their beneficiary; an example would be the goods which destroy the insects that cause malaria' (Cohen, 2006: 18). Cohen argues that Sen's concern with individual freedom, in terms of choice, leads him to use the term capability to refer to the actions of an individual in relation to midfare but that this does not describe all aspects of the dimension between goods and utilities. He further argues that Sen, 'over-estimates the place of freedom and activity in well-being' (ibid., 2006: 25). Cohen argues for 'equality of advantage' arguing this goes beyond Sen's 'athletic' notion of capability to encompass also 'states of a person which he neither brought about nor ever was in a position to bring about' (ibid., 2006: 28). However, this underplays the freedom that Sen argues is so important in evaluating an individual's opportunity for well-being freedom and achievement. Sen's notion of capability, 'gives the agent a sort of power over what happens in their life that is independent both of how their preference happens to go and of whether they enjoy the favour of the powerful' (Pettit, 2001: 16). However, where freedom is constrained by others then this social constraint would be regarded as a conversion factor in capability terms. This notion of convertability responds to some degree to Pettit's concerns about Sen's view of freedom (Pettit, 2001). Perhaps 'pure' freedom is unattainable, but the CA draws attention to the fact that individuals are only as free as social, economic, cultural and personal factors allow them to be.

Functionings

It has been argued that, 'Sen characterises functionings differently at different times' (Cohen, 2006: 21). Cohen points out that the term is used by Sen to refer both to activities, such as being able to do certain things, like read, as well of states of being like 'being well nourished' (2006: 21). In Sen's earlier writings *potential functionings* was the term used to refer to elements in an individual's capability set and *achieved functionings* was the terms used to refer to the states of being and doing actually achieved by an individual (Sen, 1985). In later work, Sen explained that,

> *the capability set would consist of the alternative functioning vectors that she can choose from. While the combination of a person's functionings reflects her actual achievements, the capability set reflects the freedom to achieve: the alternative functioning combinations from which this person can choose.* (Sen, 1999a: 75)

Later still, the term potential functioning became synonymous with 'capability' and continued to refer to elements in an individual's capability set. More recently, the term 'functioning' became commonly used by Sen and others to refer to what had previously been known as 'achieved functionings'. The term capability which had once referred to an individuals' overall capability set has more recently been used to refer to individual elements within the capability set (Sen, 2009). However, throughout Sen's work he has placed an emphasis on the importance of the alternative combinations of functionings an individual may achieve and these are referred to as 'functioning n-tuples' (Clark, 2005: 4). Williams has argued in relation to Sen's emphasis on combinations of functionings that, 'choosing to realise some capabilities may involve huge opportunity costs, which implies we should focus on "sets of co-realisable capabilities"' (Williams, 1987: 100). The changing terminology and multiple conceptualizations by others, particularly of capabilities, make the territory of the CA difficult to negotiate and clarity is needed in the methodological application of these concepts.

Freedom

Gasper and Stavern take up Sen's conceptualization of freedom in relation to feminist economics. They argue that in economics the tendency has been to consider negative freedom in terms of freedom from, 'constraints on one's choices in the markets' such as poverty, hunger or coercion (Gasper and Staveren, 2003: 139). Gasper and Staveren further suggest that Sen has attempted to focus attention on positive freedom which in comparison constitutes, 'the ability to attain desired ends' (ibid., 2003). Qizilbash (1996) also criticizes Sen for failing to give an adequate account of negative freedom [freedom from control, coercion] as opposed to freedom to do and be. Qizilbash argues that, by contrast, Nussbaum's notion of 'external capability' is able to express positive and negative freedom. Perhaps the counterargument to this is the use of the concept of conversion factors by Sen and others (Robeyns, 2005a). In other words, an individual is free to do and be as they wish within the constraints imposed by conversion factors.

Furthermore, Qizilbash argues that, 'the '*means* to freedom must matter' and he offers the example of a poor person stealing from the rich (Qizilbash, 1996: 146). Although the poor person's capabilities may be enhanced by the stolen commodities, the means by which his capabilities are expanded are morally questionable. Pettit's position concurs with Qizilbash on this point arguing that although the functioning of two individuals, or the same individual over time, may appear to be the same, the means by which they achieve the functioning may differ (Pettit, 2001).

Gasper and Staveren comment that Sen incorporates some values into freedom but leaves open what should be included despite suggesting that freedom is the primary framework for advantage (ibid., 2003). They go on to argue, Sen's overemphasis on freedom may draw attention away from the critical importance of social relations and personal relationships in the well-being of humans (with particular reference to women) (ibid., 2003). However, the CA recognizes the contribution of a range of conversion factors in supporting and constraining the development of an individual's capabilities. This encompasses the opportunities and benefits derived from social relations as Gasper describes.

To list or not to list?

Sen's CA has been criticized for lack of specificity in terms of the actual capabilities to be expanded or evaluated (Terzi, 2005; Walker, 2006b). There is an ongoing debate within the CA regarding the necessity and value of attempting to list capabilities either universally or in specific contexts. Nussbaum, as one of the first major proponents of the CA, supports the general notion of using capabilities as the space of comparison for purposes of development and social justice. However, she differs from Sen in arguing that, 'Sen's "perspective of freedom" is too vague' and that 'commitments about substance' are necessary. Nussbaum argues that in order to achieve substance it is necessary to, 'specify a definite set of capabilities as the most important ones to protect' (Nussbaum, 2003: 33). Nussbaum endorses a list of ten 'Central Human Capabilities' which she regards as fundamental entitlements and a minimum threshold for all societies shown in Table 2.4 (Nussbaum, 2005b: 43).

Table 2.4 Nussbaum's list of Central Human Capabilities

Central Human Capabilities	Description
Life	Being able to live a life of normal length
Bodily health	Being able to have good health
Bodily integrity	Being able to move freely, secure against assault
Senses, imagination and thought	Being able to use the senses to imagine, think and reason … informed and cultivated by adequate education
Emotions	Being able to have attachments to things outside ourselves
Practical reason	Being able to form a conception of the good and to engage in critical reflection about planning one's life
Affiliation	Being able to live with and towards others, to recognize and show concern for other human beings
Other species	Being able to live with concern for and in relation to animals, plants and the world of nature
Play	Being able to laugh, to play, to enjoy recreational activities
Control over one's environment	Being able to participate effectively in political choices. Being able to hold property

Source: Adapted from Nussbaum, 2005b: 43.

> *Some items on the list may seem to us more fixed than others . . . In this sense, the list remains open-ended and humble; it can always be contested and remade. Nor does it deny that the items on the list are to some extent differently constructed by different societies. Indeed, part of the idea of the list is its multiple realizability; its members can be more concretely specified in accordance with local beliefs and circumstances. . . . . The threshold level for each of the central capabilities will need more precise determination, as citizens work towards a consensus for political purposes.* (Nussbaum, 2005a)

Nussbaum's version of the capability perspective has been seen as limited and biased towards political frameworks and legal constitutions (Clark, 2005). Nussbaum has been clear that her list is not absolute or finite and it is open to discussion. Nussbaum clearly conveys the massive injustices in the world, in relation to the capabilities she identifies, and she graphically draws attention to intolerable levels of human suffering. Her decision to focus her energy on persuading governments to at least debate if not endorse her list is perhaps a strategy to get the injustices she sees onto the political agenda as efficiently as possible. Nussbaum may be commended for this even if the initial list she drew up had not been subjected to the rigorous processes of public discussion and debate that both Sen and Robeyns propose (Sen, 2005a; Robeyns, 2005b). Nussbaum concludes,

> *To get a vision of social justice that will have the requisite critical force and definiteness to direct social policy, we need to have an account, for political purposes of what the central human capabilities are, even if we know that this account will always be contested and remade.* (Nussbaum, 2005b: 58)

On the other hand Sen finds, 'one canonical list, based only on theory and usable for every purpose' is 'problematic' (Sen, 2005a: 335). Sen has repeatedly explained how pinning down set lists of capabilities fails to acknowledge the diversity of different sociocultural contexts and denies the possibility of public deliberation on what should comprise a list (Sen, 2004; Clark, 2005). In relation to the development of a list of capabilities for a specific context, Sen comments, 'I see Martha Nussbaum's powerful use of a given list of capabilities for some minimal rights against deprivation as being extremely useful . . . For another practical purpose we may need quite a different list' (Sen, 2005b: 159). Sen refers to his own use of lists in specific circumstances, namely in the development of the human development index and in his work with Dreze, addressing hunger and public action in India (ibid.). Hence, it may be argued that it may be of value to develop a specific list of capabilities to be developed through formal education in a particular context.

However, Sen is careful to emphasize the key role of democratic deliberation and public reasoning in developing any such list. He also underlines the need to reflect on any specific list that might be developed to take account of changing circumstances, noting that a fixed list, 'would deny the possibility of progress in social understanding, and also go against the productive role of public discussion, social agitation and open debates' (Sen, 2005b: 160). This point is absolutely critical to the pursuit of social justice and there are two separate forces for change. The first critical point is that the hegemonic views of a society may change over time in ways which may allow the expansion of capabilities for a wider range of groups in the light of increased social understanding. There are numerous examples of this historically and in different contexts; for example, suffragettes in England in the early twentieth century, civil rights activists in the United States in the 1960s and anti-apartheid campaigners in South Africa. Thus substantial intra-paradigm divergence has arisen around the question of whether or not we should specify a list of essential human capabilities (Sen, 2005a). Sen, does not try to predetermine capabilities but says they should be context-specific, recognizing for example that different cultures may have different ways of valued living (and dying). He highlights the need for a constant process of negotiation and renegotiation, for example, as societies' values change or demographics alter (Sen, 1999a).

Ingrid Robeyns warns that a list could be biased, for example, in terms of gender or limited and proposes a set of criteria for identifying capabilities (Robeyns, 2005b). She, 'argues against the endorsement of a definitive list of capabilities and instead defends a procedural approach to the selection of capabilities using five criteria' (Robeyns, 2005b: 63). In response to concerns regarding list-formation, Robeyns has proposed a 'procedural approach' to select capabilities in a specific context using five criteria (ibid., 72–3). She suggests that when drawing up a context-specific list of capabilities or functionings that the list should be 'explicit, discussed and defended'. In addition, Robeyns argues for a clear method which is sensitive to context. Robeyns further suggests that initially an 'ideal' list of capabilities or functionings should be created but that this should be followed by 'drawing up a more pragmatic list' which takes account of methodological, sociopolitical and other constraints. Finally, Robeyns suggests that any list should 'include all important elements' but 'not be reducible to other elements' (Robeyns, 2005b: 72–3). In further rebutting the criticism of paternalism, Robeyns argues it is the degree of paternalism which matters. From a capability perspective, if a government intervenes to enhance an individual's capability set, it is important to ensure as far as possible that it still remains up to the individual to choose the functionings they wish to pursue. While Nussbaum's listing may be imperfect, in the light of the discussions on the merits of her list, Clark agrees with Gasper that Nussbaum's list may provide, 'a starting point for discussions in each society' (Clark, 2005: 7). However, whether others agree on this depends fundamentally on whether they align themselves with Sen or Nussbaum's views regarding the possibility of a list of human capabilities.

The individual and social structures

Sen argues that the CA takes more account of distribution of advantage within the family compared to alternative approaches. Pogge (2002) argues that capability theorists and resourcist theorists do not differ on 'distribution within the family'. He argues they have a shared commitment to normative individualism and therefore both are bound to look at an individual's share of resources (but this is not the same as share of capabilities). Pogge comments, 'Whether a criterion of social justice takes account of intra-family distribution depends not on the metric it employs ... but on its interpersonal aggregation function: Equalitarian, prioritarian, and sufficientarian criteria of social justice all do, while sum-ranking and averaging criteria do not, take account of intra-family distribution' (ibid., 179). However, Pogge equates inequalities of resources with inequalities of capabilities but this is a fundamentally flawed argument. This is because a resource metric is not a proxy for capability since it does not account for the variable ability to convert resources into capabilities (Sen, 1992: 27). Therefore even if a resourcist takes account of the unequal share of resources within a household this will still not tell them how able an individual is to convert those resources into capability.

This has been found to be the case, for example, in terms of familial gender and adult/child comparisons and draws attention to gender and aged-related inequalities within the family. While it is desirable for individuals to enjoy great freedom in determining, developing and pursuing their chosen capabilities (and hence functionings) their ability to do this will be limited in certain ways due to the social conditions of humanity. Some may need more support than others in developing and expanding their capabilities and recent attention has been drawn to the possibility of enhancing individual capability through carefully planned group participation (Stewart, 2005; Ibrahim, 2006). Arguments have also been put forward for what have been termed 'group capabilities' although this remains a contested area as some argue this shifts the focus away from the individual as the unit of analysis (Alkire, 2008). The CA does acknowledge that the individual is placed in a social context and this underpins Sen's argument that capabilities need to be context-specific (Sen, 1992, 2005a). This implies the social interaction of individuals in society and the relevance of culture, history, norms, values and expectations in the development of capability. For example, the provision of more education places will not make a difference to girls' education if the culture of the society in which they live is not supportive of girls' education. Hence, the CA draws attention to the need to secure the capability for education (that is to say, the real freedom to fully participate) and not only the right and infrastructure for education in a given society.

Pogge (2002) argues that resourcists do tend to look at the standard needs of an individual while a CA would look at the specific needs and endowments of an individual. Therefore resourcists are not sensitive to personal heterogeneities. Pogge (ibid.) uses two examples to attempt to illustrate how the resourcists can take account of human diversity. The first example of a pregnant or lactating woman, Berges (2007) argues is shown to be weak because contrary to Pogge's argument, a lactating woman and infant is not the same as a woman and an infant. That is to say, the lactating woman has additional special needs before, during and after pregnancy. These needs may, for example, affect her health, ability to participate in education or work and her future ability to earn a living. The second example Pogge (2002) uses is that of, 'past and present social injustices'. For example, an individual may be malnourished due to poor maternal health. However, Berges argues that in order to compensate someone for past injustices 'somebody must accept responsibility for that injustice' (Berges, 2007: 21). Secondly, she argues that it would be impossible to determine who should be eligible for compensation – some will miss out and others will cash in on such a system. While Pogge claims that resourcists could take account of equal treatment of men and women in an institution (with regard to resources) he also concedes, 'the capability theorists are way ahead of most resourcists, thanks to the great efforts by Sen, Nussbaum and others. But I see no reason to doubt that resourcists can do as well. They should certainly make the effort' (Pogge, 2002: 178). Pogge offers high expectations of the way that resourcists' evaluations of advantage can be improved but this is yet to be seen.

The CA has been criticized for being too individualistic to the detriment of wider social commitments and concerns (see, for example, Robeyns, 2005a). Critics have argued that there needs to be further thought given to the extent to which individual freedoms can remain unfettered and without social regulation of some kind. Furthermore, Robeyns points out that there are different kinds of individualism and it is 'ethical' individualism which is important in relation to the CA. In this sense she argues that we do need to consider each individual's position because, for example, there may be significant differences between the capability sets of individuals even within the same family, doing the same job and so on (Robeyns, 2002). Sen's focus on ethical individualism emphasizes the need to look beyond group characteristics such as class, gender or ethnicity (Sen, 2006a).

The individual and social relations

The CA has been criticized for under-emphasizing the role of social interaction in the generation of capabilities. Cameron and Ojha explain Dewey's position that, 'human relationships are in a continuous process of creation . . . transactional processes envisage the creation of both individuals and groups in society through the processes of transmission' (Cameron and Ojha, 2007). They note that Habermas' notion of communicative action and Bourdieu's notions of *habitus* and *doxa* are also relevant in the context of social interactions (ibid., 2007). Sen does take account of an individual's variable capacity to develop capabilities due to conversion factors which may include the products of social interactions. As noted earlier with reference to Berges' work (2007), a girl may not have the capability to be educated, not for lack of a school, but because her parents do not wish her to go to school. Here the social interaction of the girl with her parents clearly plays an important role in the development, or in this case constraint, of her capabilities. However, Sen does not develop a substantial theory of the nature of social interaction and this is where there is a potential weakness. Sen is, however, explicit that the capability framework needs to be augmented with context-specific theory and social relations may differ from one context to another (Sen, 1992, 2005). Having said this, Cameron et al. offer at least three alternative sets of conceptual tools with which to augment understanding of capabilities in relation to social interactions by drawing on Dewey, Habermas and Bourdieu (Cameron and Ojha, 2007). I take up Bourdieu's sociological theorization and its relevance to the CA in Chapter 3.

Under-theorizing the role of education

Walker (2006b) has noted that education has been, 'under-theorized in the CA' and this observation is supported by Flores-Crespo (2007). Conversely, Saito comments that,

> . . . despite the fact that Sen's capability approach has received substantial attention from philosophers, ethicists, economists and other social scientists, it has not yet been critically examined from an educational perspective. (Saito, 2003: 17)

This comment helps to illustrate the rapidity of growth in interest in the CA across many disciplines including education. Moreover, together, the comments show that the challenge is as much for educationalists to take up the task of developing the CA in education as it is for capability theorists to provide insights into how this might be done. Hopefully, this will lead to a growth in scholars with expertise in both areas. Since Saito's paper was published there has been steady growth in specific publications dealing with the application of the CA to matters of education.[9] Walker's observation about the lack of theorizing of education in the CA has been partially addressed by recent work by Terzi (2005), Walker and Unterhalter (2007), Hart (2007, 2009), Biggeri et al. (2011) and Lessmann et al. (2011).[10] However, operationalizing notions of capability within educational institutions as well as in the realms of educational policy is still in the early days. The research presented here raises many theoretical and methodological issues which pave the way for future research.

From the perspective of the capability approach, it cannot be assumed that time spent in an educational institution (be it a school or university) is commensurate with the expansion of capabilities and hence well-being (and agency) freedom. For example, if an individual is encouraged through their schooling to accept a lower social position (e.g. based on gender, class, race, ability) then this does not enhance their well-being or agency freedoms and achievements. In other words, not all schooling is good for well-being (of adults or children). In addition, the experience of formal education in schools clearly differs immensely from one individual to another, even within the same institution.

In the introduction to this book, I referred to a school where the head teacher's car was petrol-bombed. At that school I had a variety of responsibilities including teaching mathematics. Students were placed in ability-based classes and I was assigned to teach 11B5. This was the lowest of five ability groupings across in the whole of Year 11 (students aged 15–16 years). During my induction for teaching this class the head of mathematics referred to the class as, 'the monkey cage'. No syllabus or textbooks were supplied for teaching the class and when I enquired about what aspects of the syllabus had been covered the previous year I was told it did not matter as the students would not remember anyway. I was also told there was no point in giving 11B5 homework as they would not do it. Finally I was informed none of the students would be entered for the GCSE[11] mathematics examination at the end of the year as they had no chance of passing it. The experience of the 11B5 students was very different from the experience of the 11B1 (highest achieving) students being taught by the head of department and yet they were students in the same school, the same age and with the same entitlement to an education. This example underlines first, the importance of avoiding making assumptions about the value of education to a given individual in a particular context. Secondly, it underlines the importance of drawing a distinction between schooling and education. Schooling may be conceived in terms of enrolment and years of schooling whereas education can be related more closely to what is learned in formal institutions and beyond. This may include, for example, becoming politically conscious, an attribute not guaranteed by the act of schooling itself. Both the experiences of schooling and the capabilities and functionings accrued through education may be subject to bias. Bourdieu, Freire and others have illustrated how social inequalities may be reproduced through education systems (Friere, 1972; Bourdieu and Passeron, 2000) and there is great scope for the application of the CA to deepen understanding of these issues.

Conclusion

The CA presents new challenges for educational policy, practice and research as it drives us to reconsider our dominant ontological and epistemological stances particularly in relation to the nature of well-being and human flourishing. It offers a new space to evaluate what is of value in education. The CA has been subjected to numerous criticisms and several of these relate to the way the approach may be applied in a research context. Care must be taken over the explication of key concepts noting their changing use by different capability theorists and over time in the literature. This process will be facilitated by clarity of personal position in relation to Sen's resistance to, and Nussbaum's endorsement of, a universal list of human capabilities. Furthermore, the criticisms have emphasized the need for ontological clarity in the way the individual is conceived in relation to social structures as well as to fellow human beings. Finally, with particular reference to education, this chapter has highlighted the challenges to positioning the role of education clearly within a capability perspective. The challenges associated with operationalizing the approach, particularly with reference to capability measurement, are central to research in this field and are followed up further in Chapter 4 on evolving theory into method drawing on the conceptual work of both Sen and Bourdieu.

3

Blending Sen and Bourdieu

Introduction

Amartya Sen and others have acknowledged that the capability approach offers a framework to be complemented with additional theories that are context-specific (see for example, Sen, 1999a, Robeyns, 2005a; Walker, 2006b). In developing the conceptual framework for my research on aspirations I drew on Pierre Bourdieu's work to help theorize the relationships between individual students and school, college and higher educational institutions. This led to the development of the Sen-Bourdieu analytical framework (SBAF) I have applied to the research described here.

Pierre Bourdieu (1930–2002), the French sociologist, produced a vast body of work in his lifetime and this book focuses on just a small fraction of that work. In particular, this chapter aims to highlight the ways in which Bourdieu's sociological analysis can complement Sen's CA. First of all, Bourdieu introduces the idea of different forms of *capital* rather than just the economic form of capital used elsewhere. His conceptualization of capital enriches the understanding of the body of commodities and resources that may be converted into what Sen terms, *capabilities*, that is the freedom to pursue ways of being and doing the individual has reason to value. Secondly, Bourdieu's work complements Sen's CA by offering a more dynamic interactive understanding of the conversion factors helping and hindering the development of capabilities. This understanding stems from Bourdieu's conceptualization of individual *habitus* in relation to fields of action. These concepts are illuminated further in the following discussion.

Bourdieu and the concepts of habitus, capital and field

It has been argued that, Bourdieu did not write anything explicitly about 'education policy' (Rawolle and Lingard, 2008: 729). However, he did concentrate on issues relating to 'education and social reproduction' and there is much that can be learned from the application of Bourdieu's ideas to understanding why, for example, 'widening participation' in higher education in England is such a monumental task (Lingard, Taylor and Rawolle, 2005: 663). Naidoo argues that, 'at the heart of Bourdieu's work on higher education has been his desire to expose higher education as a powerful contributor to the maintenance and reproduction of social inequality' (Naidoo, 2004: 457).

In particular, Bourdieu's conceptions of habitus, field and forms of capital aid understanding of the way policies and institutions can contribute to reproducing inequalities as well as overcoming them (Bourdieu, 1986). These three Bourdieurian concepts are widely referred to in educational and sociological studies and there are many interpretations of Bourdieu's work (indeed his own interpretations were somewhat fluid). Therefore an overview will be given alongside working definitions of Bourdieu's concepts of habitus, capital and field in order to facilitate the discussions that follow. It is not possible to give a full account of the depth and richness of Bourdieu's work, this has been dealt with in his own works and by others.[1]

Habitus

> *The habitus is necessity internalized and converted into a disposition that generates meaningful practices and meaning-giving perceptions.*
>
> (Bourdieu, 2010: 166)

Bourdieu drew attention to what he called the 'habitus' of an individual which is related to the cultural and familial roots from which a person grows. Bourdieu explained that, habitus, 'operates below the level of calculation and consciousness' and that the, 'conditions of existence' influence the formation of the habitus which is manifested in the agent's 'tastes', practices and works thus constituting a particular lifestyle (2010: 167).

Habitus is constituted by an individual's embodied dispositions manifested in the way they view the world. An individual's habitus is developing from the beginning of life in relation to the social milieu of their home and family life and, 'through observation and listening, the child internalises "proper" ways of looking at the world, ways of moving (bodily habits) and ways of acting. Children thus acquire the "cultural capital" associated with their habitus' (Reed-Danahay, 2005: 46).

Bourdieu highlighted two key aspects of habitus, particularly relevant to understanding young people's relations with the field of HE. Bourdieu remarked that an individual's position in terms of social relations in the field will be influenced by their ability to perform in appropriate ways in a given environment (field) by alignment with the recognized 'tastes' or 'preferences' associated with that social space. In addition, the individual needs to be able to distinguish which of the tastes, practices and preferences of others are representative of the particular field.

'It is in the two capacities which define the habitus, the capacity to produce classifiable practices and works, and the capacity to differentiate and appreciate these practices and products (taste), that the represented social world, i.e. the space of lifestyles, is constituted' (Bourdieu, 2010: 166). Hodkinson has observed that,

> *lifestyle and habitus are inseparably interrelated – one is the manifestation of the other. They evolve, partly through choice and partly through changing circumstances, as life progresses. They are constrained and enabled by the social and cultural conditions within which a person lives, which are, in turn, influenced by the actions of that individual.* (Hodkinson, 1996: 147)

There is evidence that, even though it is not the norm, individuals who may be deemed 'disadvantaged' by their habitus can, for example, gain entry and be accepted in elite educational institutions. Bourdieu describes his own life as one where coming from a less privileged French rural background he was still able to be successful at the highest levels of the French education system. He suggested that individuals could escape their disadvantaging habitus by seeing chances and taking them. Contrary to critics comments, it would seem that even Bourdieu himself accepted that habitus is not totally deterministic (Reed-Danahay, 2005).

Thus, what is unclear is the extent to which habitus becomes a determining factor in an individual's future direction. Indeed Bourdieu himself suggested that it was unrealistic to think of a person's life as a journey following a single path but rather that a life may be comprised of multiple and possibly chaotic trajectories. For example, family breakdown, parental drug abuse or incarceration as the result of criminal behaviour may also contribute to chaotic life trajectories. Carmen Mills has argued that the relationship between social reproduction and habitus is not inevitable and it can be argued that Bourdieu was aware of this from his own experience. In a film documentary entitled, *La Sociologie Est Un Sport de Combat*, Bourdieu meets with residents in a deprived urban area in France (Carles, 2001). He acknowledges the residents' agentic power in bringing about social change through resistance and struggle. I now turn to another key concept in Bourdieu's sociological framework, that of the different forms of capital.

Capital

'It is in fact impossible to account for the structure and functioning of the social world unless one reintroduces capital in all its forms and not solely in the one form recognized by economic theory' (Bourdieu, 1986). Bourdieu argued that an individual's social position is influenced not only by economic capital but also by other forms of capital including social, cultural and symbolic capital and his work is useful in considering social difference in more complex terms (Bourdieu, 1986). Economic capital may be generated through inherited wealth, family income or engagement in the economy for financial return. Social capital is accrued through social networks, the family and wider community interactions. Symbolic capital is manifested as individual prestige and authority (Bourdieu, 1986). In terms of cultural capital, Bourdieu explained,

> *Cultural capital can exist in three forms: in the embodied state, i.e., in the form of long-lasting dispositions of the mind and body; in the objectified state, in the form of cultural goods (pictures, books, dictionaries, instruments, machines, etc.), which are the trace or realization of theories or critiques of these theories, problematics, etc.; and in the institutionalized state, a form of objectification which must be set apart because, as will be seen in the case of educational qualifications, it confers entirely original properties on the cultural capital which it is presumed to guarantee.* (Bourdieu, 1986: 7)

The idea of cultural capital is particularly relevant to rethinking the position of young people from different backgrounds regarding their perspectives on higher education and this issue is raised in further chapters. Bourdieu also drew a distinction between acquired and inherited capital. He remarked, 'the possessors of strong educational capital who have also inherited strong cultural capital . . . enjoy a dual title to cultural nobility, the self-assurance of legitimate membership and the ease given by familiarity' (2010: 74). Hence it is not easy to fix a person's social position and potential simply by considering their level of qualification, amount of money in their bank account or the area where they live.

The conversion of different forms of capital

Rather than thinking in terms of social class, perhaps it may seem more appropriate to consider the advantage that accrues to individuals with certain kinds of capital. In this sense an individual may be deemed more or less 'well off' or 'advantaged' dependent on their portfolio of economic, cultural, symbolic and other forms of capital. However, Bourdieu noted that this would overlook a crucial problem. Bourdieu argued that despite the fact that individuals from all walks of life may accrue cultural capital via education credentials what mattered was their differential ability to convert cultural capital into other forms of capital. Hence two individuals achieving the same qualification from the same institution may yield different 'rates of profit' from their 'scholastic investment' (Bourdieu, 1986: 243).

The conversion of capital into capability

In considering the notion of advantage, from Sen's capability perspective, Bourdieu's forms of capital may be seen as commodities that might be converted into capabilities. Sen's CA highlights a second crucial issue in determining a person's advantage based on the accumulation of different forms of capital. It is necessary to consider the extent to which different forms of capital can be converted into capabilities, that is to say, the freedom to pursue ways of being and doing the individual has reason to value. Indeed, Bourdieu's forms of capital can be seen to hold variable 'subjective' as well as 'objective' values contingent on both the field of action and the perspective of other agents in that field (Bourdieu's concept of field is illuminated further later in this chapter).

Inter-generational transfer of capital

Bourdieu theorized that capability may be accumulated through inter-generation transfers of different forms of capital from adults to their offspring. This was linked to the possibility of a family drawing on one form of capital in order to generate another form. For example, economic capital might be converted into cultural capital through the purchase of books and resources as well as participation in culture-rich activities. Marjoribanks later claimed that Bourdieu placed a strong emphasis on the amount and kinds of capital that, for example, an individual's family had and how this allowed an individual to secure advantage (Marjoribanks, 2002). However, Marjoribanks argued that family capital is not sufficient to guarantee the advantage of an individual. He argued that what was crucial was the combination of, '*capital* volume and adult-child interactions' and the opportunities an individual had to enable them to access the capital accrued within the family (Marjoribanks, 2002: 7).

Not all children are able to access family capital and, for example, this is borne out by a recent study by Serrokh on the lives of children living and working on the street in Bangladesh (Serrokh, 2011: 181). The argument can be extrapolated to other fields such as school, community and so on. Hence, in order for a child to benefit from family capital (or school/community capital) it is necessary for a process of transfer or conversion to take place. Thus it cannot be assumed that any or all offspring will benefit from their family's capital. Regarding school achievement, Marjoribanks concluded:

> *in families, the potentially valuable social capital related to a child's successful schooling includes, (a) the amount and quality of interest, support, encouragement and knowledge other family members have about education and (b) the extent that such resources are transmitted to the child in interactions with family members.* (Marjoribanks, 2002: 12)

Marjoribanks' argument resonates well with the capability approach where expanding capabilities depends on the conversion of commodities into capabilities. Recent work by Virogito and Salas (2011) resonates with Marjoribanks' analysis. They looked at the adaptation of parental expectations of their offspring's educational achievement. They found that parents adapted their preferences in relation to peer group expectations and reported from their literature review that some children appear to adapt their effort dependent on anticipated educational achievement. Parent expectations may therefore be associated with educational attainment of children.

Not all children are situated in a family setting and for those in families the context and dynamic are not static. For example, Padron and Ballet (2011: 166) refer to the transitional status of children, using the example of children 'not yet on the street'. This idea of transitional status can also be applied to the family setting where children experience shared-custody arrangements intermittently lodging with different parents and respective partners. I recently met a young female who described the dislocation of having two biological parents, three step-mothers and two step-fathers in addition to step-siblings. Other circumstances leading to the separation of children from their families temporarily or permanently include domestic violence, war, illness, death and criminal actions. Thus even where children are living long term with one or more parent(s) the nature of the relationship with parents is not guaranteed to be nurturing. Moreover, relationships are likely to fluctuate over a young person's life course (e.g. as they seek independence and potentially encounter conflict with parental views on contentious issues). In other words we cannot take the familial status of children to exist, to have longevity or consistency.

Activation of capital

Even if an individual may be able to accrue different forms of capital from their family, Laureau and Horvat (1999) have argued for recognition of the difference between the *possession* and *activation* of capital and shown that despite large volumes of economic, social or cultural capital this does not guarantee the achievement of desired outcomes. For example, it is also necessary to learn how to apply different forms of cultural capital in different fields. Knowing when and how to deploy particular forms of capital, and being skilful and confident to do, requires learning unwritten rules, and yet, is vital for maximizing the activation of capital. Erickson has argued that in the private sector, 'the most widely useful cultural resource is cultural variety and social network variety is a better source of cultural variety than class itself' (Erickson, 1996: 217). Thus, I would argue there is at least a two-stage process required to convert the commodities of 'family capital' into individual capabilities. The first stage requires the conversion of family capital commodities into individual capital commodities. Thus the second stage requires the conversion of individual capital commodities into capabilities (Figure 3.1). A further intermediate stage relates to the possibility of converting one form of capital into another in order to ultimately develop a capability.

Assuming an individual is able to successfully convert family or school capital into individual capital the capability approach still questions traditional notions of advantage and thus highlights the importance of the *freedom* to achieve valued ways of being and doing as well as achievement itself. The concept of 'capability' helps to demonstrate that achieving the possession of individual capital in itself is not an indicator of freedom to achieve well-being. An individual may be well educated, rich and knowledgeable of high culture but may not be able to achieve the valued functioning of being well liked because they lack the ability/

Figure 3.1 Two-stage process of converting capital to capability

knowledge of how to use their capital commodities effectively to achieve this goal.

So, from a Bourdieurian perspective education may contribute to an individual's advantage by enhancing their capital portfolio and the possibilities of transforming one form of capital into another (although the latter does not automatically lead to capital growth). The kinds of capital that are valued in any given society might in combination be said to create a 'cultural arbitrary' (Bourdieu and Passeron, 2000: 9). In other words there is not necessarily a scientific logic to the dominant culture but rather it is something determined arbitrarily in the interests of the powerful and at the expense of the less powerful in society. As Bourdieu and Passeron argued,

> *the major thrust of the imposition of recognition of the dominant culture as legitimate culture and, by the same token, of the illegitimacy of the cultures of the dominated groups or classes, comes from exclusion, which perhaps has most symbolic force when it assumes the guise of self-exclusion.* (Bourdieu and Passeron, 2000: 42)

It is a subtle form of disempowerment when an individual excludes themselves from opportunities (such as participation in higher education) because of the imposition of an inhospitable 'other' culture. Why would individuals want to put themselves in a position where, as Bourdieu puts it, 'they easily cross the borders, but with empty suitcases – they have nothing to declare . . .'? (Bourdieu in Harker, 2000: 843).[2] Bourdieu's concept of the 'cultural arbitrary' is useful in highlighting the ways in which the current policy of widening participation may marginalize certain social groups and individuals because their aspirations do not immediately fit with the dominant legitimized goal of pursuing higher education. Thus, despite a child's growing capital portfolio they may be unable or at least constrained in converting capital into capability. I turn now to discuss the concept of field which is the third element in a trio of Bourdieurian concepts drawn upon in the SBAF I developed for this research.

Field

Bourdieu's concept of *field* comes from the French 'le champ' which has been used to describe, 'an area of land, a battlefield and a field of knowledge' (Thompson, 2008: 68). Perhaps the middle definition is closest to Bourdieu's idea of a social competitive space. Bourdieu identified his concept of field in part as, 'a configuration of relations' between individuals and institutions which are essentially mediated by different forms of capital (Bourdieu, 1992: 72). However, drawing on Sen, this does not take account of the variation in individual capability to convert individual capital into capability as described earlier. Hence the CA illuminates the finer nuances of Bourdieu's field dynamics. On the other hand, Bourdieu's work illuminates the relationship of the individual to the social world in a context-specific way. Thus, the capability approach benefits from Bourdieu's concept of field. This is in the sense that although the individual remains the unit of evaluation they are positioned within a wider sociocultural context.

The concept of field is dynamic. Bourdieu and Wacquant proposed that, 'a *field* is a game devoid of inventor and much more fluid and complex than any game that one might ever design ...' (Bourdieu and Wacquant, 1992: 104). Following on from this, Grenfell and James have argued that government policy interventions, can, 'change a *field* of knowledge by the imposition of definitions of legitimacy and the re-grounding of institutional relations, and thus structures' and this has crucial implications (Grenfell and James, 2004: 513).

Bourdieu's notion of field is helpful in conceptualizing the nature of the field of higher education. He proposed that, 'There are as many fields of preferences as there are fields of stylistic possibles ... the total field of these fields offers well-nigh inexhaustible possibilities for the pursuit of distinction' (Bourdieu, 2010: 223). Thinking about the range of institutions, courses, places and spaces of HE, Bourdieu's description of the field highlights the distinctions to be made and the possibility that individuals select particular features of HEIs in order to reflect their tastes and preferences.

In the context of Bourdieu's concept of field, WP policy in England can be viewed very much as an interventionist strategy in the sense that it attempts to go against the natural order of dominant fields of power and education. While some have critiqued Bourdieu for being overly deterministic it is possible to see how such interventionist strategies could over time shift the balance of power within a given field. As noted earlier Mills (2008) has argued for the 'transformative potential of Bourdieu's theoretical constructs'. She suggests that, 'teachers can draw upon a variety of cultural *capitals* to act as agents of transformation rather than reproduction' (Mills, 2008: 79).

Bourdieu argued that, 'the earlier a player enters the game and the less he is aware of the associated learning' (2009: 67). According to Bourdieu, '"the feel for the game" is what gives the game a subjective sense – a meaning and a raison d'etre, but also a direction, an orientation, an impending outcome, for those who take part and therefore acknowledge what is at stake (this is *illusio* in the sense of investment in the game and the outcome, interest in the game, commitment to the presuppositions – *doxa* – of the game)' (2009: 66). Applying this to a young person contemplating entering higher education, where they have a parent or significant other who has experience of HE this may offer insights and a 'feel for the game' that place the individual at an advantage compared to others without such insights. The field is an arbitrary social construct and 'consensual validation . . . is the basis of collective belief in the game' (ibid., p. 66). Such collective belief in the HE field commences long before the individual reaches adulthood for many young people raised in a family with a tradition of HE participation. Different individuals will be more or less able to develop what Bourdieu referred to as, 'a feel for the game' in relation to the field of higher education (Bourdieu, 2009: 66). This will depend, in part on the individual's experience of the game, or at least their access to knowledge and understanding of the game.

In the student interviews from the S2 study, reported in Chapters 5 and 6, there is evidence of the institutional misrecognition of young people who choose not to apply to HE when they have the academic potential to do so. This failure to subscribe to expected norms of the education field leads to what Bourdieu describes as, 'the countless acts of recognition which are the small change of the compliance inseparable from belonging to the field, and in which collective misrecognition is ceaselessly generated' (2009: 68). This idea of recognition has been noted elsewhere (Berlin, 1969; Griffiths, 2010: 3). The absence of recognition or the misrecognition of an individual can have a damaging effect, leading to exclusion and alienation and this is illustrated by some of the young research participants' experiences.

Bourdieu recognized that sub-fields may exist within a larger field, so for example higher education within education. Looking at the landscape of higher education in England it could be argued that using Bourdieu's concept of field there is not one single field but several sub-fields of higher education within the larger field. In other words it is becoming more difficult to talk about higher education as a monolithic entity and it seems that different institutions potentially reflect different socio-cultural environments or fields to use Bourdieu's conceptualization. In the past inequalities in cultural capital with respect to educational achievement could be construed mainly in terms of participation or non-participation in education. Higher education was reserved for a select few with the overall participation rate in HE at just 3% in 1950 increasing to 33% in 1997 (Chitty, 2009: 203). However, the massification of higher education in England has dramatically changed the marketplace with more providers and an implicit hierarchy of courses and institutions (Gewitz et al., 1995; Reay et al., 2005). This means that inequalities in relation to cultural capital can no longer be construed in terms of a binary understanding of participation or non-participation in HE due to many inequalities unfolding within and between institutions and the types of HE on offer (Brennan and Osborne, 2008). In this sense higher education institutions have strengthened their position as producers of cultural capital although the field of education is uneven with some institutions and courses commanding greater cultural capital currency than others. As Bourdieu points out, 'the structure of the *field*, i.e. the unequal distribution of *capital*, is the source of the specific effects of *capital*, i.e. the appropriation of profits and the power to impose the laws of functioning of the *field* most favourable to *capital* and its reproduction' (Bourdieu, 1986: 246). Thus although CEP conflates widening participation in HE with progress in developing social mobility, Bourdieu's insights illustrate the flaws in this assumed connection.

A Bourdieurian perspective on conversion factors

An individual's self, identity, aspirations and ultimately capabilities are developed in and through interaction with different fields. Indeed, individuals experience the interaction of diverse cultural norms, values, and power relations in the various fields they encounter. For example, bi-lingual skills may be developed in a multicultural home environment whereas in an educational setting an individual may be expected to use an 'additional language' to communicate rather than their primary language. The complex interaction of social circumstances in the development of the individual has been recognized in a range of sociological work (Bourdieu, 1986; Reay, 2001; Archer et al., 2003).

Figure 3.2 illustrates a conceptual model (based on the S1 and S2 research findings and drawing on the work of Ball et al., Robeyns, Bourdieu and others) which aims to highlight the dynamic interplay of key factors which influence the conversion of aspirations, capital and commodities into capabilities (Ball et al., 2000; Bourdieu and Passeron, 2000; Robeyns, 2005a). Stephen Ball et al.'s (2000) sociological work on young people's careers was helpful in developing my conceptualization of conversion factors as identified in the CA. Ball et al. identified three key 'arenas of action' or 'centres of choice' which they present using a Venn diagram illustrating the overlap between different arenas of young people's lives. The three arenas they identify broadly relate to family, work/education and leisure (Ball et al., 2000: 148).

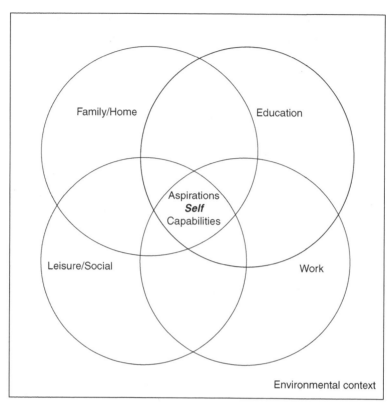

Figure 3.2 Framework of conversion factors influencing the development of aspirations and their conversion to capabilities and functionings

The four fields of education, family, work and social life/leisure identified are placed within a broader environmental context to draw attention to the interplay of these broader arenas and their roles in the development of the individual. Pierre Bourdieu's theory and frames of reference regarding his notions of habitus, capital and field were invaluable in this respect. Each arena or field may vary in its importance to a given individual at a particular point in time. For example, one student in my case study had moved to the United Kingdom from Somalia and spoke of the contrast of studying in a peacetime context compared to the conflict they had experienced in their home country.

Policy tends to overlook the way young people themselves perceive the different fields they participate in and the relative priorities they give to their roles in each. Education policy assumes a major role for education whereas a young person may perceive a different set of priorities foregrounding, for example, the fields of work, leisure or family rather than education. In relation to this point, the S2 survey data presented in Chapter 6 illuminate young people's engagement in the fields of paid work and domestic labour.

The individual's power relations with others in a given field may also vary and impact on other arenas. For example, if a young person feels under pressure from their employer to work extra hours this may impact on their position in the field of education by making it more difficult to meet the demands of college or school work. On the other hand the additional income from working may enable an individual to acquire symbolic capital in relation to the field of leisure relating to, for example, fashionable clothes, music and other symbols of youth culture. The conceptual framework acknowledges the individual's symbiotic, dynamic and changing relationship with the different fields they encounter. The research findings from studies S1 and S2 presented in this book draw attention to the interaction of individual habitus with social structures formed in and through interaction in different fields. This analysis moves forward from Robeyns' (2005a) stratified analysis of the three 'conversion factors' she describes as environmental characteristics, social characteristics and personal characteristics. While Robeyns (2005a: 99) indicates that it is necessary to consider, 'the whole social and institutional context that affects the conversion factors and also the capability set directly' she does not offer a theoretical approach for addressing this task. In addition, although Robeyns does specify that, 'material and non-material circumstances' may shape an individual's opportunity set over and above goods and services, she does not identify capital in this context. Hence the theoretical framework developed here, drawing on Bourdieu's concepts of habitus, capital and field, is able to supplement earlier analysis in this respect.

A synthesis of Sen and Bourdieu's key concepts

The synthesis of Sen's capability approach with Pierre Bourdieu's three concepts of habitus, capital and field led to the development of the SBAF. This allowed new connections to be made between the concepts of commodities, capital and capabilities. The theoretical synergy allows new questions to be asked about the nature of aspirations. Understanding of the individual habitus and the accumulation and activation of family capital help to illuminate the conversion factors influencing both aspiration formation and the transformation of aspirations into capabilities. The CA has been formulated historically from an economic perspective and the term, 'commodities' is used to describe the goods to be converted into capabilities (Sen, 1999a).

Bourdieu's work illustrates how individuals have access to different forms of capital through social interaction in different fields (Bourdieu, 1986). Bourdieu's interpretation of capital can be seen to extend economic views of commodities to incorporate cultural and symbolic capital as social commodities. Conversely, using the capability approach to understand the nature of conversion factors allows a reinterpretation of the way in which capital is transferred between individuals, particularly in the family. In addition, the Bourdieurian understanding of capital augments the capability approach and welfare economic notions of commodities. This theoretical synergy between Sen and Bourdieu is explored further in the later chapters of this book.

Conclusion

Sen's CA offers some ethical principles to apply in approaches to developing and evaluating systems of education. Bourdieu's sociological concepts provide an ideal partner to these organizing principles by offering tools for in-depth analysis and understanding of the social context in which education takes place. Bourdieu's 'logic of practice' offers valuable insights into the very physical movement of young people between family and education-oriented fields. The 'game' is played out quite visibly through these transitory movements of students to and from their homes and formalized places of learning. Bourdieu's concept of habitus opens a door of perception into the less visible world of agents' minds and decision-making processes. Bourdieu has been criticized for being overly deterministic, identifying elements of the habitus as unconscious and the societal structures as enduring constraints leading to the social reproduction of inequalities between social classes. However, Bourdieu's conceptualization of game-playing in the field is dynamic rather than static. Perhaps more importantly, Bourdieu's work offers us understandings of human action and interaction that allows the unconscious to become conscious. From this perspective, he indicates that through consciousness, resistance, struggle and change are possible. The challenge, I venture, is to decide whether the risks of consciousness, and the potential pursuit of change and resistance, are worth taking. This depends, at least to some extent, on whether policymakers and practitioners are willing to support the struggle of young learners. Sen's CA tells us more about the kind of equality we might wish to strive for in the pursuit of social justice. This is not only related to matters of social class and economic advantage but draws on a far more comprehensive view of the nature of human flourishing and an individual's freedom to pursue ways of being and doing they have reason to value.

Sen goes to some length to highlight the way in which individual freedoms impact on the possibilities for just social institutions and structures as well as vice versa. His position implies that, rather than attempting to produce a perfect institutional structure (an infinite task), it is more fruitful to focus on the lives people are *actually* living and to use this as the focus for reducing inequality (Sen, 1992, 2009). This contrasts with others such as Deneulin who argues that more attention should be given to 'transforming unjust structures' (Deneulin et al., 2006). The CA raises concerns about the relationship of the individual and the state. This is particularly with regard to how much autonomy and agency an individual should have to develop capabilities due to the potential impact on others and the constraints of social arrangements. Sen argues, 'There is deep complementarity between individual agency and social arrangements. It is important to give simultaneous recognition to the centrality of individual freedom and to the force of social influences on the extent and reach of individual freedom' (Sen, 1999b: xii).

Bourdieu's notions of habitus, capital and field are helpful in understanding the social influences referred to by Sen. The dissonance of personal habitus in a given field where one individual is asked to enter a field of unfamiliar sociocultural territory puts them at an immediate disadvantage. The question arises as to whether a particular field of action, such as education, can be reconstituted to be less threatening to individuals by reducing the dissonance between habitus and field *and therefore increasing capability*. In consequence we may ask whether low dissonance is more likely to create a setting where individuals can convert their capitals into capabilities.

Thus, the SBAF deepens understanding of the processes involved in the development of an individual's capabilities. Our freedoms are limited in the sense that from the beginning of life we do not choose our race, birthplace, nationality or gender. In other words we are not in a position to choose some of the fundamental variables upon which discrimination and inequality have been based for centuries. Individuals are born into different circumstances and the effects of this cannot be completely erased. In synthesizing the thinking of Sen and Bourdieu we may be able to develop an approach to social justice where policy makers and practitioners working with children and young people strive to ensure that as far as possible individuals are free to choose a life they value. This would need to involve acknowledging the inequalities produced by the interaction of different individuals' habitus in the broad field of education. The

SBAF is applied to the research presented in this book with regard to three key challenges. First, it is used to inform the challenge of developing an appropriate research methodology for exploring the concepts of aspirations and capabilities. Secondly this framework is used to understand the development and nature of aspirations. Thirdly the framework facilitates examination of the socially contextualized processes influencing the development of aspirations through to their transformation to capabilities. Bourdieu argued that, 'it is only by making a second break, this time with the illusion of the neutrality and independence of the school system with respect to the structure of class relations, that it becomes possible to question research into examinations so as to discover what examinations hide and what research into examinations only helps to hide by distracting inquiry from the elimination which takes place without examination' (Bourdieu et al., 2000: 141). The synthesis of Sen and Bourdieu's perspectives allows a new order of questions and enquiry to emerge that challenges the status quo and normative perceptions of educational processes.

4

Evolving Theory into Method

Introduction

Bourdieu's sociological concepts have been widely applied and there is a rich body of work to draw upon in developing a research methodology from a Bourdieurian perspective. There are, of course, challenges, but in this chapter I focus particularly on the application of the CA to empirical research as this is still very much an emerging area of expertise. First of all some points are made about the peculiarities of the CA on a generalized level, highlighting challenges as well as practical reflections. Then in the second part of the chapter the research methodologies are described for the two studies (S1 and S2) presented which explore young people's aspirations and capabilities.

Defining the evaluative space

Sen identifies 'capability' as a very important concept although he does not attempt to operationalize the concept for the purposes of research. It is deliberately left to the individual researcher to decide how best to approach their specific subject area (Sen, 1999a). The methodologies developed drawing on the capability perspective require a different kind of question to be asked about what constitutes quality and success in and through education. The capability approach asks us to reconsider what kind of equality we are pursuing and also whether equality is the most worthy goal of policy. 'The evaluation of inequality cannot but be purpose-dependent, and the important need is to provide an appropriate match between (1) the purposes of inequality evaluation, and (2) the choice of informational focus' (Sen, 1992: 71).

Researchers and theorists alike have been grappling for some time with the issue of how to measure capabilities especially as they are less tangible than functionings. The measurement of capabilities requires a different kind of data and informational focus compared to the measurement of functionings and more traditional indicators of development. Kuklys concluded from her survey of the literature that few attempts had been made to operationalize Sen's concept of capabilities (Kuklys, 2005: 9). She argued that, 'while theoretically attractive Sen's approach is difficult to operationalise empirically' (ibid., 2005: 7) and her observation echoes previous work by Sugden (1953, 1993) who highlighted disagreement about 'the nature of the good life' and how to value capability sets leading him to question how far Sen's framework is operational. This position has led to suggestions that functionings may need to be evaluated as a proxy for capabilities (Walker and Unterhalter, 2007: 16). Kuklys identified problems relating to deciding, first, what functionings are to be measured and, secondly, how this is to be done. Often research is driven by available datasets and limited funding and this is especially the case for large-scale international research on development issues such as poverty, health and education. A further difficulty that has been noted is the difficulty of meeting informational requirements due to a lack of relevant social indicators in many places (Alkire, 2005).[1] Kuklys' work also draws attention to the problem of comparing multi-dimensional measures and all of the issues she highlighted are compounded further when working in the 'space of potential achieved functionings [capabilities]' rather than achieved functionings (Kuklys, 2005: 7–8).

Research and the practical application of the CA in education has evolved rapidly over the last few years. A substantial body of methodology literature is building up with regard to the application of both Sen and Nussbaum's capability approaches. Recent contributions from Walker and Unterhalter (2007), Lessmann et al. (2011) and Biggeri et al. (2011) offer particularly helpful insights.

Terzi argues, 'the capability to be educated is fundamental and foundational to different capabilities to lead a good life'. She suggests a list of basic capabilities for educational functionings (2007: 37). However, it is unclear whether Terzi's list of basic capabilities for educational functionings has been derived through a democratic process. A capability perspective in education encourages evaluation to look beyond years spent in education or level of study to consider the risks and benefits to an individual's well-being and agency as a result of participation in education. Vaughan argues that educational processes can be viewed as functionings in themselves as well as being precursors or conversion factors in the development of future potential functionings (Vaughan, 2007: 114). For example, it could be argued that being able to read or write enables the expansion of other capabilities. However, such a measure does not take account of whether the teaching materials are a form of indoctrination or even in the primary language of the students.

Achieved well-being tells us little about the distribution of resources, opportunities and an individual's capabilities in converting resources and opportunities into achievements (Sen, 1992). Different individuals may be more or less able to make use of the same resource. As Robeyns writes, 'not everyone has the same rate of return on education. Given the same amount and quality of education, not every child or adult will to the same degree be able to use this education for income-generating activities' (Robeyns, 2006: 73). For example, Janet Raynor undertook research with adolescent girls in Bangladesh, vividly portraying some of the many real constraints acting on girls' capabilities to be educated. Barriers included personal safety while travelling to and from school, facilities for maintaining female hygiene at school and the reinforcement of the ascribed lower status of girls through schooling (Raynor, 2007: 186). The capability approach demands that quantitative indicators of educational achievement are substantiated with more detailed analysis of the nature of children's participation in educational processes in relation to notions of freedom, equity and social justice.

In another example of CA research on education, Melanie Walker, drawing on empirical data from a South African study, puts forward a provisional list of educational capabilities with a special focus on gender equality in South Africa (2007: 189–90). She readily notes that the suggested capabilities are not weighted and the issue of valuation of the various capabilities (regarding, for example, autonomy,[2] knowledge and social relations) is not addressed. Thus, although progressing the idea of developing a list of capabilities for gender quality, Walker leaves fertile territory for further work.

Williams (2002) comments on the difficulty in ranking the capabilities people have reason to value. He argues it is difficult to show the same respect for all individuals while suggesting inequalities in some capabilities are more important than others. Sen has tried to show how ranking of capabilities may be possible using partial orderings but this has not convinced all his critics. For example, Qizilbash argues, 'Sen fails to give a complete account of interpersonal comparisons' (Qizilbash, 1996: 147). More recent work by Comim (2008), Anand et al. (2009) and others shows more optimism in addressing the issue of making interpersonal comparisons based on both capabilities and functionings.[3]

Mario Biggeri (2007) has focused on the child as whole rather than specifically formal educational experiences and he thus brings some useful insights to exploring the nature of child well-being from a capability perspective. Reporting findings from empirical research undertaken with children in India, Italy and Uganda, Biggeri identifies issues specifically relevant to children's capabilities. These are broadly related to the influence of parents and other adults on the development of children's capabilities, factors linked to the life cycle and maturity of children, and the potential of children to acts as agents of change in society in adulthood. Biggeri reports a useful attempt to operationalize the CA for work with children. Specifically the researchers attempt to overcome the issue of adapted preferences.[4] This is done by asking children to reason reflectively about the opportunities children in general should have throughout life, rather than asking about the individual's own life.

In concluding this review of the empirical application of the CA to research in education, eight key questions that I think are useful in orientating the researcher are summarized in Table 4.1, together with some key points to consider.

Table 4.1 Summary of key issues for research using a capability approach

Research issue	Points to consider
1. What is the purpose of the inequality evaluation? (Sen, 1992)	This question can help to identify what kind of equality is of interest.
2. What is the choice of informational focus? (Sen, 1992)	Is the individual or a group the unit of evaluation? Sen identifies four possible points of informational focus relating to well-being freedom, well-being achievement, agency freedom and agency achievement.
3. Should there be a threshold for any specified capabilities?	Sen and Nussbaum have divergent views. A threshold minimum may have an instrumental value in helping to inform policy and practice.
4. Are functionings to be measured?	Which functionings? How will they be measured? (threshold, individual episodes, over time, repetition) What are the limitations?
5. Are capabilities to be measured?	Consider evaluating the capability to aspire (CTA) and the capability to realise (CTR) aspirations as starting points for evaluating an individual's full capability set. Consider language and mode of communication of concepts to research participants.
6. Is functioning an adequate proxy for capability?	Functionings do not reflect the individual's full capability set and the intrinsic freedom to choose.

Table 4.1 Cont'd

Research issue	Points to consider
7. Is a list of context-specific capabilities to be generated?	Possibly follow Robeyn's procedural approach (2005a). Create opportunity for democratic deliberation of suggested capabilities facilitating a strong voice for all stakeholders.
8. Are capabilities to be weighted?	How can the differential weighting of capabilities be justified?

In the light of the issues raised, in the following section an overview is given of the methodology used for the two studies I undertook to explore the nature of aspirations and their connections with capabilities.

Applying the capability approach

Applying the capability approach to the study of young people's aspirations was challenging because, first, the concepts and language were unfamiliar to the young people and educational practitioners with whom I worked. Therefore the research strategy needed to incorporate a preliminary phase that aimed to find a vocabulary for communicating the necessary capability concepts. Secondly, it was challenging to operationalize the concepts of capability and well-being freedom in relation to the research questions.

Study S1 – Bradford

The fieldwork for study S1 was undertaken at an 11–18 state comprehensive school in south Bradford in 2003–4. The pseudonym Northmead is used to refer to the school. The S1 study aimed to explore first of all how students perceived their aspirations and needs. Secondly, S1 aimed to further understanding of how widening participation policy could support the aspirations of students and their needs in achieving them.

Background

Bradford has an unusual demographic profile with a high proportion of ethnic minorities and a large population from low socio-economic groups (SEGs). The population of Bradford is very multicultural with proportionally four times as many Asians and five times as many Muslims as in the national population. A very large number of school-leavers from Bradford who went on to higher education at the time of the S1 study remained in Bradford. The students either went to Bradford University, Bradford College or commuted to Leeds or Huddersfield while continuing to live at home with parents. In some schools over 90 per cent of students continuing to higher education stayed in Bradford (Bradford LEA, 2003).

At the school where the S1 study took place, situated in South Bradford, a third of the students were eligible for Free School Meals (FSM) and this was typical of the local area. In the sixth form at the same school around two-thirds of students were eligible for Educational Maintenance Allowances (EMA) which are means-tested on parental income. Bradford also has a relatively young population compared to national demographic trends with considerably more young people under 30 (National Census, 2001). Relatively few students go on to higher education and unemployment is above average. Table 4.2 gives some basic national comparisons regarding employment, qualifications and home environment and, although now dated, this reflects the demography at the time of the S1 study (2003–4).

Table 4.2 Socio-economic data comparison for the S1 study

Area	No qualifications 16–74-year-olds (%)	Employment of 16–74-year-olds (%)	Homes without central heating (%)
England	30	60	8.5
Bradford	35	56	23
South Bradford	38	40	N/A

Source: National Census, 2001.

Population and sampling

The population for S1 included all students in Year 10 (aged 14–15) and all Year 12 students (aged 16–17) studying for either Advanced Vocational Certificates of Education (AVCE's) or Advanced Subsidiary (AS) qualifications at Northmead. Year 10 was chosen because it included a wide cross-section of students in a year group prior to Year 11 when students can legally choose to leave school.[5] It was likely that this cohort would have a range of needs and aspirations perhaps more diverse than in later years. Year 12 students who were studying AVCE and AS courses formed the target group for post-16 Aimhigher Widening Participation activities at Northmead and were chosen mainly to see if there were any significant differences in the dynamic of aspirations and needs between Year 10 and those students who stayed on beyond the compulsory school-leaving age.

Research strategy

Initially informal discussions were held with students in years 9, 11 and 13 (aged 13–18) at Northmead in order to operationalize the concepts of 'aspiration' and 'need'. Students brainstormed the meanings of the terms and considered other words which they felt had similar meaning. Further discussion revealed that students identified different types of aspirations and needs relating to the short, medium and long term. Students appeared to perceive different degrees of control over the achievement of aspirations and longer-term objectives seemed to be associated with greater uncertainty. When considering what students need in order to achieve their aspirations I divided this into broadly two aspects. One aspect considered what factors may help an individual achieve their aspirations and the other considered what barriers may prevent an individual from achieving their aspirations.

S1 Preliminary group interviews

Four group interviews were conducted at Northmead as pilot work for both the questionnaires and interviews. Group interviews (small groups of 6–8) were conducted with Year 10 and 12 students to explore their perceptions of the concepts of 'aspirations' and 'needs' and to facilitate the construction of a questionnaire suitable for this population. They provided useful experience in communicating with young people and 'tuning in' to their sociocultural environment. The groups consisted of six to eight students each, one male and one female group from each year group. A semi-structured questioning approach was used and the emphasis was on the exchanges between myself and the interviewees as well the exchanges between participants. The aim was to explore the concepts of aspirations and needs by encouraging free group discussion (Litoselliti, 2003).

S1 main study

A self-completion questionnaire was designed to gather data on how students perceived their aspirations and needs in relation to the development and achievement of their aspirations. A range of variables were used as indicators of socio-economic background defined by eligibility for FSM,[6] receipt of EMA and whether a parent had been to university (Kysel, 1992: 88; Foskett et al.,

2003). This was seen as preferable to other methods such as postcodes and parental occupation since quite a few students have more than one address and occupations are notoriously difficult to link to income and social class. The survey was completed by all students in Year 10 at the school and also all Year 12 studying for AVCE's and/or AS qualifications as described above. It aimed to explore student perceptions of aspirations and needs at a broad level and also to identify individual students for in-depth interview. The survey was comprised of mainly quantitative Likert-scale and fixed response questions with a small number of open questions (Oppenheim, 1996). In total 239 students completed the S1 survey which generated an 82% response rate. Fifty-three per cent of the sample were female and 47% male. Thirty-one per cent of the survey participants were eligible for FSM and 71% were eligible for EMA which are both means-tested as described earlier. The relatively high proportions of students receiving benefits in the sample population is indicative of the multiple socio-economic deprivation of the catchment area for Northmead. Individual interviews with Year 12 students aimed to follow up on the survey data to enrich understanding of how students perceived their aspirations and needs in achieving them.

S2 study – Sheffield

S2 concentrated on identifying the factors that reduce or enhance an individual's well-being freedom and hence their capability in relation to realizing aspirations. Four indicators were identified which could illuminate factors which influence an individual's well-being freedom. They include, first, the perceived agency of the individual; secondly, the range and significance of perceived barriers and constraints; thirdly, the range and significance of perceived needs and, fourthly, the adaptation of preferences by young people.

The S2 study was conducted in Sheffield, England from 2006–8. The study aimed to understand the nature of participants' aspirations and the factors that helped and hindered the transformation of aspirations into capabilities in response to widening participation policy in England. The S2 study built on the findings of the S1 study. Further key aims were to learn more about young people's experiences and participation in education in relation to notions of equity and inclusion. There was a particular focus on students' ideas about HE and their decision-making processes regarding post-school and college transitions.

Background

Sheffield is a large city with a population of over 500,000 situated in South Yorkshire, England. There are two universities in the city, the University of Sheffield and Sheffield Hallam University. Together they have a total student population of over 50,000. Sheffield has an industrial past, becoming famous for the production of steel and cutlery which was exported worldwide before falling into economic decline in the 1980s and early 1990s. Over the last few decades the city has redeveloped with new businesses being attracted to the area. Like other large cities in England, Sheffield is socio-economically divided with affluent residential areas situated in the south-west of the city and households with multiple social deprivation being predominantly situated in the north-east of the city. Sheffield was selected for the S2 study because the contrast between the two sides of the city is more extreme than elsewhere. It was felt this provided a strong context to explore the generic and unique features of aspiration formation and their transformation into capabilities. In 2005, the Higher Education Council for England (HEFCE) published a report on 'Young Participation in Higher Education'. The report showed that the Yorkshire and Humberside region, where the city of Sheffield is situated, nationally had the second lowest Young Participation Rate (YPR) including all forms of HE.[7] Research by Kay and Walker (2006), highlighted that Brightside 'had the lowest participation rate in England' while 'Sheffield Hallam constituency had the third highest participation rate in England' (Kay and Walker, 2006: 6). Young people in Sheffield Brightside were much more likely than their Sheffield Hallam counterparts to be eligible for means-tested Free School Meals (an indicator of socio-economic status) and much more likely to have recognized Special Educational Needs. Less than one in three 15-year-olds in Sheffield Brightside achieved five or more A*-C's at GCSE in 2005 compared to more than 2 in 3 of their Sheffield Hallam counterparts (Kay et al., 2006). HEFCE estimated that in this region only around 1 in 4 young people went on to HE at age 18 or 19 and a significant number of these did not achieve a qualification at this level (HEFCE, 2005). In the north-east constituency of Brightside, only 6% of 18-year-olds accepted places in HE in 2002–4 despite this area having 19% of the Sheffield Year 11 cohort.[8] By stark contrast, just 12% of the city's Year 11 cohort lived in the south-west constituency of Sheffield Hallam and yet 33% of 18-year-olds from this area accepted HE places in 2002–4 (www.dfes.gov.uk, accessed 12 June 2006).

S2 population and sampling

At the time of the S2 study (2006–8), the geographical layout of post-16 educational institutions in Sheffield was such that the only schools with sixth forms were situated in the south-west of the city in Sheffield Hallam and the neighbouring areas. The north-east of the city had two large sixth form colleges which both had links with secondary schools in the Brightside and Hillsborough areas. Thus, although students could choose where to study, the vast majority attended their local school sixth form or college reflecting the socio-economic make-up of the surrounding areas.

The S2 study involved four schools and colleges. Sites included two school sixth forms in the Sheffield Hallam area (Goldsmiths and Speedwell) and two sixth form colleges in the Brightside area (Riverdale and Sherwood). The sites cannot be seen as statistically representative of secondary schools in Sheffield generally or indeed elsewhere. However the aim of the S2 study was to provide more detailed understandings of what I have termed, the 'capability to aspire' (CTA) and the 'capability to realise' (CTR) aspirations by looking at these two contrasting areas within the same city.

S2 research strategy

Focus groups, a large-scale survey, group and individual interviews were used to learn more about the aspirations of sixth formers and the opportunities and support they have in exploring and pursuing these aspirations. Using the SBAF, the findings were considered in relation to current UK government policy to widen participation in higher education.

Preliminary S2 study

The group interviews were conducted as pilot work for both the questionnaire survey and interviews. Bogdan and Biklen (1992: 100) have found that group interviews can be useful in generating a wider range of responses than in individual interviews and this was what was required for the development of the survey. This method has also been found useful for working with young people where the aim is to encourage participants to, 'challenge and extend each other's ideas and to introduce new ideas into the discussion' (Cohen et al., 2003: 287).

The group interviews provided the opportunity to become familiar with the research sites and to talk informally with students and staff about my research area. It was important to develop a common language for communicating with young people of different abilities about the concepts I wanted to explore in my research relating to, for example, notions of aspiration, opportunity and barriers to achieving aspirations. The group interviews provided useful experience in communicating with young people and 'tuning in' to their sociocultural environment. In terms of my substantive research topics I was able to learn a great deal about the kind of terminology and questioning that the young people could relate to. For example, the role of Connexions Advisors[9] emerged as a major feature of young people's lives at school or college in terms of addressing (or not addressing) their needs in relation to their aspirations. The data generated helped in the construction of the main survey instrument by providing insights into appropriate language for the age and ability groups targeted by the research.

In total, 84 students took part in group interviews for S2 made up of 59 Year 12 students and 25 Year 10 students. This included 53 females and 31 males. 28 were from Sheffield Hallam and 56 were from Brightside and the surrounding area. The interviews were conducted over a four-week period from mid-June to mid-July 2006.

In the group interviews I explored different strategies to learn about how young people see their futures (and hence their aspirations) based on previous work in this area. I explored young people's perceptions of their ideal and expected futures (Marjoribanks, 1998); their possible, impossible and feared selves (Oyserman and Markus, 1990) and their hopes and fears for the future (Seginer, 1988). As an introduction to the group interviews I used different forms of stimulus material to facilitate this process and an example is shown in Appendix I. Drawing on work by Caviglioli and Harris (2001) I also used mind mapping to encourage young people to think about different topics. Participants were given a sheet of paper with just the think bubble and asked to map out their ideas in note form. I have included an example of a higher education mind map in Appendix II. I have previously found that young people often feel more confident speaking in a group situation if they have been given a little time to gather their thoughts initially. I used a semi-structured questioning approach with the emphasis on the exchanges between the interviewees and myself as well the exchanges between participants. I was interested to see what areas the young people introduced in relation to the research areas and tried to be flexible in response to their contributions. The overall aims were to explore factors influencing the development and realization of participants' aspirations and to find a tangible way of assessing capabilities in relation to aspiration.

Three school sixth forms agreed to take part in the pilot. Sixth form pastoral staff were each asked to obtain individual survey responses from around

20 young people in Year 12. In total around 60 surveys were completed. The schools were situated outside of the research area to avoid sample contamination with one situated in Bradford, one in South Wales and one in Essex. This was convenience sampling based on personal contacts with school sixth forms but included contrasting socio-economic areas reflecting the contrasting research sites used for the main case study.

Main S2 study

A sample of 580 young people took part in the survey drawn from the two schools with sixth forms in south-west Sheffield (jointly referred to as Westside) and two sixth form colleges in north-west Sheffield (jointly referred to as Eastside). Over 50% of the year cohort in each institution were included in the sample and the samples aimed to be broadly institutionally representative in terms of age, gender, ethnicity, socio-economic factors, ability and intention to continue to HE. A survey response rate of over 90% was achieved in each institution.

In order to generate possible questionnaire items relating to the S2 aims questions used in previous research were considered[10] (National Centre for Social Research, 2002, 2003; Farmer, 2003; Hart, 2004; Yeshanew et al., 2005; Equal Opportunities Commission, 2006). The questionnaire consisted mostly of closed questions with a few open questions. The closed questions mainly required students to give responses using a Likert scale. In order to assess socio-economic background a range of variables were used as 'traditional' indicators defined by eligibility for FSM, receipt of EMA and whether a parent had been to university (Kysel, 1992; Foskett, Dyke and Maringe, 2004). This work was reviewed by considering a variety of forms of social difference rather than solely focusing on social class. For example, Marjoribanks' (1998) work and the HEFCE study of Young Participation (2005) utilized broad ranges of indicators which were helpful in informing the development of a number of other social difference indicators. Alongside traditional indicators of socio-economic status such as FSM eligibility, for example, questionnaire items were included to indicate variations in young participants' involvement in paid work, personal income from paid work and domestic labour. I also sought information on the accumulation of family cultural *capital* in terms of familial experience of HE. The questionnaire was refined following piloting in three school sixth forms situated outside of the research area to avoid sample contamination (N=60).

The student questionnaire was used to identify individual students from each year group who were willing to volunteer to participate in individual follow-up interviews in the main study. A combination of 23 male and female participants, including some planning to go on to high education and others who were not, took part in the individual interview phase.

In 2007–8 interviews were undertaken (during the academic year following the survey completion) and consisted of a short telephone interview. In some cases communication was mainly by email since the young people had left school or college since the start of the study. Interviews aimed to find out what individual interviewees had actually gone on to do once they left school or college. It was difficult to contact all young people who had take part in the original interviews but a response rate of over 50% was achieved.

Reporting data from the S2 study

Each of the four institutions in the S2 study was given a pseudonym. The two schools with sixth forms in the affluent south-west of Sheffield are referred to as 'Goldsmiths' and 'Speedwell'. Together, they are jointly referred to as, 'Westside'. The two colleges situated in areas of multiple social deprivation in the north-east of Sheffield are referred to as, 'Sherwood' and 'Riverdale'. Together the two colleges are jointly referred to as, 'Eastside'.

In reporting data from the S2 study the term 'significant' is used throughout the analysis to denote statistically significant differences between the specified groups. See Appendix III for a table of statistical analyses carried out on the S2 survey data. For ease of reference Appendix IV contains a summary of the 23 interviewees that participated in the S2 individual interviews. Information is given regarding their institution, HE intentions, whether they were eligible for EMA or FSM and their ethnicity.

Overview of the S2 dataset

Over 90% of the survey sample (N_2=580)[11] was aged from 17–18 years with the remaining students being 19 years old and mainly based in the two colleges. The sample was fairly evenly split in terms of gender with 45% males and 55% females. The majority of students (72%) described their ethnicity as 'white UK' with the remaining individuals spread across several ethnic groups including 8% who described themselves as 'Asian' and 6% who described themselves as 'black'.

The ethnic groups used in the analysis are white, black, Asian and other ethnic groups. These groupings were determined after discussion with the group interviewees. There was significant variation in the mix of young people from different ethnic backgrounds in the four institutions studied. The variable for ethnicity was recoded into four main ethnic groups including self-defined whites, blacks, Asians and a fourth category of all individuals who had identified themselves as being from other ethnic groups. Missing values were omitted from the calculations.

Almost half (48%) of the general population indicated that they were eligible for EMA. Nine per cent of the survey sample reported that they were eligible for Free School Meals with significant variation across the institutions. Regarding family educational background, two out of three young people in the overall sample knew other members of their family who had studied at university. However, less than one in three students in the general sample indicated having a father who had been to university and the figure was similar with regard to maternal education.

The following three chapters discuss findings from the S1 and S2 studies. Chapter 5 concentrates on the findings related to understanding the nature of aspirations and their formation. Chapter 6 connects with Chapter 5 by examining the conversion factors influencing the transformation of aspirations into capabilities. Then in Chapter 7 consideration is given to the factors influencing young people's agency in choosing HE or alternative pathways once they leave school or college.

The Nature of Aspirations

Introduction

The nature of aspiring is different, though related to 'imagining' which has been explored by Nussbaum (2001) and others. Imagination is a creative, ethereal concept which may be neither goal-oriented nor related to the self. Individual aspiration, in contrast, is both goal-oriented and concerns the future of the self or the agency of the self in relation to goals concerning others. Whereas imagination may be helpful in developing the *capability to aspire* (CTA) it is not a substitute in these respects. Understanding the nature of aspiring tells us more comprehensively about the freedom an individual has to develop capabilities and to choose to pursue a future they have reason to value.

It was found from the S2 study that aspiring can be viewed in two different ways. On one hand, aspiring can be seen as a *functioning* or in other words as a state of being or doing. In this sense, the process of aspiring can be constructed as an active endeavour undertaken through abstract thinking and developed further through verbal, written or other forms of creative and physical expression. However, the freedom and possibility of aspiring can also be viewed as a *capability* which individuals may enjoy to differing degrees. In this sense we can look at an individual's capability to aspire as a freedom in its own right and as a gateway to enabling further future capabilities and functionings. This is a significant point because if an individual has limited opportunities to develop their aspirations freely, through external expression as well as unfettered private thoughts, then their freedom in choosing ways of being and doing (well-being and agency achievement) they have reason to value in the future is likely to be compromised.

The *capability to aspire* and the functioning of *aspiring* are different. The constraints young people face mean at times they are not free to aspire although they may still have a limited range of aspirations. It has been argued that the notion of adaptation can be applied to aspirations as well as to preferences (as discussed in Chapter 2). The functioning of aspiring to certain (more widely accepted) futures may be more acceptable than others and so these may be the aspirations (moulded or adapted) that prevail while other less conventional 'latent' aspirations never have the opportunity to emerge. For example, a young person may be very interested in seeing circus skills performed, but this interest never has the possibility of evolving from interest to related aspirations (e.g. becoming a circus performer), due in part, to the influence of social norms. So an individual may demonstrate the *functioning of aspiring* by saying that they aspire to go onto higher education but they may have experienced limited *capability to aspire* to other ways of being and doing they may have reason to value. Thus Sen's conceptualization of an individual's '*capability set*' is partially determined by what I have termed an individual's '*aspiration set*' and for this reason the capability to aspire can be viewed as a meta-capability.

The relationship between aspirations and capabilities

Not all aspirations are converted into capabilities and fewer still are realized as functionings, immediately or at all. This understanding contrasts with the way the government constructs aspirations as a linear process where functionings are constructed as *determined* by and *constrained* by aspirations. The strategy of aspiration-raising, under the auspices of widening participation, is used as a means to encourage young people to function in a certain kind of way, in other words, to apply to university. By contrast, Sen's conceptualization of capabilities leaves the functioning choice open to the individual and does not assume that a capability will necessarily become a functioning. The capability to aspire may be nurtured or constrained through relations with others and therefore how the individual is socially situated is critical in influencing the 'capability to aspire'. An individual's aspiration set in turn underpins the possibilities for the development of many future capabilities. Thus, building a bridge connecting aspirations and capabilities in an analytical framework can inform both theory and practice.

The functioning of aspiring

Previous research and policy have constructed the notion of aspiration as relating primarily to educational and career-related issues (Marjoribanks, 1998, 2002; DfE, 2009). Past and present governments in the United Kingdom have tended to adopt a deterministic approach towards raising aspirations, orienting learners towards the pursuit of credentials in the form of qualifications driven by national economic and social concerns. The evidence from S1 and S2 regarding the variety of aspirations expressed by students suggests that moral judgements are being made about which aspirations should take preference.

In the next section of this chapter findings from the S1 study illuminate the multi-dimensional nature of aspirations. Key factors which helped and hindered the realization of aspiration are identified. Following this, analysis of the S2 data extends the findings from S1, culminating in the development of a model of an individual's aspiration set.

The S2 findings indicated that young people have variable opportunities to explore and develop their aspirations. This was strongly associated with their orientation towards HE application. Those students who indicated that they planned to apply for HE generally had access to greater institutional support in school or college. Key conversion factors influencing the CTA are identified. Later in this chapter, these factors are explored further through the voices of the young people in the S2 study.

Study S1 – Bradford

Understanding aspirations

In the following section findings from the S1 study on the complex nature of aspirations are presented. These findings provided the foundations of the S2 study which is presented thereafter. Appendix IV contains a summary of profiles for the individuals interviewed in S2 for reference.

The nature of aspirations

It was concluded from S1 that 'aspiration' is a *dynamic and multi-dimensional* concept. Students described hundreds of different aspirations relating to many aspects of their lives and extending beyond purely educational and career aspirations. Aspirations identified related to career, educational, financial, environmental, religious, community, social status and identity goals. In general, young S1 research participants attached high levels of importance to all of the aspirations identified. The findings indicated that individuals simultaneously held a range of aspirations and the definition of aspirations as 'high' or 'low' becomes increasingly problematic when this is taken into account. The Coalition's widening participation policy for England devalues aspirations that are not related to pursuing a higher education by implying that alternative aspirations are somehow lower in a socially constructed hierarchy. Ranking aspirations as 'high' or 'low' is both difficult and controversial as they frequently do not fit readily onto a hierarchy of qualifications or length of time in education as is traditionally implied by government interpretations of 'high' and 'low' aspirations. Whereas it would be possible to say that a degree is a higher level of qualification than a General Certificate of Secondary Education (GCSE), based on a hierarchy of validated qualifications, it is very difficult to rank different types of aspirations against one another. For example, who is to say that wanting to be a good Muslim is a higher or lower aspiration than wanting to leave home against parents' wishes to study at university? Similarly, who is to say that aspiring to be a dog handler is a higher or lower aspiration than wanting to work in catering? While individuals were able to rank their own aspirations as more or less important to one another the findings indicated that it is problematic for others to rank an individual's aspirations as being 'high' or 'low' as the aspirations did not comprise a single scale or hierarchy of valued ways of being and doing.

In promoting human flourishing, it may be beneficial to support young people in generating a broad capability set containing a minimum number of opportunities for an individual to pursue ways of being and doing they have reason to value. In order to meet Sen's criteria of the importance of being able to choose between alternative combinations of functionings an individual has reason to value this requires a minimum of at least three elements within the capability set but more would clearly be encouraged. In this case, the specific capabilities to be expanded are not prescribed. Rather the argument is that well-being freedom stems from an individual developing a capability set from which they can choose between alternative combinations of functionings they have reason to value.

The S1 findings showed evidence of students tending to have several concurrent aspirations that ranged across the short, medium and long term. For example, a student might want to 'pass GCSE's' but also want to 'get married and have children' while 'becoming stronger in faith'. Similarly, there was evidence that students often hold conflicting aspirations within one area of aspiration such as career or family life. This is epitomized by one student participant who stated, 'I would like to be an accountant or tattoo artist'. Individual's responses showed that often a number of their aspirations were connected in some way. For example, a student may aspire to pass their driving test in order to achieve a personal aspiration of greater independence. Educational aspirations frequently centred on achieving certain grades and qualifications in order to pursue particular career aspirations. Increasing confidence and maintaining motivation were frequently cited personal aspirations and in the interviews students connected these aspirations to the achievement of educational and career aspirations.

Changing nature of aspirations

The S1 survey findings (N_1=239) showed evidence that many students' aspirations had changed considerably. Around one third of the questionnaire sample reported that their aspirations had 'changed a lot' over the previous year (with the groups most likely to change aspirations including boys, Asians and Year 12 students).

The reasons for aspiration changes are complex and difficult to explain being dependent on a range of factors. The S1 interviews suggested that the interviewees' aspirations had all been subject to some degree of change and this was echoed by many of the S2 interviews. For example, one young person in S1 commented, 'I wanted to be a hairdresser, and then I wanted to be a mathematics teacher, and then I wanted to be an English teacher, and then I wanted to be a lawyer and now I'm a bit unsure what I want to do'. It seems that sometimes aspirations change over time and sometimes students accept and reject the same aspiration a number of times. For example, Paula, an S1 interviewee commented, 'Sometimes I don't want to go to Uni' and then a week later I do, do you know? Just change me mind all the time . . .'. The degree of change also seems to vary from being frequent and extreme to more minor modifications.

The primary explanations for aspiration change given by the six Year 12 (aged 16–17) individual interviewees in S1 related to three broad areas. First, family aspirations and restrictions were influential in shaping and changing young people's aspirations. Secondly, interviewees' perceptions of their subject ability at school or college, their examination results and their perceived aptitude for particular careers were also reported as significant in shaping aspirations. Finally, work experience opportunities, organized through school and colleges offered insights into different careers either strengthening or weakening careers aspirations in those specific areas. Clearly, the small number of interviews in S1 means that generalizations cannot be made from these findings regarding the primary causes of aspiration change on a large scale. However, the important finding is the dimension of change among young people's aspirations and the frequency and degree of change across the whole sample. This dimension of change is not reflected in government policy directives in England. The government's widening participation agenda stands at odds with the phenomenon of change in aspirations since the policy is oriented towards students maintaining particular academic educational aspirations (e.g. to study at university) from as early as primary school age.

There was evidence from the small S1 individual interview sample that there were reasons perceived by young people as positive and negative influences on their aspiration changes. The reasons for change can be depicted as 'conversion factors' in the development of aspirations drawing on Sen's CA. The finding that different aspirations are often connected and the finding that students generally rated all types of aspirations highly have important policy implications. They suggest the importance of taking a holistic view of individuals and their aspirations, because achieving career aspirations may depend on achieving educational aspirations which in turn may hinge on certain personal aspirations such as gaining more confidence.

Agency and aspirations

The S1 findings indicated that while sometimes individuals may develop aspirations of their own volition in other cases they are persuaded towards particular aspirations by others. In the interviews there was evidence of some teachers guiding students towards or away from certain aspirations. There were also instances where an individual's aspirations conflicted with the wishes of significant others, and parents in particular. The way in which aspirations are generated, together with factors which help and hinder students, may have an effect on the agency an individual has to achieve their aspirations and this is illustrated further in Figure 5.1.

The degree of agency an individual has in achieving their aspirations seems to depend on a range of factors including factors which help and hinder them as well as their sense of ownership of the aspiration. Four broad levels of aspirations were identified in relation to agency. *Independent* aspirations which a student reached of their own volition were seen as giving the individual the greatest degree of agency in relation to their aspirations. *Shared* aspirations had a lower level of agency for the individual because they were shared with others such as parents or teachers and so the exact nature of the aspiration and how it might be achieved were more open to negotiation. The third level of aspiration identified

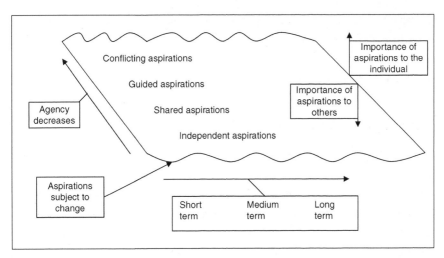

Figure 5.1 Dynamic multi-dimensional model of aspirations

Source: Hart, 2004: 66.

in terms of individual agency was a *guided* aspiration where the individual was guided towards certain aspirations. Finally, the level of aspiration with the lowest agency for the individual which was identified in the findings was *conflicting* aspirations, where the individual did not agree with the aspirations significant others had for them (Hart, 2004).

In terms of policy implications it would seem that encouraging individuals to identify their own aspirations may be a more ethical approach rather than guiding students towards aspirations predetermined by government policy. Over the last few years there has been a notable shift in policy emphasis to give greater consideration to the role of vocational training, apprenticeships, internships and employer's training responsibilities alongside HE opportunities. However, this expansion of post-16 routes has been driven by the economic 'crisis' and the perceived needs of economic growth rather than concern for individual well-being. The achievement of a balanced range of opportunities for young people beyond HE is far from fruition and the Coalition government in England has remarked on entrenched disparities that have failed to yield to previous policy initiatives (Gove, 2008; DfE, 2009; BIS, 2011a, 2011d).

Study S2 – Sheffield

Study S2 provided an opportunity to examine the nature of aspirations identified in S1 in greater detail. In the following section a typology of aspirations is described, drawing on examples from the S2 survey and interview data. In particular, aspirations were considered in relation to Sen's notion of capability and well-being freedom. This revealed a fundamental connection between the development of aspirations and the expansion of an individual's capability set.

A typology of aspirations

The data from S2 indicated that the aspirations young people openly express are not necessarily their only aspirations and they may not reflect their 'true' aspirations.[1] Four principal types of aspirations were discerned from the S2 study findings. These consisted of *revealed, concealed, adapted* and *apparent* aspirations. In addition, stages in the development of aspirations were identified, moving from *latent* (not yet formed) aspirations to *true* (actual) aspirations. In the middle stage of development true aspirations may be adapted or changed later potentially leading to the transformation of these aspirations into capabilities. Progress of aspiration development through the stages is not guaranteed and some aspirations may either fail to thrive in the early stages of formation or fail to be transformed into capabilities in the later stages.

Each is discussed in turn with examples from the S2 survey and interview data. The aspiration typology that I have developed is linked to and draws upon social choice theory that identifies revealed and adaptive preferences and I am indebted to the prior scholarship in that field (Berlin, 1979; Sen, 1982; Elster, 1983; Arrow, Sen and Suzumura, 1997).

Revealed aspirations

Revealed aspirations are those aspirations an individual has shared with others.

In terms of the overall S2 survey sample (N_2=580), three out of four (77%) young people reported wanting to go onto higher education. This was comprised of 55% who said that they wanted to go straight on to university, on completion of current studies, and a further 12% who reported that they would like to go on to university following a gap year.

One in twenty young people surveyed reported they would like to get a job immediately following completion of their current studies at school or college. Four out of five (82%) of those students intending to seek immediate employment were attending the Eastside Colleges. Among these students, Eastside students were significantly more likely to ideally wish to seek employment directly on leaving college.

Table 5.1 illustrates the *functioning* of aspiring by indicating some of the expressed aspirations reported by the young interviewees. 'Expressed' aspiration is the term used to describe the range of aspirations revealed to me in the course of the individual interviews. These expressions may include previously revealed, concealed and apparent aspirations and hence the term 'expressed' aspirations is used as an overarching term to reflect the various types of aspirations, specifically in the research context. It also shows how some individuals expressed concurrent aspirations, more general or more specific aspirations, such as finance, family and geographically focused aspirations. Less-focused aspirations, such as, 'having fun' might be achieved in different ways. Others, such as, 'becoming a midwife overseas', require specific entry qualifications, training and experience.

An example of revealed aspirations is used to illustrate how a combination of factors may help to support an individual in developing and realizing their aspirations. The confidence to reveal aspirations becomes one part of a much bigger picture. The example concerns Rosa (white, female, Speedwell) who at the time of the interview was studying for six A2 subjects having successfully

Table 5.1 Expressed interviewee aspirations from S2

Individual/ Institution	Examples of expressed aspirations
Sarah Goldsmiths	To be a jazz performer.
Lisa Speedwell	To join a dance company and travel internationally.
John Speedwell	To live at home. To continue caring for his grandmother.
Michael Speedwell	To 'learn and earn', working his way up in a healthcare role.
Rita Riverdale	To have 'fun' and 'play'. To travel around the UK. To move, work, learn to drive and buy a van. Possibly go to university to study later in life. To study at Swansea University because it is by the sea.
Salma Sherwood	To be an animator. To become a primary teacher.
Aisha Sherwood	To be a midwife overseas. To go to Sheffield Hallam University to do adult nursing diploma.
Martha Sherwood	To join the Police Force. To undertake an apprenticeship in retail.

completed six AS Levels in Year 12. In terms of family life, Rosa talks about the support she has received from her mum and extended family, although she has not seen her father since she was 6 years old. For example, her mum helped to collect information about higher education. Rosa's grandparents are both from a teaching background and her aunt is a geologist and they have all been 'quite involved' in supporting Rosa. Rosa also talks about the individualized support and inspiration she has received from teachers at school. For example Rosa describes how in Year 10 she had, 'a wonderful Chemistry teacher . . . and I understood everything . . . I decided the subject is wonderful and I had to carry it on . . .'. Another teacher supported Rosa's aspiration to self-study English Language in addition to her school studies. In addition, Rosa described how she was able to get access to a quiet study area at lunchtime, commenting, 'I know the Technology staff very well'. Rosa aspired to study Chemistry at Oxford University and in the future she said she would consider studying for a PhD in Chemistry. In the follow-up interview, in 2008, Rosa reported that she was enjoying being in her second year at Oxford and she had submitted a manuscript for her first novel to a publisher. In this example, Rosa was not afraid to reveal her aspirations and she had the support of family members and staff at school. She also described how she actively sought out additional information from Connexions Advisors[2] at the Connexions Centre in central Sheffield (not in school) as well as seeking guidance from several HE institutions before deciding on Oxford. Rosa attributed her success to hard work, good revision technique and a 'wonderful' teacher as well as to her own 'ability'. The example helps to illustrate a combination of factors which have helped Rosa to succeed in realizing her aspirations, linked to her preparedness to reveal her aspirations. While Rosa may have succeeded without all of the support she received the example helps to illustrate how the balance of possibilities of realizing aspirations may be tipped by these factors.

Concealed aspirations

Concealed aspirations are aspirations that have not been shared with others. The survey asked participants if they ever felt afraid to tell people about their aspirations for the future. It also asked whether individuals had aspirations they had never shared with anyone else.

Overall 45% of the S2 survey (N_2=580) sample had at some time felt afraid to tell others about their aspirations. Around 10% of the whole sample reported that they 'always' or 'often' felt afraid to tell people what their aspirations are for the future (N_2=580). A further one in three (35%) said they 'sometimes' felt afraid to tell other people about their aspirations. This could be seen as an indicator that the relationships young people have with significant others, together with their senses of trust and confidence, may be important in them expressing their aspirations. The ability and opportunity to communicate freely emerged as significant factors. Fear of sharing aspirations affected both male and female students across socio-economic backgrounds, institutions, across ethnicity and whether or not they intended to apply for higher education.

However, female students were more likely to indicate being fearful of sharing their aspirations compared to male students. Mann-Whitney tests established that there were no significant differences regarding fear of sharing aspirations based on eligibility for EMA/FSM, a proxy for socio-economic background, or higher education intentions and Kruskal-Wallis tests established no significant differences in fear of sharing aspirations based on ethnicity or institution. In other words, gender was the sole marker of increased likelihood of reporting being fearful of revealing aspirations. A Spearman's correlation of students' reporting, 'feeling confident about achieving aspirations' and 'feeling afraid to tell people about aspirations' showed a significant inverse relationship. That is to say, those who were least confident to achieve their aspirations were significantly more likely to feel afraid to tell people about aspirations they held.

In the following example, Amy (white female, Goldsmiths) had indicated on the survey that she had aspirations she had not shared with anyone and that she sometimes felt afraid to talk about her aspirations. She explained,

> *It was when I was younger, it was really stupid. It was to do with acting and it was that I wanted to be a film actress which was my number one thing so it was a bit stupid but I wanted to be a film actress, that was like someone like Julia Roberts and be really inspiring to people and like win an Oscar and things . . . it's all about luck really or not so much about . . . I don't know, it's just very unlikely for me to be good enough to do that for a start and for anyone to actually, you know, want to watch me on TV sort of thing. So it's a bit, I dunno, I just think it's very unlikely that it would happen.* (Amy, white female, Goldsmiths)

The extract shows that although sometimes aspirations may be expressed in quite general terms, such as the desire to work in the music industry at other times they may be quite specific, such as wanting to be a famous Hollywood actress. In this case, Amy has not had the chance to explore and nurture this aspiration and the discourse she uses is quite negative in her construction of self. By viewing the aspiration as 'stupid' and 'very unlikely' for her to achieve, Amy attempts to rationalize why she will not be able to realize this aspiration. Amy's fear limits the way in which she shares her aspiration and with whom. Presenting an aspiration as, 'very unlikely to happen' may set up a self-fulfilling prophesy if actors in the fields in which Amy interacts do not take the initiative to help Amy to explore her aspiration further. Later in this chapter, a further extract from Amy's interview reveals how there are a number of factors influencing the way she constructs her aspirations.

The S2 survey also asked, 'do you have any aspirations that you have never shared with anyone else?' This was a separate, though related, question to the question discussed above which asked, 'Do you ever feel afraid to tell people what your aspirations are for the future?' Young people decide not to share their aspirations with others for a variety of reasons, including, but not limited to fear. The responses showed that around one in four students (24%, N_2=580) overall indicated that they had aspirations they had never shared with anyone else. This is an indication of unshared aspirations rather than fear of sharing aspirations. There were no significant differences based on institution, gender, eligibility for FSM or intention to go onto HE regarding likelihood of having unshared aspirations.[3] Further data analysis showed that 107 (25%) of students who indicated that they intended to apply to higher education also reported having aspirations they had never shared with anyone else. Similarly, 21 (28%) of those students not intending to apply for higher education indicated that they also had aspirations they had never shared.

If young people do not share their aspirations with others it makes it more difficult to offer support and help and therefore these individuals may be further disadvantaged in achieving their aspirations. It also suggests that while individuals may appear to be realizing their aspirations by applying for higher education (in line with UK government widening participation strategies) they may also be harbouring concealed aspirations that they have not had the opportunity to develop and pursue. This is not to say that such individuals do not aspire to a higher education but that the process by which they have come to this decision may have excluded the development of a range of other aspirations they have reason to value. For example, James (white male, Goldsmiths) who revealed an aspiration to apply for HE also expressed the contrasting concealed aspiration of wanting to become a ski instructor. However, he felt that this would not fit in with either his teacher and family expectations.

Adapted aspirations

Young people's aspirations often appeared to be in flux and subject to review and change. More than four out of ten (42%, N_2=580) of the young people in the S2 sample reported that over the last year they had changed their mind about their future plans for when they leave school or college. A range of reasons were given with, for example, 12% of young people in the S2 survey reporting that they did not know how to achieve their aspirations.

The following extract, from Amy's interview, helps to illustrate how a variety of factors may influence whether an individual adapts or changes their aspirations. Amy identified three key reasons why she had changed her aspirations. She said she could not afford her original idea of studying at the Royal Academy of Dramatic Arts (RADA) in London as she could not afford to move to London and pay for the course. She also said she lacked motivation and felt under pressure from her parents to do science, 'because it's better'. She also felt under pressure from her parents to stay at home. In the context of the constraints Amy identified she decided not to pursue an acting career explaining,

> I used to want to be an actress desperately, that's what it was. I spent most of my life when I was younger doing plays and like. I was very much into 'I am going to be an actress one day'. I used to read plays constantly and just put everything into it and last year, well the start of last year was when I decided look it's not really realistic and I can do more useful things with my life than act and things like that. I mean although it's a really amazing thing to do I just think that Science is a bit more important. (Amy, white female Goldsmiths)

At Goldsmiths school there was a very strong ethos of encouraging sixth form students to apply for higher education. The weekly 'Guidance' lessons led by tutors from the sixth form pastoral team focused on progressing students through the difference stages of the Universities and Colleges Admissions System (UCAS) process. It is possible that this cultural environment was influential in the way Amy constructed her chances of success in different areas she was interested in.

Amy rationalizes her adapted preference to study science rather than acting by suggesting that science is more important and more useful than acting. Amy's comment invokes a discourse of hierarchies of knowledge in which the sciences are placed above the arts. There is also an implicit assumption that a three-year science degree and subsequent science career will be easier to achieve than a successful acting career. This strategy helps to make the decision to pursue science rather than acting a positive choice rather than a disappointment. It also fits in with Elster's description of adapted preference where an individual changes the attribution of weights to different choices especially where two choices initially appear to have similar weights. This strategy also helps to reduce tension and what Elster terms, 'anticipated regret' in relation to what is lost by not selecting the rejected option (Elster, 2000). Amy did not have the chance to convert her aspiration to be an actress into a capability and therefore her choice to apply for a science degree is not made from a range of valued alternatives. The interview indicated that Amy had limited opportunities to explore her aspirations in-depth and to develop an informed view of the risks and possibilities of her different aspirations. Conflict with others is a particular issue for vulnerable individuals (e.g. minors, elderly, the sick). The role of conflict with significant others raises the issue of power. Bourdieu and Passeron have noted that one of the most insidious forms of power is where individuals decide not to strive for certain goals because they deem themselves ineligible and thus become complicit in the exclusion (Bourdieu and Passeron, 2000). There is a concern that individuals may retain a *sense* of autonomy and control, but where they are making decisions within a range of choices limited by others.

Apparent aspirations

The term that I use to describe expressed aspirations that do not reflect an individual's true aspirations is 'apparent' aspirations. Expressed aspirations may not reflect the individual's aspirations but rather may reflect the expectations and aspirations of significant others and this is reflected by the term 'apparent'. An individual may indicate that they want to go onto higher education, even though they do not want to, because they feel it is the aspiration their parents or teachers want them to have. Although apparent aspirations do not reflect an individual's 'true' aspirations, they can actually lead to the adaptation of 'true' aspirations by individuals. For example, the following extract gives an example of how a young person may go along with the expectations and aspirations of others, even if they differ from their own. Katie is a white female from Goldsmiths school. Katie is unusual in the sense that she lives in Eastside but goes to school in Westside. She is an able student who has been predicted to achieve A grades in all of her A2 examinations:

CH:[4] What were your feelings about applying for higher education at that point?

Katie: Well I didn't really know what I wanted to do, but I just sort of applied because like you were supposed, if you know what I mean, do you know like just everybody were doing it, so I just applied really . . . we all had a little individual meeting like after we've got our results and that from our [AS Level] exams and they just said like what do you want to go to Uni', and at first I said no, and she was like 'oh well that's gonna be a waste if you don't go' so then you feel like you've got to don't you?

CH: Right, and how did that make you feel then?

Katie: Maybe I weren't like bothered by it but I just, I don't know it just felt like I had to apply so I did.

CH: Right.

Katie: For something that I didn't want to do.

Katie was in the process of applying for a higher education place through school at the time of the interview although she did not aspire to go onto HE once she left school. Looking at Katie's actions alone would suggest she aspires to university but her own story indicates this action reflects the aspirations of others rather than herself. Katie explained that she felt she had to apply for university even though she did not actually want to go onto HE after leaving school. From a capability perspective this indicates a lack of well-being freedom and agency freedom and it also shows a limited capability to aspire. Hence the term 'apparent' aspiration is adopted. Amy was a member of the adult and under-19s British Kick-Boxing Teams and she regularly competed internationally. Her aspiration was to pursue and develop this interest. She commented,

what I really like doing is my kick boxing and I like fight in the Great Britain team so really I just want enough money to be able to go away when we go to fight. It's not, like my job, I'm not really like career focused really like some people know they want to be like a teacher or whatever . . . but I'm not really fussed. I'll just have a job. (Katie, white female, Goldsmiths)

Kick-boxing is not recognized as an Olympic sport and so the opportunities to gain funding and professional coaching are limited. Individual capability to realize sporting aspirations at an advanced level are constrained by funding policies and this is rarely acknowledged in considering young people's development and well-being. Indeed, if Katie had been a gifted male footballer her outlook for sponsorship and recognition might have been very different.

Changing aspirations

Current government policy focuses attention on a linear model of aspiration growth which concentrates on educational and credential-based achievement. The hegemonic discourse deflects attention from the dynamic and often changeable nature of young people's aspirations. Thus it cannot be assumed that once a young person has expressed an aspiration that this will remain constant over time. This has implications both for policies aiming to drive forward specific aspirations as well as for more holistic strategies to develop both an individual's capability to aspire as well as capabilities to realize aspirations. A key concern of the S2 research, with regard to change, was to understand more about the extent to which change is occurring as a natural evolutionary element of the aspiration process and whether change is occurring as a result of positive or negative conversion factors. Inadequate careers guidance was identified by many young people as a key impediment to the development of their aspirations. The following group interview extracts are indicative of the feelings expressed by interviewees in the S2 study:

> *Student 1: Our careers people are pretty useless really . . . when I was in Year 11 I wanted to be a pilot . . . I did the research . . . they had no way of encouraging me . . . then I decided I wanted to do architecture and they just told me to put 'architecture' in Google. . . .*
>
> . . .
>
> *Student 2: I did a quiz [in careers] and it told me to be a daycare assistant and I just shrugged my shoulders . . .*

In some cases young people were looking for specialized advice about specific careers and felt let down when Connexions Advisors were unable to provide adequate support and information. In other cases individuals were unsure of what they wanted to do and were looking to the Connexions Advisors to help them identify pathways that would suit their interests and abilities. Students felt disappointed when they were given quizzes and computer-generated activities that they felt were not well tailored to their personal qualities.

Key findings on the nature of aspirations

Reflecting on the S2 data on young people's *revealed* aspirations helps to demonstrate the functioning of aspiring. However, this may only present a partial view of what I have termed an individual's *aspiration set* and this is illustrated in Figure 5.2.

I propose that *concealed* (unshared) aspirations may also form important elements of an individual's aspiration set. Furthermore, both revealed and concealed aspirations may also include a sub-set of '*adapted* aspirations'. Adapted aspirations may be found in both the revealed sub-set of an individual's aspirations set and in the concealed sub-set. An individual's aspiration set is thus illustrated by the following formula:[5]

$A = A_R \cup A_C$ where,

A	=	An individual's *aspiration set*	$= (r + ra + pr + pra + c + ca)$
A_R	=	An individual's revealed aspirations	$= (r + ra + pr + pra)$
A_C	=	An individual's concealed aspirations*	$= (c + ca + pr + pra)$
r	=	An individual's revealed aspirations (not adapted)	
ra	=	An individual's revealed aspirations (adapted)	
pr	=	partially revealed aspirations	
pra	=	partially revealed adapted aspirations	
c	=	An individual's concealed aspirations (not adapted)	
ca	=	An individual's concealed aspirations (adapted)	

* partially revealed aspirations can also be construed as partially concealed aspirations.

The aspiration set formula is explained in three stages for clarity. First, within the sub-set of revealed aspirations (A_R) an individual may hold aspirations related to different fields of their life. For example, they may have aspirations relating to family, education, work and leisure. Also within the sub-set of concealed aspirations (A_C) an individual may hold aspirations related to different fields of their life. Indeed, some aspirations may overlap different fields, for example, regarding education and work and, while some aspirations may relate solely to the individual, others may be linked to the wider community and broader agency goals (Appadurai, 2004; Burchardt, 2009). Secondly, it is over simplistic to categorize aspirations as either revealed *or* concealed. Hence, the intersection between revealed and concealed aspirations acknowledges that some aspirations may be only 'partially revealed' and this is represented by the symbol A_P. One kind of partially revealed aspiration is where an individual chooses to reveal an aspiration to some but not others. For example, an individual may reveal an aspiration to friends but not to teachers or parents. Another kind of partially revealed aspiration is where an individual reveals part of their aspiration but not the whole aspiration. For example, an individual may reveal an aspiration to pursue higher education studies but not their aspiration to apply to prestigious institutions such as Oxford and Cambridge universities. The third aspect of the formula relates to the positioning of adapted aspirations within both the revealed and concealed aspirations sets. Indeed, adapted aspirations may also be elements in intersection between revealed and concealed aspirations. Adapted aspirations are represented by the symbol A_A. In the light of this explanation of the aspiration set formula, the Venn diagram in Figure 5.2 helps to further illustrate the composition of the individual's aspiration set.

Earlier in this chapter four levels of aspiration were identified in relation to individual agency. Recalling the model in Figure 5.1, these levels are considered in relation to the idea of an individual's aspiration set. Table 5.2 summarizes both the different kinds of aspirations identified in study S2 and the levels of agency identified in the S1 study (Hart, 2004).

Revealed aspirations may include aspirations with each of the levels of agency described in Table 5.2. Concealed aspirations may be more likely to be independent compared to revealed aspirations but they may also relate to each of the other levels of agency in Figure 5.2. In addition, individuals may hide aspirations that they feel may be in conflict with significant others. However, as noted above individuals could, for example, be concealing aspirations from parents that they have shared with other individuals. In other words, this is a

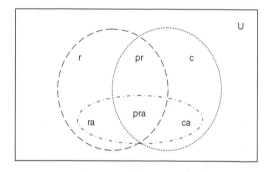

Key

U	=	Universal set of all possible aspirations
A_R	=	An individual's revealed aspirations (shown by dashed line)
A_C	=	An individual's concealed aspirations (shown by dotted line)
$A_R \cap A_C$	=	An individual's partially revealed aspirations
A_A	=	An individual's adapted aspirations (shown by dotted dashed line)

Figure 5.2 Venn diagram to show the composition of an individual's aspiration set

Table 5.2 Summary of aspirations and levels of individual agency

Type of aspiration	Level of agency	
REVEALED	INDEPENDENT	agency decreases
CONCEALED	SHARED	
ADAPTED	GUIDED	
APPARENT	CONFLICT	↓

partially concealed aspiration. Similarly, one individual may be guided towards an aspiration by another individual but they may keep this aspiration concealed from others. For example, an individual's family may guide them towards applying for a place at an elite university but the individual may conceal their 'guided' aspiration from friends.

At each of the different levels of agency an individual may adapt their aspirations. Independent aspirations may be adapted, for example, because an individual does not know how to pursue their goal. 'Shared' and 'guided' aspirations may be adapted in relation to expectations of others such as teachers, family and friends (Elster, 1983; Bridges, 2006). Conflicting aspirations may be adapted in the light of the real or potential barriers posed by others. For example, while some individuals experienced direct parental conflict, other individuals may adapt their aspirations rather than be exposed to anticipated conflict.

Finally, apparent aspirations do not represent aspirations in an individual's aspiration set as they are aspirations imposed on the individual by others. Hence, an apparent aspiration would not be an independent or shared aspiration. Apparent aspirations are likely to represent either guided or, more likely, conflicting aspirations. One further permutation may be that an individual expresses the apparent aspiration they think is expected of them rather than because they have been guided or coerced through the actions of others.

Figure 5.3 shows the complexity of the relationship between an individual's agency and revealing their aspirations, partially or fully. The process freedom of being able to express aspirations without prejudice has an intrinsic value. Value is related both on the one hand, to the capability to aspire and, on the other hand, to the capability to express aspirations. However, there is no guarantee that revealing aspirations will necessarily increase an individual's agency and result in the transition from aspiration to capability. Indeed, revealing aspirations that

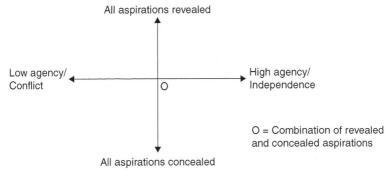

Figure 5.3 The relationship between individual agency and aspiration

conflict with the expectations of significant others may impede the realization of that particular aspiration.

Thus, in terms of policy implications, acknowledging the fact that a young person may not reveal all their aspirations and what we see may be the 'tip of the iceberg' is crucial. A positive ethos in this regard leaves the door open for individuals to share previously unshared aspirations in the future should they wish to do so. The current HE widening participation policy ethos is linear, moving individuals towards the goal of higher education in a uni-directional fashion. Once the young person is 'signed up' the possibility of other trajectories stemming from unshared aspirations is closed down. From a capability perspective this unnecessarily limits a young person's well-being freedom.

The capability to aspire

Analysis and reflection on the S2 data found that there are a range of factors influencing the generation and exploration of aspirations among young people. This is shown in the flowchart in Figure 5.4 illustrating the process by which an individual may convert commodities and different forms of capital (A) into aspirations (E) through a range of 'conversion' factors (B). This is explained below.

In discussing the theoretical framework of the capability approach, Ingrid Robeyns offers a schematic representation of the conversion of

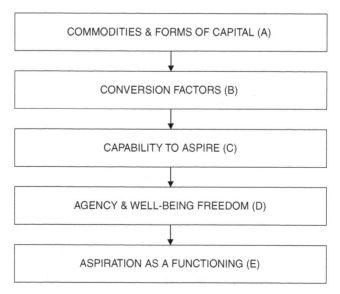

Figure 5.4 To show the capability to aspire and conversion to the functioning of aspiring

commodities into capabilities (Robeyns, 2005a). Robeyns relates the conversion factors to personal, social and environmental characteristics. Personal characteristics include physical and mental attributes of the individual; social characteristics include policies, social norms and power relations; environmental characteristics refers largely to infrastructure and public goods (2005a: 99). Robeyns' model is lucid although it is limited in its acknowledgement of the interplay of personal, social and environmental conversion factors. The inclusion and distinction of Bourdieu's *forms of capital* in the flowchart in Figure 5.4 draw attention to the different forms of resource upon which individuals may be able to draw including different forms of capital, as described by Bourdieu (1986). This conceptualization supplements the more economic understanding of commodities used in much of the literature (Pogge, 2002; Robeyns, 2003).

Referring to Figure 5.4, commodities (A) include primary goods and other resources such as access to knowledge via the internet. An individual may be able to convert family or school capital into individual capital and the latter may be later converted into individual capability. This process of conversion of commodities and forms of capital (A) is encompassed in Figure 5.4 by conversion factors (B). Conversion factors may relate to individual physical and mental capacities as well as to multiple aspects of the fields encountered by the individual and their symbiotic relationship with the *habitus*. The field interactions of significant others including family, friends, teachers and employers will also affect the individual's potential to covert commodities and capitals.

The impact of the various conversion factors acting on an individual's capability to aspire will be such that some individuals enjoy high levels of freedom to aspire while at the opposite end of the continuum other individuals may experience low capability to aspire (C). This meta-capability to aspire in turn affects the degree of well-being freedom and agency freedom (D) an individual has in deciding how to develop their aspirational capacity in terms of the functioning of aspiring (E). The flow diagram in Figure 5.4 is extended in Chapter 6 as the discussion turns to consider the conversion of an individual's aspirations into capabilities.

Conversion factors and the capability to aspire

In the S2 study conversion factors were identified, relating to the fields of family, education, work and leisure that may influence the extent to which individuals are able to convert commodities into the 'capability to aspire'. In S2 young people frequently experienced a range of constraints on their aspiration preferences.

For example, young people were often influenced by expectations of parents, teachers and friends. In addition, many students felt their choices would be affected by their predicted and achieved examination grades. Many young people surveyed said they lack information about options such as work-based training or other alternatives to higher education. The overall impression is one where despite conscious and unconscious constraints the majority of young people surveyed felt they retained freedom and control in decision-making processes regarding aspirations. However, this perceived freedom is set within limits and attention has been drawn to the deceptive nature of perceived freedom (Freire, 1972; Lukes, 1974; Elster, 1983; Bourdieu and Passeron, 2000). For example, Steven Lukes (1974) describes the 'third face of power' where individuals' desires are shaped and manipulated. Hence, although individuals feel they are making a free choice, those choices have been shaped by others. In relation to the government agenda to widen participation in HE this may be manifested by practices effectively asking young people to choose which HE institution they wish to apply to and not whether they want to apply. The area of choice is shifted away from the crucial issue. Jon Elster's concepts of manipulation and pre-commitment reinforce this point (Elster, 1983).

Conversion factors related to the field of family

Previous research has identified economic and cultural capital and parent–child relations as significant in young people's decision-making and educational aspirations (Marjoribanks, 2003). In S2, four key factors were identified from the study data which affected the extent to which parents were able to support their children and which may contribute towards young people's capability to aspire. The overall support young people had from parents and other family members in developing and realizing their aspirations was affected by (i) family background, in terms of economic and cultural capital, (ii) living arrangements, (iii) the nature of adult–child relationships in the family and (iv) family structures.

Family background

Wider family economic capital may give young people access to support they may not otherwise have. This may include, for example, food, shelter and clothing but also access to a quiet study area, internet access, telephone facilities and transport to explore opportunities. Being well nourished and living in a warm home may contribute to an individual's capability to aspire by giving individuals the opportunity to think beyond their basic needs. Reduced family economic capital can have a significant impact on an individual's circumstances and potential to aspire to and realize different kinds of futures. In the S2 group interviews one Year 12 male student explained how he wanted to have a career as a model. He had achieved some local success and was required to provide a portfolio in order to progress to the next stage of securing a contract with an agent. However, he did not have access to the £400 it would cost for a professional photography shoot and therefore felt unable to pursue his aspiration. In some cases students seemed to self-limit their aspirations based on what they felt was affordable to them and their family. Assessing economic capital becomes more complicated when account is taken of young people's income from paid work and other allowances such as EMA. In a few circumstances, a young person from a relatively poor socio-economic background may have greater access to economic capital than a person from a wealthier background. This may relate particularly to disposable income accrued through work in the labour market.

Not all young people benefited from their home environment in the same way. For example, a number of students undertook paid employment in order to contribute towards family expenses. For example, John (white male, Speedwell) worked an average of 20 hours a week in an electrical shop in addition to his 'full-time' studies at school. He contributed some of his earnings to cover household expenses supporting his mother and grandmother with whom he lived. Although John had considered applying for a university place he explained he would stay at home if he did apply for HE to save his mum the 'thousands of pounds' it would cost his mum to provide care for his grandma if he was not able to help. Thus John's aspiration formation is contingent on the social context in which he is emotionally, physically and financially connected.

There was widespread variance in the level of support, knowledge and helpfulness of discussions with parents experienced by young people. Both the S2 interview and survey data showed that often young people felt their parents lacked the knowledge to support them in achieving their aspirations, highlighting the uneven distribution of cultural capital between families. In addition, the majority of survey participants found it easy to talk to mothers (86%) and fathers (77%) about their aspirations which may in turn affect their ability to convert familial cultural capital into individual cultural capital. The interview data offered further insight into the different forms of cultural capital that some young people were able to accrue from their parents. Young people perceived that the ability of parents to discuss their children's aspirations was influenced by their parents' knowledge of different ways of life. The possession or lack of cultural and academic capital was significant in the way young people were able to interact with parents particularly with regard to aspirations regarding HE.

For example, Adam (white male, Goldsmiths) was able to draw on his father's experience as a head of a university department. Adam explained, 'I've never had any proper need for that much guidance . . . my dad's pretty knowledgeable about it all because he's in the university system'. The variable advantage of young people's relations with the HE field is examined further in Chapter 7.

In the S2 sample, 29% of participants had a father who had a university education and 27% had a mother with a university education. However, there was a substantial contrast across institutions with Westside students more likely to have university educated parents compared to Eastside parents (52% compared to 14% of fathers and 45% compared to 16% of mothers respectively).

In an example of transfer and activation of social capital, Martha (white female, Sherwood) explained that she had been thinking about a career in the police force. I asked her where she got this idea from and she said that both her father and brother were in the police force, explaining, '. . . it just seems like such a fascinating job, like I've been into work with my dad a few times and it's always different; there's never the same job twice'. In both Adam and Martha's cases it is possible that their parents have influenced their aspirations and they both benefit from the inside knowledge that their parents can offer them in their respective areas.

Living arrangements

Students experienced variable support depending on which adults lived in their households and whether they were able to maintain contact with parents no longer living with them. Some individuals benefited from the added support of step-parents while others suffered from a lack of meaningful interactions with parents. The findings suggested that an individual's family structure and living arrangements could have a significant impact on an individual's capability to aspire particularly in relation to the contact young people have with significant others in the family. While some students benefited from drawing on the knowledge, experience and understanding of several family members others suffered a deficit in this respect. Thus living arrangements may have a significant influence on an individual's CTA and ultimately their capability set.

Robyn explains that her step-dad does not have, 'much input into my life' and that he became a joiner following an apprenticeship and therefore does not have any higher education experience to draw on. However, Robyn goes to her dad's house once a week and says that her step-mum has tried to encourage her to apply for higher education. She describes her step-mum,

> *Yeah my step-mum, she's quite but she's quite biased towards University. She thinks that because I'm like clever I should be going sort of thing but I go over to my dad's once a week and like I'll talk to her and she'll like, she's quite supportive and she'll like ask me about things and but she's quite like a chatty person and she's summat to do with Law, I think she's, I don't know, a solicitor or summat so she's quite educated and she knows sort of what she's talking about a bit more but like I said she's quite pushy towards University . . .*
> (Robeyn, white female, Goldsmiths)

The above example illustrates the somewhat idiosyncratic nature of young people's opportunities to gain support from family members in exploring and developing their aspirations.

Adult–child relationships in the family

Relationship dynamics may influence the overall quality of interactions regarding nurturing an individual's capability to aspire. This has been supported by prior research arguing that adult–child interactions are significant in influencing whether capital is transferred from parents to their children as discussed in Chapter 3 (Marjoribanks, 2002). In the S2 study 95% of the survey sample reported relatively high levels of opportunity to discuss aspirations at home (N_2=580). The majority of students (78%) felt their parents were involved in helping them to make decisions about the future. However, parental involvement is not necessarily good, for example, students who reported that their aspirations conflicted with their parents' ideas for the future were significantly more likely to agree that their parents were very involved in helping them to make decisions about the future.[6] So, being involved as a parent is not always positive for the offspring. In the following interview extract, Rowan (white female, Riverdale College), explains how it is hard for her to discuss her college work or the possibility of going on to university with her parents:

> *My parents never like went to college or a University, so they don't really know what it's all about, and how hard it is and stuff like that, they just . . . they show interest, they ask me if I've had a nice day and have I got any work to do, but they don't really understand what it is that I'm doing, because they never, they left school and that was it so they don't know just how hard work is, and my*

brother didn't go to college so it's like I'm the first one and they just don't know a lot about it . . . They don't understand. (Rowan)

. . .

It's just a case because they don't know what it is and like University they haven't got a clue, they just said 'you go for it, you do what you want to do' but they don't really know enough about it to sit down and actually talk to me properly and say 'well look at this', you know, give me advice because they never went so . . . they don't really have the knowledge to help me make my decisions. . . . (Rowan, white female, Riverdale)

In Rowan's case, her parents show interest in her studies but she feels they are unable to support her in decision-making. She placed an emphasis on their lack of knowledge of the possible futures she may pursue. Yet Rowan's parents may have valuable knowledge and understanding of Rowan's personal qualities and interests that could form a starting point for discussion. In this next example, Eddie describes his situation at home,

I mean I've seen other people's parents, seen the way they are with their kids and I can't talk to my parents about anything. That's how I feel. I can't talk to my mum or my dad and my dad's hardly around. (Eddie, black male, Sherwood)

Eddie said he did talk to his elder brother in London, although his brother pointed out his parents would react badly if Eddie did not fulfil their aspirations for him to go to university. In this case where relationships are strained even if a family has significant economic or cultural capital the transfer of capital from family to individual is not guaranteed. Thus strained family relationships may impede the transfer and activation of family social and cultural capital. Ultimately, capability expansion is contingent upon living arrangements, family relationships and the transfer and activation of different forms of capital within the family.

Family structure

In terms of family structure, both the survey and interview data indicated that young people experienced a wide range of family support and in some cases parents (particularly fathers) were completely absent. For example, explaining his relationship with his father John commented,

He left when I was about one and I've not really seen him since. I actually found him in the Yellow Pages when I was 12 and like I've seen him but I

started seeing him for like a year then it just got too much because like he had his own family and that and now I only see him like birthdays and Christmases and stuff . . . he hasn't got any impact at all. (John, white male, Speedwell)

John had lived at home with his mother and grandma since his parents have separated. His elder sister and younger brother lived with his father. John said he did not see much of his siblings except on special occasions. The S2 interviews illustrated the differences in parent–child interactions. The influence of this factor on possibilities for inter-generational capital transfer has also been noted by Marjoribanks (2002).

Conversion factors related to the field of education

In this section three key institutional factors related to developing an individual's CTA are discussed. These include, conflict with teachers, institutional support and opportunities to talk about aspirations in the school or college environment.

Conflict

Conflict potentially reduces an individual's well-being freedom both in the capability to aspire in the first place and in the capability to realize aspirations in the future.

Although often individuals may develop aspirations of their own volition, in other cases individuals are persuaded towards particular aspirations by others (Hart, 2004). There was evidence in the S1 study of selective reinforcement of particular aspirations by teachers, Connexions Advisors and parents. At times this resulted in conflict between young people and their significant others. More than one in ten (11%, n_2=570) of the S2 survey participants felt their aspirations conflicted with their teachers' ideas for their future. Around one in five (21%) of them felt their aspirations conflicted with their parents' ideas (N_2=580). Five per cent (31) of the overall sample indicated that they experienced both parental and teacher conflict in relation to their aspirations. Conflict was significantly higher between teachers and students not intending to apply for a higher education place. Students were also more likely to report encountering conflict with teachers and parents compared to conflict with friends (7%) and girlfriends/boyfriends (8%).

The idea of conflict with others as a factor that may lead to adaptive preferences goes beyond Elster's analysis of adaptive preferences. Elster describes 'Manipulation' where individuals are manipulated into adopting the desires others want them to have (Elster, 1983). Elster uses 'Pre-commitment' to explain the way certain options are made unavailable in the hope that the individual becomes committed to an existing option (ibid., 1983). Where conflict arises between significant others, such as teachers or parents it is possible that Elster's Manipulative and Pre-commitment strategies to shape a young person's aspirations have either not been tried or have failed.

Voicing aspirations

Griffiths et al. argue that, 'empowerment through voice' is an essential element of achieving social justice through education (Griffiths et al., 2006: 358). The findings indicated that 87% of young people in the S2 survey sample found it helpful to talk about their aspirations with other people and the findings were similar across all institutions. However the opportunities to talk were variable. Around one in six of the S2 survey participants (18%) indicated in addition to lacking enough *opportunity* to talk to their teachers about their aspirations they also did not find it *easy* to talk to teachers about their aspirations. A Spearman's correlation indicated a strong positive relationship between opportunities and ease of talking to teachers about aspirations.

Students from Eastside were significantly more likely to have enough opportunity to talk to Connexions staff compared to their Westside counterparts. Conversely, Westside students were more likely to agree they had enough opportunity to talk to peers about their aspirations with their greater opportunities to talk to peers being statistically significant. There was no significant institutional difference in relation to opportunities to talk at home.

In the following example, Robyn (white female, Goldsmiths) explains how talking with a particular teacher has been helpful. Robyn mentioned one teacher at school who was a friend's form tutor and explained that she felt he, 'wants like what's best for people so I like talking to him about it, and he will like give me like suggestions and things, and saying that he'd be happy to act as like a referee, you know, like for a job and things like that so he's been quite supportive'. She contrasted this support with her Guidance teacher, who had tried to encourage her to go to Guidance[7] lessons because she might then change her mind and decide to go to university. Robyn said she just wanted him to, 'leave me alone'.

Wegerif et al. (2004) have explored an innovative approach to developing student voice through the 'Thinking Together' approach. It is based on research that suggests that some social groups are excluded from classroom talk and the ability to communicate and reason together can be enhanced through active intervention. Practical classroom activities have been devised to develop primary school children's language and thinking skills and there may be merit in exploring this approach further in developing young people's capabilities to aspire and in discussing and reflecting on their aspirations.

Support

The survey findings provided evidence that, on the whole, students enjoyed attending school or college, felt well supported and knew staff who would go out of their way to help them. More than eight out of ten students surveyed reported that they liked the atmosphere of their school or college (N_2=580). Across all institutions, 90% of students (N_2=580) felt well supported by their school or college at the time of the survey. There was some variation with figures dropping to 75% for students at Speedwell School. In this example from the S2 interviews, Amy describes her sixth form experience at Goldsmiths School:

> *I think it's a really good school. I think that the teachers are amazing about what they do and as schools go, I mean I've seen a lot about other schools on TV and things and I think this is definitely one of the best. I've been very lucky to go here. I think generally like all the way through school I've been sort of supported by all the teachers and things and yeah I've just been really happy here and things so it's really been cool.*

In Chapter 6 further institutional conversion factors are elucidated in relation to individuals' capabilities to realize their aspirations.

Conclusion

Contemporary education policy initiatives tend to focus on young people's revealed aspirations many of which have arguably been imposed by others. When we are examining the functioning of aspiring we are actually seeing *revealed* aspirations, and not necessarily the whole picture of the range of aspirations held by an individual. Therefore although revealed aspirations (the functioning of aspiring) may seem apt as a proxy variable for 'the capability to aspire' there are substantial limitations to this means of appraisal. The new insights derived by a focus on the capability to aspire and the varying levels of agency young people have in developing aspirations offer deeper understanding of the potential for human development in and through education. The S2 study findings showed evidence of a number of key factors which influenced young people's capabilities to aspire relating to family (lack of knowledge), school and college (bias towards HE), Connexions (poor untimely guidance) and peer pressure.

The freedom to aspire and the functioning of aspiring both have important roles to play in human development. Current policy neglects the capability to aspire and adopts a narrow view of the functioning of aspiring based on policy-relevant aspirations. The multi-faceted nature of aspirations is reduced solely to revealed aspirations, bundling 'true' and 'apparent' aspirations into one pot. This chapter has explored the merits for expanding the conceptualization of a space for evaluating well-being and human development. This expansion takes account of the role of the freedom to aspire as a meta-capability and the functioning of aspiring as a precursor to many future capabilities. Developing an individual's capability to aspire is not a time limited process but an ongoing project that can be expanded and enhanced by removing barriers to this meta-capability.

Aspirations are contextualized and formed in relation to different fields and relational positions within those fields. Processes of negotiation and renegotiation of aspirations occur as part of both planned and spontaneous events, triggered by the young person but also by opportunities created by others. In particular, family habitus and parent expectations played a significant role in young people's CTA. Expectations worked both to encourage and support some young people while others were pressurized to a greater or lesser degree by the expectations of parents.

Aspiration building is a reflexive and iterative process. Crucially, aspiring is a valuable functioning in itself, irrespective of (i) whether the capability to achieve the particular aspiration becomes possible or (ii) whether the aspirational goal becomes a functioning at some point in the future. A narrow policy focus on raising educational aspirations does not acknowledge the substantial range of aspirations that constitute an individual's full aspiration set. Helping individuals to become more aware of their full aspiration set (both in educational settings and elsewhere) has the potential to contribute to more progressive education policy. Chapter 6 continues with a closer examination of the processes influencing the transformation of aspirations into capabilities.

The Genesis of Capabilities

Introduction

This chapter examines the processes influencing the conversion of elements in an individual's *aspiration set* into elements in their *capability set*. It is argued that the notion of 'capability' is a useful way of conceptualizing the transition space between aspirations and the realization of related goals. Whereas an aspiration represents a desire to achieve a particular valued functioning, a capability represents a genuine freedom to achieve that particular functioning. The findings from S1 and S2 both showed evidence that while students often had multiple aspirations and often ambitious career plans there often seemed to be a significant gap in the transition to realizing aspirations. While some aspirations are converted into capabilities reflecting the 'capability to realise' the aspiration, other aspirations fail to be converted into capabilities. For example, evidence is presented in this chapter indicating that while many individuals may aspire, for example to a higher education, they lack the capability to realize their aspiration. Applying the Sen-Bourdieu analytical framework (SBAF) to the analysis of factors influencing the aspiration-capability transition illuminates several key issues that may be addressed by future education policy and practice. It is argued that by focusing on capabilities, as well as aspirations, attention is directed to the vital step of transforming aspirations into capabilities, that is to say, real opportunities to achieve desired goals. Identifying key potential conversion factors in this process can help to inform progressive education policies and practices that endeavour to promote human flourishing.

Linking aspirations and capabilities

The capability set is not a sub-set of the aspiration set but certain elements in each set can be said to overlap where an aspiration (A) has been converted into a capability (C). Strictly speaking, the aspiration and capability elements in A∩C are not one and the same but there is a clear connection between each aspiration in this intersection and the capability into which it is transformed.[1] Elements in the capability sub-set, C – (A∩C), arise without the active aspiration of the individual. For example, some capabilities come into being by virtue of the environment in which an individual exists rather than as an outcome of individual aspirations. For example, the capability to live in a healthy environment, war-free zone or affluent country. These capabilities may not arise from specific individual aspirations but still constitute ways of being and doing the individual may have reason to value.

In this chapter, the S2 study analysis of conversion factors affecting the transformation of aspirations into capabilities is formulated around the fields of family, educational institutions and work as described in Chapter 5. Consideration is given to the role of an individual's *habitus* in mediating the conversion factors acting on the transition space between aspiration and capability. The dominant conversion factors young people encountered tended to be related to home, school, careers information and guidance, predicted grades, learner concept and application processes for employment and higher education. The role of structures and *doxa* in the various fields are also examined in this transition space with a view to learning what more may be done to expand young people's capabilities in relation to their aspirations.[2]

Changing aspirations and adaptive preferences

Both what might be regarded as positive and negative reasons were given for changing aspirations. For example 38% of young people in S2 said they had changed their aspirations due to having a 'better idea' and 19% said a 'better opportunity' had come up (N_2=580). However, referring again to work on adaptive preferences by Sen and others it is not necessarily the case that because individuals seem positive about changing their aspirations that this is necessarily linked to a high level of well-being freedom (Sen, 1992; Bridges, 2006). Motivation continued to be highlighted as a pivotal factor for many students with almost one in five (19%) of the overall S2 sample indicating that they had changed their aspirations due to 'lack of motivation towards the original plan'. Another emerging theme related to lack of support and appropriate guidance with one in five (19%) S2 survey participants changing aspirations in part due to needing more specific careers advice. Fourteen per cent of the S2 survey sample changed their aspirations to keep their parents happy. Finance, achieving grades and parental expectations were also each reported as key reasons for changing aspirations by more than one in eight of the S2 survey participants.

Those individuals reporting a lack of support from home were more likely to report lack of support from school and lack of specific careers advice as key reasons for their changing aspirations. Students in receipt of the means-tested Educational Maintenance Allowance (EMA) were statistically significantly more likely to change aspirations due to lack of finance, motivation, home and school support and their perception of whether they could achieve the grades they needed to achieve their aspirations. In addition students in receipt of EMA were more likely to report changing aspirations due to lack of specific careers advice and due to not being able to afford to do what they wanted. These findings reflect the impact of having lower stocks of cultural and economic *capital* to draw upon. These findings illustrate how certain kinds of students are more likely to 'fall through the net' through the experience of multiple negative conversion factors. The failure to achieve adequate support appears to be linked to socio-economic status, ethnicity and institutional habitus.

Conversion factors influencing the genesis of capability

The flowchart illustrated in Figure 6.1 extends the flowchart presented in Figure 5.4 in Chapter 5 (p. 98). The 'Conceptual Framework of Aspiration Formation and Conversion into Capabilities and Functionings' highlights the significance of the 'capability to aspire' and the functioning of 'aspiring' as critical precursors to the development of many capabilities. It shows that conversion factors (F) culminated in three key possible outcomes for those individuals who are able to convert their aspirations into the 'capability to realise' and these are illustrated in Figure 6.1 (J, K, L). They are able to exercise their well-being/ agency freedoms (I) in deciding whether to convert their capability into a functioning, for example, going to university (J). If they do pursue this option then the achieved functioning will contribute towards their agency/well-being achievement although it cannot be guaranteed that this will be a positive contribution. For example, a young working-class individual may aspire to go

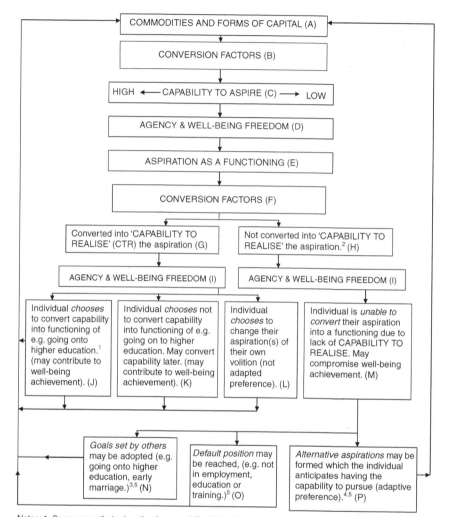

Notes: 1. Some argue that education is a capability in itself and that having a higher education therefore expands a person's capabilities. However, this depends on the nature of the higher education experience.

2. If conversion factors are insufficient this results in a lack of individual agency and well-being freedom blocking the conversion of aspirations into capabilities and then functionings. This in turn compromises well-being achievement.

3. This may or may not lead to valued ways of being and doing (functionings). Non-aspirational goals could lead to alienation.

4. Adaptive preferences may be valued less highly than original aspirations by the individual and therefore lead to lower well-being and agency achievement.

5. Degree of well-being achievement varies across these three pathways.

Figure 6.1 Aspiration formation and conversion into capabilities and functionings

to university and through a combination of positive conversion factors may go on to achieve a university place. However, the reality of being a student in higher education may not fulfil expectations and therefore the individual may experience reduced well-being achievement despite accomplishing a desired functioning. In any case once a particular functioning is achieved this may open the pathway to the generation of further aspirations or capabilities and the conversion cycle begins again.

Other individuals with the 'capability to realise' certain functionings may choose not to pursue these functionings but nonetheless they are exercising well-being and/or agency freedom in this process of decision-making (K). Similarly, some individuals who have the capability to realize their aspiration(s) may simple decide that despite the possibility of conversion to functioning they have changed their mind or would prefer to do something else (L).

In the case where an individual is unable to convert their aspiration into a capability this will lead to reduced well-being and/or agency freedom(s) and may compromise well-being/agency achievement (H). There are three main possible outcomes of this scenario. An individual who is unable to realize their aspiration by conversion to a capability (M) may adopt goals set by others (N). For example, Robyn, who wanted to work abroad rather than go to university ultimately changes her aspiration to fit in with the cultural norms of her institution and applies for a university place. A second outcome could be that a 'default' position is reached through lack of capability to realize any alternative aspiration (O). So for example, Robyn may be unsuccessful in achieving her aspiration of working abroad and therefore ends up being unemployed due to a lack of any achievable alternative aspirations. A third outcome of the lack of capability to realize an aspiration is the formation of alternative aspirations which may be deemed to constitute 'adaptive preferences' (P).

In this case the individual begins the cycle again with the capability to aspire being influenced by the prevailing conversion factors. For example, an individual may wish to apply for a university place but fails to complete the application form due to difficulties writing the required personal statement. The individual may adapt their aspiration and decide to seek employment as an alternative to higher education, explaining that they have just changed their mind.

It may be helpful to expand the evaluative space within the capability approach to consider the role of aspirations alongside capabilities and functionings. While the particular example of aspirations in relation to higher education is examined here, as a case in point, the conceptual framework has much more general applicability in evaluating notions of advantage and social justice. The theory could be used to inform the development of evaluative strategies in future work on human development. In this expanded model of the evaluative space of capabilities, education has an important dual role as a conversion factor first enabling, the formation of aspirations in the first place and secondly, in the subsequent conversion of aspirations into capabilities.

The conversion of aspirations into capabilities emerges as a vital process mediated by multi-dimensional conversion factors emerging in and between different social spaces or fields. The conversion factors influencing the CTA sometimes reflect the conversion factors which influenced the formation of aspirations in the first place but there may also be differences. For example, a young person may aspire to work abroad when they leave school but find themselves ostracized by peers and staff for not following the institutional norm of applying for a university place. This may make it difficult for them to access the relevant information needed to convert their aspiration into a capability and in addition may lead to feelings of disenfranchisement and alienation.

Study S1 conversion factor analysis

A range of factors emerged from the S1 Year 12 interviews which seemed to create barriers to students achieving their aspirations. Key factors identified related to education, family, work and social fields. In the S1 survey (N_1=239) for each of the factors of money, ability and motivation around one in four students responded that they thought these factors would definitely or probably stop them from achieving their aspirations. Just over 20% of the S1 survey sample said they thought the factor of friends would definitely or probably stop them achieving their aspirations. Eighteen per cent of students thought school factors would definitely or probably stop them achieving their aspirations and 15% of students thought the same for home-related factors. In addition, a number of positive conversion factors were also identified in S1. Many of the students across the whole S1 sample felt that increased confidence and motivation together with continued encouragement and support would help them achieve their aspirations. Personal skills such as communication and planning were also identified as factors which would help. However, it was clear that the level of support students received varied greatly within and across institutions.

In S1, individual students on the whole were significantly more likely to report that money, ability and motivation might present barriers to the achievement of their aspirations compared to home, school and friends-related factors. There were no significant differences between money, motivation and ability in terms of the likelihood of them presenting barriers to individuals when considering the whole sample. The findings indicated that many students were conscious of a range of barriers that may affect the likelihood that they would achieve their aspirations. School factors and friends-related factors were both more likely than home-related factors to be barriers to students in achieving their aspirations. When boys and girls' responses were compared similar numbers reported that home and school might stop them achieving their aspirations. However, boys were significantly more likely to say that they thought factors related to friends would either definitely or probably stop them achieving their aspirations compared to girls. Significantly more boys than girls indicated they thought money would be a barrier. Ability was more likely to be seen as a barrier to achieving aspirations by females and by non-HE applicants compared to males and HE applicants respectively.

S1 was a useful exploratory study providing the foundations for the more detailed examination of conversion factors influencing the capability to realize aspirations pursued in S2. The S2 survey built on S1 by asking more specific sets of questions related to key conversion factors identified in the earlier study. In addition a set of questions was asked to learn about why young people change their aspirations and this aimed to ascertain both factors that helped and hindered young people in pursuing their aspirations.

Study S2 conversion factor analysis

Family and home-related conversion factors

The S2 survey asked individuals a series of questions designed to understand more about factors relating to home and family circumstances that may help or hinder the transformation of aspirations into capabilities. As discussed in Chapter 4, survey items were devised in the light of student participation in focus groups. Table 6.1 indicates the proportions of young people reporting a range of different constraints in the achievement of their aspirations.

The factors affected significant numbers of students ranging from 5% of students helping with a family business to 26% students finding it difficult to find a quiet place to study at home. Some of the factors in Table 6.1 relate to the possession, inter-generational transfer and activation of family economic and cultural capital. For example, young people from lower income families may be less likely to have a quiet place to study or be more likely to work to help with family expenses reflecting a lack of economic capital. Where parents lacked knowledge related to young people's HE aspirations, in particular, this can be linked to a lack of cultural and social capital.

Table 6.1 Family-related barriers to achieving aspirations

Reason Q. *'I'm finding it hard to achieve my aspirations because of . . .*	Whole sample Number/Percentage who agreed with this statement (N_2=580)
a). . . *The lack of a quiet place to study at home.'*	150 (26%) 1 in 4
b). . . *My parents' lack of knowledge.'*	85 (15%) 1 in 7
c). . . *Lack of support from parents.'*	78 (13%) 1 in 8
d). . . *Looking after younger brothers and sisters.'*	54 (9%) 1 in 12
e). . . *Working to help with family expenses.'*	49 (8%) 1 in 12
f). . . *Looking after parents or other relatives.'*	40 (7%) 1 in 17
g). . . *Helping with a family business.'*	30 (5%) 1 in 20

Note: Percentages rounded to nearest whole number.

Further key family factors that were significant in the conversion of aspirations into capabilities were parental involvement in young people's decision-making, their knowledge, support and expectations. Lack of parental support is not easily attributable to a lack of cultural or economic capital although both may play apart. The four most prevalent home-related conversion factors, as shown in Table 6.1, are discussed further with examples.

A quiet place to study

The example of one female student is used to illustrate the kinds of difficulties young people experienced regarding finding a place to study. Robyn is a young white, female student who lived in Eastside and commuted daily to attend Goldsmiths School on the other side of the city. Her parents had divorced and had new partners at the time of the study. Robyn lived with her mum, step-dad and two younger sisters although she maintained contact with her dad too. Robyn explained why she found it hard to find a quiet place to work at home,

> *Well there's my mum, my step-dad and my 2 little sisters, they're 12 and 10 but as you can imagine they're not really the most considerate of people so. I'm in [the] attic as well and it's like got ladders with a hatch so it's not really . . . I've got like curtains coming across but I haven't got a door or like anything so like all the noise just travels straight up to my room and there's like telly's and everything. It's just a bad environment to work so . . . I mean I do ask them, I tell my parents and say 'oh like can you just keep kids quiet for a bit' and they tell them to but they just don't listen to them so I just prefer to work like away*

from that environment . . . it would be even worse if I worked downstairs, you know like where the computer [is] in the kitchen . . . because everyone's in and out, in and out so . . . . (Robyn, white female, Goldsmiths)

Robyn's description of her home environment helps to illustrate some of the challenges young people face in trying to find a space to study effectively at home and may reflect a lack of economic capital manifested by overcrowded accommodation. These kinds of constraints remain largely invisible considerations in government policy and measures of success at both the school and individual level.

Parental knowledge

In the S2 survey one in seven young people reported that their parents' lack of knowledge was preventing them from achieving their aspirations. While other students gained insights into higher education as a result of their parents' experiences Steven's experience stands in stark contrast illustrating a lack of familial cultural capital. Steven was a white male at Riverdale College. He was eligible for an EMA allowance indicating that his family had a relatively low household income. However, on the survey Steven indicated that it was both his parents' lack of knowledge and also his own difficulty in staying motivated that were making it harder for him to achieve his aspiration to go on to university once he left college. Steven described how he felt that he made decisions about his future more or less by himself saying of his parents,

Like they don't really understand it much because like they've never been to university themselves or owt like that so they don't know what it's about and everything. . . . Like they just asked me what I'm going for, like what university I'm like thinking of going to and what sort of grades I'll need. That's like all the things like they asked us. They don't know much about it like because I just get on with it myself really. (Steven, white, male, Speedwell)

It is possible that Steven's lack of motivation is partly a result of the lack of cultural capital and the way this plays out in the influence on Steven's habitus. Steven is having to negotiate the prospect of entering the field of higher education without help from his family in his understanding of the field. This may lead him to have a 'tense' rather than 'effortless' relationship to this potential future (Bourdieu and Passeron, 2000: 161). The negotiation of the HE field is considered further in Chapter 7, particularly with reference to the dissonance that may be apparent between the individual's habitus and the HE field.

Parental support

The S2 data showed one in eight young people felt they had difficulty achieving their aspirations due to lack of parental support and it became evident from the interviews that families had different ways and means of supporting young people. For example, while some parents lacked knowledge (cultural capital) of different future opportunities for their children they offered positive emotional support and opportunities to discuss ideas. Other parents were able to offer financial assistance (economic capital) for pursuing a higher education or practical help such as taking their children to look around universities in distant locations. The latter depended on a number of factors including what I have termed, '*time*' capital.

Young people's interactions at home were examined with regard to the way they influence their aspirations, capabilities and choices with regard to higher education application. Young people experienced different kinds of support and interactions with family and friends regarding their post-school/college choices and decisions. Significant factors relating to the field of family centred around four areas including overall support, parents' expectations, academic capital and economic capital.

Seventy-three per cent of young people in the sample felt that, 'my parents are keen for me to go to university'. Westside students were most likely to agree with this statement and, proportionally, Goldsmiths students expressed the most agreement overall. In terms of family background, those students hoping to go on to higher education at the time of the survey were statistically significantly more likely to have parents who were keen for them to go onto higher education.

Parent expectations

The expectations of others seemed to play an important role for many in their desire to pursue a higher education. For example, 40% of the overall sample wanted to go to university in order to, 'live up to family expectations' and 47% in order to 'make my parents happy'. There is a blurred line between parent encouragement and parent pressure that was revealed in the interviews, especially regarding higher education pursuits.

For example, James' parents expected him to fulfil their middle-class expectations by him striving for a prestigious university place. James (white, Goldsmiths) described feeling that his parents wanted him to fulfil their expectations and live up to what he perceived as a taken-for-granted middle-class career pathway. While James said he did not compare himself to his brother (a Cambridge undergraduate), he thought that his parents did. He explained:

> *I try and separate myself from him, you know, I wasn't interested in applying to Cambridge, I wasn't interested in doing the activities he does but my parents were always like that. They were always like saying, you know, the first day he went to Cambridge they were like 'one day you'll be able to go there' and they're always trying to push me to be like him but I've never wanted to be, you know, be like him and sometimes I feel they get a little bit disappointed that I'm kind of different, you know . . . they're very keen for me to go to university and I don't think any other option is ever given to me by them to, you know, yeah.*
> (James, white male, Goldsmiths)

James' comments show the way that parental expectations are pressurizing him towards application for a place at a prestigious university. There is clearly some tension in the parent–child relationship and yet at the same time James has not felt able to address this openly with his parents. The expectation that he will progress to university is compounded by the highly academic nature of Goldsmiths School where the institutional habitus is clearly orientated in favour of progression to HE. James' lack of well-being freedom in this situation and the silencing of his feelings about his future are concealed in school performance data that simply records the numbers of students moving into HE after leaving school.

In a second example, Steven said his parents had not talked to him about any other possibilities other than going on to university saying,

> *They're pretty keen for me to go, because they didn't go to college sort of thing, so they're pretty keen for me to go to higher education. . . . They don't want me to like be stuck where they are, because like my Dad's like in a job where it's like all dying out, because he's like a grinder, but it's like a trade that's sort of dying out, and my Mum's like a secretary sort of thing, but they don't want me to be like stuck where they are . . . well, what my Dad said like he keeps getting made redundant every few, like he's been like made redundant in the last few years about three times so like he don't want me to like go into like industry sort of thing. My Mum just doesn't want me to like be stuck like at the lower part of like of a business sort of thing like a secretary or 'owt like that. She wants me to like get higher.* (Stephen, white male, Speedwell)

Steven uses the word, 'stuck' repeatedly to describe his parents' aspiration that he should strive to move out of the sociocultural field into which he was born.

In Steven's case his parents viewed higher education as a means of escaping their difficult socio-economic circumstances and as a route to a more stable future. However, this requires Steven to leave the comfort of a field with which he is familiar and to enter a new and unfamiliar field which may challenge his habitus.

Financial support

Around six out of ten (62%) of the S2 survey participants felt their parents would support them financially if they went on to university although a similar proportion (58%) reported being worried about getting into debt if they went to university. The same proportion (58%) was worried about the cost of going to university. There were significant group differences based on institution, EMA eligibility and higher education intentions. Students from Westside were more likely to have parents willing to support them financially and the same applied to those not eligible for EMA and those intending to apply for university compared to their counterparts. Students eligible for EMA were statistically significantly less likely to feel that their parents would be able to offer them financial help if they went to university compared to other students.

An individual's family history in relation to attitudes and experiences of debt can impact on young people's feelings about accumulating debt if they progress to HE. These feelings can be so strong that the decision of whether or not to participate in HE is partially or even predominantly determined by them. Talking about the cost of university John explained,

> But I don't wanna have it hanging over me. I'd rather take a low loan or not have to take a loan out at all. . . . Like I really that's one thing I hate, owing money. I can't . . . even if it's just little amounts that I pay back straightaway because I hate it. I just feel guilty. I just don't like it.

John uses a highly emotive discourse to describe his feelings in relation to debt. Research participants in both S1 and S2 commented on their negative attitudes towards debt. This related particularly to individuals from deprived socio-economic backgrounds where they had experienced the negative consequences of parental debt. Young people from families with low economic capital are thus potentially disadvantaged in the HE field where the rules of the game or *doxa* are constructed around middle-class cultural norms. Individuals from families with higher economic capital may feel more secure in the HE field even though they accrue financial debt as they may be able to call upon the family economic capital if necessary. This extract suggests that John's concerns are related to deeply rooted cultural experiences and attitudes and that just knowing the facts about sources of financial aid for HE is not enough.

Practical support

Some students also gained practical support from parents, for example, being taken to university open days or shadowing a parent at work. For example, James revealed that his parents had helped to write his university application form for him ensuring a strong application. 'I mean I knew it was good because my parents helped me write it. I mean I knew it was a really, really good personal statement' (James, white male, Goldsmiths). In James' case he has a strong stock of familial cultural capital to draw on leading him to have a more 'self-assured' disposition towards the prospect of entering the field of higher education. In helping James to write his application, James' parents have the opportunity of transmitting 'linguistic capital' to their son as well as inside knowledge of the field. This leads James to develop an attitude of 'ease' towards his prospective field and to understand the tactics pertinent to entering the 'game' of higher education (Bourdieu and Passeron, 2000: 161; Bourdieu, 2009, 66–8).

Emotional support

Another important aspect of parental influence on offspring was emotional support. I asked Helen what she thought her parents and neighbours would think about her going to university and she said, 'I just think they'll be proud'. Hearing that she had been offered a university place Helen said, 'Like me mum rang everybody and stuff like that and they're all like really pleased that I've managed to do it'. Helen expressed delight that her mother had so openly shown support for her daughter's achievement. In this instance it is possible to conceptualize the transference of positive emotional capital. The public support shown to Helen by her mother's actions makes Helen feel joyful and excited at the idea of going to university. This helps to offset some of the anxieties she expresses elsewhere in the interview about whether she would fit into the new environment of HE. However, where parents are intensely involved in directing young people towards particular pathways, whether HE or otherwise, it was found that this may result in a negative emotional transfer.

This resonates with work by Diane Reay where she found that, in relation to their children's schooling, 'guilt, anxiety, frustration, as well as empathy and encouragement were the primary motifs of mothers' involvement' and that, 'seemingly positive emotions could sometimes have negative repercussions for children' as well as there being, 'no simple correlation between positive emotions and emotional capital' (2004: 58). Thus, from a Bourdieurian perspective, negative emotional influences from parents to offspring may actually create what I have termed a capital '*debt*' rather than adding value to the individual's capital portfolio.

Looking after siblings

Four female Somali students who took part in an S2 group interview each had between six and eleven siblings so issues related to care for younger siblings was one of a range of challenges they faced at home. Those students from larger families and with lower incomes were more likely to struggle to find a quiet place to work. A number of students mentioned helping younger siblings with homework and other responsibilities at home that impinged on opportunities to study. Some young people mentioned sharing bedroom accommodation with younger siblings, cramped accommodation and noisy pets. Indeed, the impact of being involved in domestic responsibilities does not just represent a physical and emotional call on a young person's time and energy. It also may influence their self-perceptions and habitus. For example, one of the Somali females commented with regard to her domestic role, 'I'm happy about it because I feel useful'. Young people often described the challenges they faced in relation to other possible scenarios. As one young Somali female pointed out, 'I left my country when I was four because of civil war' so in this context the potential burden of caring for siblings may not seem a hardship. We cannot be sure whether this individual has adapted her preferences in the face of little alternative other than to help out at home in addition to her own studies but again there is resonance with Elster's analysis of adaptation of preference (Elster, 1983).

Family conversion factors related to domestic labour

In the S2 group interviews discussions arose which suggested that young people's involvement in domestic labour may have an important influence for some people in relation to achieving their aspirations related to other aspect of their lives including, but not limited to education. The S2 survey asked young participants a series of questions aiming to learn about their involvement in domestic labour. Previous research has often concentrated on the role of paid work in relation to effects on academic studies but the group interviews revealed that many students were heavily involved in caring and other domestic responsibilities at home (Metcalf, 2003).

In many cases young people felt their involvement in domestic chores and responsibilities had an adverse effect on their studies and more broadly in relation to achieving their aspirations. In summary, around seven out of ten (70%) of the S2 sample reported that they regularly helped with housework, childcare or other chores at home. The majority estimated spending between 5 and 15 hours per week helping at home but 36 students (6%) indicated committing 16 or more hours per week. In the overall sample (N_2=580) 10% of students felt helping at home negatively affected their studies. Nine per cent of survey participants reported that their sleep was negatively affected by them doing household chores and 13% felt their social activities were hindered by the same. Females in the sample were significantly more likely to regularly help at home and on the whole black females were the most likely to regularly spend time on domestic chores. Asian females and black males shared second place in likelihood of helping at home (sample split for gender and ethnicity) with 50% of young people in these groups spending over 10 hours a week helping. Interestingly, there were no significant differences found in relation to participation in domestic labour based on socio-economic background (using EMA and FSM as proxy variables).

However, it is important not to generalize on these characteristics as the following two examples show how two white male students spent a very significant amount of time on domestic labour which was emotionally as well as physically demanding.

In the S2 study, John (white male, Speedwell) explained how he helped to look after his grandmother who was living with dementia. He lived with his mother and grandmother following the break up of his parents' relationship. John's mother worked 12-hour shifts and so between them they managed his grandmother's care needs. Since the separation of John's parents, his mother had relocated them to a small house at some distance from the school. This meant that John had to take two bus journeys each way to school taking up over 2 hours a day. John's capability to study and his social life were significantly affected by these circumstances. Yet John spoke extremely positively about his relationship with his grandmother and did not construct his caring responsibilities as a burden. Indeed, he described his grandmother as, 'the funniest person I've ever met' and conveyed the warm relationship they shared.

In another example from the S2 interviews, Michael (white male, Speedwell), identified himself as the primary carer for his grandfather who had lived 'down the street' from his parents' house. His grandfather was housebound and, as Michael's parents both worked long hours, he would visit in the morning, after school and at night to look after his grandfather. In the interview, Michael revealed that his grandfather had died the week before. He said he felt that there was no one at school that understood the significance of his loss. He described how he was still being pressurized for homework that was late and yet he was clearly still trying to come to terms with his bereavement. Michael's experience underlines the significance of the contrasts and tensions in priorities and positioning that young people experience in the different fields they encounter. The CEP emphasis on examination achievement leaves limited space for acknowledgement of this issue.

Summary of family-related conversion factors

This section on family-related conversion factors has highlighted several prevalent factors that young people report as supporting and constraining the achievement of their aspirations. Parental cultural capital in terms of knowledge and experience, economic capital relating to financial and support as well as family emotional capital were all found to be valuable. However, there were marked variations in the young people's parental knowledge and experience, particularly in relation to higher education. In addition the opportunities to receive emotional support depended on family relationships, living arrangements and compatibility of parental aspirations and aspirations of offspring. Family dynamics and structure had key roles to play in the kinds of parental pressures, expectations and opportunities for support experienced by young people.

Conversion factors related to educational institutions

Reay et al. use the term, 'institutional *habitus*' to describe, 'a semi-autonomous means by which class, raced and gendered processes are played out in the lives of students and their higher education choices' (ibid., 2005: 35). In S2 the students that appeared to be privileged by the institutional habitus were those who were able to fit in with the cultural expectations of the institution regarding the pursuit of higher education. In practice perceived ability and higher education potential emerged in S2 as distinctions through which the institutional habitus was mobilized across the student membership.

Well-being

On the whole, female students were significantly more likely than males to say they felt well supported by their institution. As mentioned in Chapter 5, more than one in ten individuals in the S2 survey sample ($N_2=580$) felt their aspirations conflicted with their teachers' ideas for their future and this can be seen as a potential barrier to the realization of aspirations as well as the capability to aspire. Fifteen per cent of the same sample reported that they found it hard to be themselves at college or school and it was significantly more likely that these participants were EMA recipients, that is to say, they were generally from families assessed as having lower income. In the S2 survey 36% reported lacking motivation in their current studies and 25% had considered dropping out of school or college. These are all indicators that suggest the level of well-being achievement among students in each of the four S2 institutions was variable and manifested in a variety of ways.

Speedwell stood out from the other institutions in the S2 sample, with students significantly less likely to agree that they felt well supported by their school and they were also less likely to enjoy coming to school compared to counterparts elsewhere. Interestingly, the example of Speedwell indicates that student well-being may not be reflected by examination achievement. Informal interviews with sixth form staff at Speedwell indicated that most students were expected to apply for higher education either in Year 13 or during the year after leaving school. Two out of three (64%) of Speedwell students had one or more parents who had studied at university and this was more than for any other institution. In fact, 77% of the Speedwell students who said they did not feel academic had at least one parent who had studied at university. Interestingly, 22 of the 34 Speedwell students who said they 'did not feel that academic', had 8 or more GCSEs graded A-C, which represents significant above national average academic achievement. The institutional (and wider) factors contributing to students' self-perceptions require further examination. Parental and institutional expectations and ethos may have a role in young people's expectations of how they should perform although this could not be inferred from the data.

However, the S2 findings do indicate that neither achievement at GCSE nor parents' education are necessarily good indicators of individual's self-perceptions or emotional well-being. Despite high levels of family cultural capital and personal academic capital these young people's well-being freedoms may be compromised. Indeed there is a growing literature focusing on changing perceptions of child well-being generally, as well as specifically in relation to education.

Expectations of HE progression

Almost two-thirds (62%) of the whole S2 survey sample felt their teachers expected them to apply to university and 33% of young people surveyed reported that one of the reasons they were applying to university was to do what their teachers expected of them. Those students intending to apply for a higher education place were significantly more likely to agree that they knew teachers at school/college that were willing to go out of their way to help them. Sixty-eight per cent of the S2 sample thought there should be more help available for options other than university. For example, Robyn (white female, Goldsmiths) did not want to apply for higher education despite the persuasive tactics of her teachers. She described feeling, '. . . *a bit demoralised really because I could really do with help and like people who aren't biased towards Uni helping me . . .*'

Those students who did not plan to apply for higher education were offered limited support to discuss alternatives with Connexions Advisors and school or college staff. Those eligible for EMA were more likely than others to feel more help should be given. Similarly non-HE applicants were also more likely than those planning to go onto HE to feel more help should be given regarding other opportunities than university. The issue of information, advice and guidance is taken up further in Chapter 7.

Financial advice and guidance

All schools and colleges in the S2 study provided a variety of financial advice in preparation for higher education but the majority of young people still seemed to struggle with these matters. The Dearing Inquiry reported that if more were known about the financial benefits of HE more would enter it (Dearing, 1996). However, financial concerns represented a significant barrier for many young people with around six out of ten individuals in the S2 survey reporting that they did not understand the system of loans, fees and bursaries available for attending university. Continuous changes to the complex systems of funding available mean that the need for additional support regarding the financial help available for HE is ongoing.

Labelling practices

Concerns around labelling students and streaming according to perceived ability have been questioned in the education literature over a long period (Lemert, 1972; Becker, 1974; Gillborn and Youdell, 2000). Evidence from the S2 study suggests that some institutional practices associated with implementing the widening participation policy strategy resulted in the differential positioning of students by staff in relation to their perceived potential to participate in higher education. A symbiotic relationship appears to develop between the learner and their institutionally ascribed hierarchical position and this has been recognized in the sociology literature over a sustained period by Bourdieu and others (Becker, 1974; Bourdieu, 1986; Gillbourn and Youdell, 2000). The separation of students into groups according to staff decisions regarding who has potential to go onto higher education may result in increased numbers applying for a university place. However, such methods do not allow all students to have the opportunity to benefit and as a result some students may be left feeling excluded (Slack, 2003). For example a student who has been placed in a 'gifted and talented' or 'Aimhigher' cohort may then take on the mantel of being a high performer and hence be motivated to work harder and achieve better grades than they would otherwise. By contrast, a learner who perceives that they are not deemed to have higher education potential due to their institutional positioning outside of the gifted and talented and 'widening participation' groups may develop a more negative attitude towards learning and achievement in school or college.

Robyn wanted to pursue a career living and working abroad in Tenerife with her Spanish boyfriend. Robyn described her disappointment with the weekly 'Guidance' lesson which was the formal channel of school support for young people in the transition from school to the wider world. She explained,

> *Especially at the start of this year it [the Guidance lesson] were all about UCAS and my guidance teacher were gonna like, she were trying to force me to apply even though I really weren't gonna go. She was like 'oh you may as well apply' and I were like, 'I don't even want to' but all the lessons were totally focused around that ... If you don't go to guidance you don't get anything. The teachers will say to my friends 'oh how's your applications going then?' and blah, blah, blah. Nobody will say to me 'oh have you found a job yet?' or whatever. They just ... it's as if I'm not like, once I've finished A-levels I'll just go into oblivion or summat. It's weird.* (Robyn, white female, Goldsmiths)

Students clearly experienced varying levels of input and institutional support in their schools and colleges. Institutions varied in their approach to counselling and supporting students in making decisions about higher education and this had profound effects in a number of cases. Robyn vividly draws attention to the lack of guidance and support available to her in developing her aspirations to work abroad once she leaves school. She described feeling, 'demoralized' and 'alone'. Robyn's boyfriend's family lived in Tenerife and so this is where she hoped to find work. She explained, '... as to what I'm gonna do I just haven't got a clue yet. I'm just gonna play it by ear ...'. Robyn described how she felt she needed further information about opportunities to work abroad and basic information about the legal and practical aspects involved. The absence of support from school made it difficult for her to develop her aspirations beyond a basic idea.

The institutional culture of labelling students as gifted and talented (in line with government policy directives) appears to lead some 'outsider' students to assume deviant identities in order to avoid alienation.[3] Overt classifications of some students as more 'gifted' or 'talented' than others can cause tension across a student population. In a further example of labelling, Eddie (black male, 'forced' by parents to apply for HE) describes the way he became labelled at school as one of the 'bad boys' at his previous school (an 11–18 Catholic school). The gifted and talented cohort had been selected prior to him (and his twin brother) joining the school mid-year and he felt that for this reason he had missed out on being considered for the gifted and talented group at the start of the year. He explained how peers used to refer to the gifted and talented cohort as, 'geeks' and explained that he joined the 'bad boys' because he wanted, 'to be part of the group'. He explained,

> ... there were the clever ones which were the geeks and they're not cool so you're like caught in between. So basically what happened we're the bad boys at school, at home we do the work ... That's what really happened. So it's like two lives we're leading ... (Eddie, black male, Sherwood)

Eddie, a black male, describes the gifted and talented cohort of students at his previous school as, 'geeks'. He recalls how he aligned himself with a sub-cultural group of, 'bad boys' in order to achieve a sense of affiliation and belonging. The tragedy here is that Eddie sees himself as an academically able student who wants to study and this is reflected in his later examination achievement at Sherwood.

Eddie had separated the identity he adopted at school to get by from his identity outside of school. Labelling himself as a 'bad boy' is seen by Eddie as a way of generating a sense of group belonging. He perceives only a limited number of choices for group affiliation within the school and feels he is excluded from the gifted and talented cohort. Opportunity for affiliation is seen by Sen as an important element in the pursuit of justice (Sen, 2009). Both Helen and Eddie's circumstances show how such opportunities may be constrained by school habitus, thus acting as a negative conversion factor. Eddie appears to adapt his preferences choosing to present himself as a 'bad boy' rather than to risk feeling alienated from his peers. His experience 'highlights disjunctures and potential rifts between learner and social identities' which Reay et al. have previously identified in their recent study of working-class students in higher education (Reay et al., 2010: 117). Reay quotes one student who says she would tell her peers she had not done the required reading when actually she had and that she had left her assignments until the last moment when actually she had started well in advance of the deadline (ibid., 2010: 115). We will return to Eddie's story in Chapter 7 when considering how young people exercise choice over their futures beyond school and college.

The institutional practices at all of the research sites favoured those who intended to apply for a higher education place over non-applicants irrespective of social background. The tutorial and guidance sessions were firmly directed towards Year 13 (17–19 year-olds) completing the UCAS process during the autumn term. Staff across all four institutions informally admitted they felt they could do more for those who were not planning to go onto higher education but this was an issue that tended to be addressed once the UCAS process was completed in the second term. The following interview extracts help to illustrate how institutional habitus can be mobilized differently for different pupils. This was particularly the case in relation to institutional widening participation practices. Israh and Jack were identified as gifted and talented students at Sherwood College whereas Helen (Jack's girlfriend) was not. These three students all went to the same 11–16 school and were all at Sherwood College at the time of the S2 study.

In the following extract Israh (Asian male, HE applicant), who was in the gifted and talented cohort explains his position in this group:

Israh: I were quite a good worker. I used to get down and work and come after school and basically used to go to library, get my homework done and hand it in whenever it needed it and then I got chosen to be in the Gifted and Talented Group . . . to be in the Gifted and Talented you need to work hard and get on, get on with your work, not cause trouble . . . but we were chosen by the standard of our grades as well.

CH: . . . and how did that make you feel then?

Israh: Quite good.

. . .

CH: Do you think you might have done better as a result in the end then?

Israh: Well I think so yeah, I reckon so yeah . . . because of thinking that we're in the Gifted and Talented Group it like makes you think that you need to work harder so we just worked harder and basically it did, it worked.

WP groupings may have both positive and negative consequences for different individuals. Maintaining motivation particularly among those who are not deemed to have 'university potential' is thus more challenging. In a second example, Jack (white male, Sherwood College, HE applicant) describes how he has benefited from being in the gifted and talented cohort both in his previous 11–16 school and while at Sherwood College. He comments on the advantages he feels he has enjoyed compared to his girlfriend, Helen, (who attended the same 11–16 school and who also went on to study at Sherwood College). She was not placed in the gifted and talented cohort and Jack highlights how their experiences have differed. While at secondary school Jack went on a Year 11 summer school to Oxford University. He also went on a two-week long residential trip to Exeter University through the National Academy of Gifted and Talented Youth (NAGTY). In addition he visited Warwick on a one-day English seminar also arranged through NAGTY. Jack said going to Exeter was his first experience of this kind commenting, 'it were the first time I'd ever done 'owt like that and I loved it'.

Jack thought that the kinds of experiences he had had would look, 'amazing on a cv' but that he had only done them because school had pushed him. He explained, 'I can't wait for University because I've been to two things where I've lived on my own in dorms with friends . . .'. In contrast, Jack referred to his girlfriend, Helen (white female) explaining,

> . . . she weren't there with top group . . . there were never like special trips arranged – like the lower ones got special trips arranged for them, higher got special trips arranged for them and she obviously felt a bit disenfranchised by the fact she couldn't do anything like that . . . She'd [Helen] never had opportunity, not even to turn it down. She's just never been given the opportunity to do stuff like that. (Jack, white male, Sherwood)

Jack's comments resonate well with Sen's argument that it is not only the choices an individual makes that constitute their well-being but also the freedom the individual has to make those choices. From a Bourdieurian perspective, Jack's additional experiences as part of the gifted and talented group have allowed him to accrue cultural capital and understanding of the *doxa* in relation to the field of higher education and even within the field of HE, Jack has gained experience of Oxford University, which may be viewed as an HE site of particular privilege.

Helen (white female, Sherwood), in a separate interview from Jack, gave her own account of her experiences. Helen saw herself as being in a 'middle group' at secondary school, neither seen as gifted and talented or 'special needs'. Helen had not been selected for either the gifted and talented cohort or the 'Aimhigher widening participation' cohort while at her previous 11–16 school. However, when she started at Sherwood College she was identified as having the potential to go on to university. Helen is now in a sixth form college where she feels she has been given much greater support and opportunities. She reflects on her current situation commenting,

> *I'm going on to higher education from thinking nobody cared about what happens to my future, and that's because people here care . . . you're not a number that's not in special needs and not in Aimhigher. You are somebody whose got talent and can go on to do stuff you want to do . . .* (Helen, white female, Sherwood)

Helen echoed Jack's comments describing the way students were seen in different terms at school such as 'special needs', 'Aimhigher' and 'people like me' who were in neither of these groups. Helen described how she thought different kinds of students were perceived by the staff.

> *CH: . . . And then you talked about the Aim Higher people so who are the Aim Higher people?*
>
> *Helen: The people that were in like the special assemblies, the people who go on trips to different Universities, people that got a teach about more to life than getting a job. So they're pushed to more of their abilities because you sort of spend [more time] with them and thought like well these people have got summat, we'll ignore everybody else below that because they're shit basically, they can't . . . what are they gonna do with themselves? They're past help . . . We'll push them [Aimhigher sudents] to make our school look amazing. It's like they don't want middle people to represent their school as the Aim Higher people.*

Helen explained that it was clear to her who was in the 'Aimhigher' group because as she put it, 'I mean they're always called for meetings and they're always on trips and they're always, always doing summat that the rest of us weren't doing'. She said that people came to talk to the Aimhigher people about going to university and also said they had the opportunity to attend university summer schools commenting,

> *Helen: I'd have loved to do a summer school me.*
>
> *CH: Did anybody ever sort of say, 'would you like to do any of these things?'?*
>
> *Helen: Never. Never got approached about anything to do with being pushed further in education.*

Helen expressed disappointment that she had not been offered the same opportunities as other students in the gifted and talented and 'widening participation' groups at her previous school. Her 'missed opportunities' were foregrounded by the positive experiences of her boyfriend, Jack who was labelled as gifted and talented. In terms of the capability approach the mechanisms at play in the scenarios described both help and hinder different individuals' conversion of aspirations into capabilities. Helen, is not able to experience the HE field in the same supported way as Jack. She has positioned herself in the field by applying to the local new university reflecting her habitus and the limits of her comfort zone. Reay et al. have noted the tendency for working-class students to, 'retain the comforts of the familiar' in their engagement with HE (Reay et al., 2010: 111). This is not reflected in data by simply looking at increases in HE participation rates such as those reported by HEFCE (2005, 2010). Jack explained how Helen had decided to apply to go to university locally commenting,

> *She was scared of leaving city, one of the reasons she chose Sheffield. Ultimately I wanted to choose Sheffield anyway but one of the main reasons she chose Sheffield she didn't want to leave the city. She dreaded the fact of going away from home. A lot of people want to get away but she didn't. She's never gone away from home . . .* (Jack, white male, Sherwood)

Four out of ten students in the S2 survey (N_2=580) said they would prefer to remain living at home if they applied for a university place. The CA highlights the possibility that studying locally may (though not necessarily) be linked to adaptation of preferences influenced by conversion factors. The expansion of an individual's capability set and their relative freedom to make choices they have reason to value are not reflected in government statistics in this respect.

Conversion factors related to paid work

The S2 findings regarding survey participants' involvement in paid work indicated that exercising the capability to work may impinge on an individual's capability to learn or to socialize with friends or to help at home. In other words an individual's capabilities are not mutually exclusive. Sen argues that although it is important to develop single capabilities, the possible *combinations* of functionings are also crucial and therefore understanding youth engagement in the labour market enriches understanding of capability expansion elsewhere (Sen, 1999a, 1999b). The significance of active involvement in the paid labour market by young people who are deemed to be in 'full-time' education has been largely overlooked in education policy and practice (Callender, 2008). Evidence from the S2 data shows that, large numbers of students are regularly engaged in paid work. At the time of the S2 survey six out of ten (61%, N_2=580) of the young people were involved in regular paid work outside the home and this was fairly consistent across all institutions. The data show that young people commit significant amounts of time to their employment with some working for over 20 hours a week. Forty-six per cent of young people surveyed reported working 15 hours or less while 16% claimed to regularly work more than 15 hours a week. Goldsmiths students were significantly more likely to spend less time doing paid work than counterparts with just 5% reporting that they worked for more than 15 hours a week. Interestingly, Goldsmiths had a school policy limiting the hours that students were authorized to work outside of school.

Across all four research sites, less than 20% of Asian female students (and 30% of Asian male students) regularly did more than 10 hours paid work a week compared to over 40% of both white UK males and females. White males were significantly more likely to undertake paid work than Asian or black males and white females were significantly more likely to work than Asian or black females. Overall white females were more likely to work than any other group. Young people were paid an average of £5 an hour and hence the potential impact on paid work to other areas of young people's lives is significant both economically and in terms of time spent.

It was found that there are diverse reasons why young people undertake these levels of paid work. In many cases the income is used to fund young people's engagement in leisure activities and to secure commodities for themselves. The most common reason for working was to earn money for leisure activities (57%, N_2=580). For these young people the access to instant disposable income (economic capital), temporarily at least, influences positional relations in other fields. The individuals acquire greater capability to, 'play the game'. Being able to buy the right clothes and accessories of youth culture helps to develop the individual's capability to 'appear in public without shame' (Williams in Hawthorn, 1987: 101). In other cases the income contributed towards essential family expenses. It was found that a quarter of young people engaged in regular paid work felt that their studies, sleep and social activities were negatively affected as a result. This serves to illustrate the interconnections between different fields of young people's lives. It underlines the significance of taking a holistic interest in the complexity of young people's priorities and agency within the different fields in which they operate. It is clear that while the field of education may be important to young people their motivation and agency will be determined to some extent by the relative impact of other fields. The data suggest that the priority and status of educational experience to any given individual is dependent on its relationship within a complex network of other social experiences. An individual's relationship to education and their desire as well as ability to participate is mediated by circumstances far beyond the educational institution. However, the form and flexibility of educational experience may be crucial in offering flexible modes of learning and engagement in furthering their education inside and outside of institutions. Understanding these processes may help to rethink educational policy and practice in ways that empower young people and facilitate higher degrees of participation in lifelong learning across a diverse range of students.

The second most popular reason was to pay for essential personal expenses such as rent, food or travel (31%, N_2=580). Students from Sherwood were more than three times as likely to work to pay towards family expenses compared to their Westside counterparts. Similarly, students from Riverdale were twice as likely to contribute towards family expenses compared to Westside students.

The young people were asked whether they thought their participation in paid work affected other aspects of their lives including studying, sleeping and socializing. Around one in four young people reported that the amount of paid work they did affected their studies, sleep and social activities in a bad way and this was reasonably consistent across institutions. This finding resonates with research into term-time working among undergraduates by Callender (2008). She studied the influence of term-time working of 1,000 undergraduates and found that working alongside studying had a detrimental effect on grades. In her study the least qualified and poorest students were most adversely affected.

Conclusion

Bourdieu's concepts of habitus, capital and field offer some valuable insights into the way in which formal sites of education help or hinder young people in the transformation of their aspirations into capabilities. The symbiotic relationship of the individual habitus with the institutional habitus of the school or college in the broader field of education plays an important role. Individuals are differentially supported in exploring and making sense of the field of HE within this broad field of education. Here young people from family backgrounds with stocks of cultural and academic capital may be advantaged although some within this group may be disadvantaged in other ways. In addition, young people in the gifted and talented and widening participation cohorts who are given access to the *doxa* of the HE field may gain some advantage in learning the rules of the HE 'game' through this means. However, any potential advantage accrued in this respect will be mediated by an individual's habitus. The students who both lack family capital and are excluded from the gifted and talented and widening participation cohorts, however, may be further disadvantaged by the attempts to elevate their peers and this was illustrated by Helen's experience. Bourdieu and Passeron have written about the interrelations connected to both structure and process. They argued that,

> ... the educational process of differential elimination according to social class (leading at every moment, to a determinate distribution of competencies within the various categories of survivors) is the product of the continuous action of the factors which define the positions of the different classes with regard to the school system, i.e. cultural capital and ethos; and on the other hand because these factors are converted and cashed, at every stage of the school career, into a particular constellation of relay factors, different in structure for each category considered. (Bourdieu and Passeron, 2000: 87)

Bourdieu et al. (2000) emphasize structure and social class in their analysis of the multiple variables that operate together creating structures and processes of inequality. The S2 findings suggest there are many potentially confounding variables at play in the conversion processes surrounding the capability to realize aspirations in relation to family, learning institutions, work, social life and beyond. What emerges is the necessity of understanding each individual's situation. Variables such as family and social background, gender and higher education (HE) intentions in terms of eligibility for EMA have shown statistically significant differences in conversion factors relating to developing capabilities. Trends relating to these variables may serve as warning flags for those who may be more likely to be disadvantaged by particular conversion processes in achieving their aspirations. However, while it was possible to identify some common factors that statistically significant numbers of young people in each institution perceived as helping and hindering factors in the achievement of their aspirations, it remains vital not to make assumptions about individuals' needs and relative advantage. The findings presented here provide a starting point for working individually with young people as well as on a more general level to understand the issues they face and to work towards strategies for improving support. Ultimately, we cannot 'second-guess' the conversion processes influencing specific individuals although an awareness of group trends in specific contexts particularly in relation to socio-economic background may be helpful in identifying areas for the development of policy and practice.

Social class inequalities endure in relation to accessing adequate support for developing capabilities. However, in addition, the S2 findings show inferior support and treatment of non-HE applicants resulting in both marginalization and isolation. Divisions and inequalities on the basis of HE application are cross-cut with further inequalities relating to class, gender, ethnicity and ability. In Chapter 7 the complex factors influencing young people's decisions in relation to entering higher education are explored in more detail.

Aspirations, Capabilities and Choice

Introduction

In this chapter the idea of choice is examined, first in relation to choices of secondary schools and then in relation to the choices young people make about whether or not to enter higher education. The examples used illustrate the narrowing of choice at each of these stages and how this is concealed within a policy discourse of expanding student choice. Moreover, it is necessary to draw a distinction between the idea of 'choice' and the idea of 'preference'. Choices are reflected by the functionings an individual actually pursues but they cannot be said to be wholly reflective of preferences. An individual may prefer one option and yet choose another as illustrated in Chapters 5 and 6 and the reasons for this disparity are multiple and complex.

Young people's choices arguably have their origins in two main points of departure. One the one hand, these relate to the different fields in which an individual interacts in connection with the individual's *habitus* and stocks of *capital*. These matters have been addressed in earlier chapters. Here attention is focused on the second point of departure, albeit that this is linked to the first. This second point stems from the ways young people engage different registers of meaning and action in their decision-making processes. The idea of registers of meaning and action draws on work by Reay et al. (2005) and it will be illuminated further here. A significant hurdle faced by young people in the S2 study related to the application procedures for HE and research evidence is presented to convey some of the difficulties individuals experienced. Following on from this, a range of examples from the S2 interview data are used to illustrate six major choice pathways pursued by young people in the study. These examples illustrate the distinction between preference and choice. Acknowledging this distinction is crucial in understanding present injustices prevalent in the education system in England that are at least in part the fall-out of government policy to widen participation in England. From a capability perspective, even if the ultimate functioning that two individuals choose appears to be the same (in this case studying at a university in Sheffield) it is the process by which they come to this decision that is important. There were at times negative reasons why an individual either chose or chose not to pursue a particular pathway. In addition, it became clear from the S1 and S2 research that an individual's habitus, perceptions and knowledge about the HE field were also very powerful in influencing decision-making processes and the way young people positioned themselves in relation to the HE field. Some key issues are raised in relation to these matters in order to highlight areas for further consideration. In light of the evidence presented some suggestions are made for how the challenges raised might be addressed in the future to improve the opportunities for young people to be free to pursue ways of being and doing they have reason to value, selected from an expanded capability set.

Archer et al. (2003) conceptualized participation in HE in terms of risks, benefits and costs of participation. Watts has echoed this theme of identifying the variable degrees of risk associated with participation in HE by different individuals. He describes the 'disproportionate sacrifices' that young people from lower socio-economic groups are expected to make on entering HE (Watts, 2006: 301). Further research has indicated that students from lower socio-economic backgrounds are more likely to have a difficult time in HE and to experience cultural barriers (Cooke et al., 2004). Reay argues that while some students 'find themselves' through an HE experience there are many others who risk 'losing themselves' (Reay, 2001: 333). It has been argued that the dissonance between an individual's identity and their construction of HE is related to the level of risk associated with participating in HE (Archer et al., 2003). However, it is also crucial to acknowledge that non-HE applicants may have aspirations to pursue alternative pathways as opposed to being overwhelmed by the risks of entering HE (Watts and Bridges, 2004). This view is supported by a report by the Sutton Trust which stated, 'not every high achieving student who decides not to apply to a leading university is making a mistake' (Sutton Trust, 2004: 9). However, a major issue which education policy in England has thus far failed to adequately address is that of supporting a range of valued alternative pathways to HE for young people of all abilities, including the most academically able.

School choice

It has been argued by Kelly that, 'Our understanding of school choice and its impact on student well-being is under-theorised, and research is inconclusive in respect of the theoretical complexities involved in the way choice is offered, understood and actualised in families' (Kelly, 2007, back cover). This is particularly the case in terms of choices regarding post-16 education as illustrated by young people in the S2 study. The S2 survey findings indicated that less than half of the survey participants reported considering schools *and* colleges when planning their future beyond Year 11 (aged 16). Less than half of all participants had considered more than two places to continue their studies. As Kelly remarks succinctly, 'the exercise of choice is different from the existence of choice' (Kelly, 2007: 11).

There is a policy rhetoric of choice in education and in theory all young people in Sheffield enjoy the possibility of successfully applying to any of the post-16 education providers in the city to further their education beyond Year 11. However, in Sheffield there are only a few secondary schools with sixth forms and these are all situated in a narrow and affluent south-west sector of the city. The less affluent north-east of the city has two sixth form colleges and no schools with sixth forms. Students attending either Goldsmiths or Speedwell sixth forms had the choice of staying in the same 11–19 school to continue their studies beyond GCSE. By contrast, the majority of young people from Eastside were forced to move to a new institution in order to continue their education beyond GCSEs as all of the schools in this area only cater for 11–16-year-olds.[1] Indeed, Reay (1998) found that increased freedom to select schools resulted in increased advantage for middle-class families in gaining places for their children at good schools compared to their working-class counterparts. A similar pattern of the illusion of choice emerged in relation to HE choices in the S2 study. A capability perspective of well-being freedom in terms of school or college choice would be able to take account of the freedom an individual has to choose between different institutions as well as the individual's satisfaction with their chosen institution (the latter being a current focus of institutional evaluation).

Higher education choices

The Nuffield Review concluded that, 'young people's decisions (over pathways, courses or employment) and the factors that affect them are complex and poorly understood' (Nuffield Review, 2005: 12). The government commissioned

Browne Review on the future sustainability of higher education recommended substantial increases in fees for undergraduates but with fees not repayable until a graduate achieved over a threshold salary (Browne, 2010). On this basis, the Browne Review concluded that, 'for all students, studying for a degree will be a risk-free activity' (ibid., 3). However, risk has been construed only in economic terms and even then in a limited way. It was clear from the S2 data that students perceived multiple risks as well as benefits in their potential participation in HE and this resonates with previous work (Reay, 2001).

Overall, seven key areas were identified from the S2 survey and interview data as being particularly influential in individuals' constructions of self and decision-making in relation to understandings of higher education. Each area is addressed in the ensuing discussion and the numbers are used to indicate their position in Figure 7.1.[2] The key areas include the four *fields* of education,

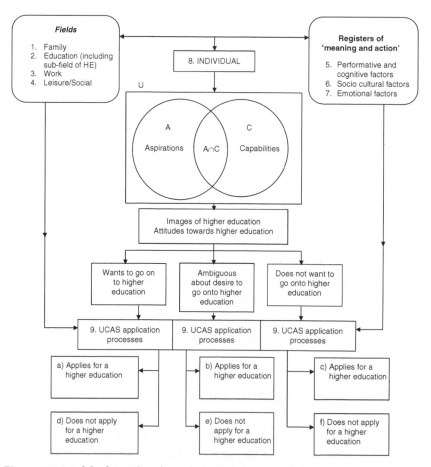

Figure 7.1 Model of social and psychological processes influencing young people's choice pathways regarding application to higher education

family, work and social life and leisure as described in Chapter 5. It is argued that interactions and differential positioning in these fields contribute to an individual's self-perceptions and are seen as crucial in the transition of aspirations into capabilities. In addition, individuals develop preferences and make choices in relation to higher education in and through their social interactions and the application of different 'registers of meaning and action' to their experiences, actions and choices (Reay et al., 2005).

Two registers of meaning and action identified by Reay et al. (2005: 19) are evident, together with a third new register linked to emotional factors, developed in the light of the S1 and S2 data analyses. It is argued that a young person's images of, and relationship to, higher education develop out of the interplay of an individual's interactions in different fields, and the influences of these interactions on the three registers of meaning and action. For clarity, the registers of meaning and action are illustrated separately in the following sections, but clearly there are overlaps between the different registers.

Six alternative scenarios in terms of the young people's decision-making processes regarding HE are indicated in Figure 7.1 (a-f). It shows the diversity of possible decision-making pathways young people may follow but is indicative rather than exhaustive of all possibilities. The S2 findings indicate that the functioning of decision-making is not adequate to indicate well-being freedom or achievement.

Three registers of meaning and action

Cognitive/Performative register

The cognitive and performative register of meaning and action relates to an individual's tendency to select institutions and courses of higher education by matching their academic performance (Reay et al., 2005). The S2 findings illustrated that alongside academic performance, young people also took into account their teachers' and their own perceptions of their abilities and their teachers' predicted grades for them. Regarding this register of meaning and action, interview data reflected some students' desires to connect their higher education choices with their perceived, achieved and predicted abilities. The cognitive and performative register is reflected by individuals asking the question, '*can I do it?*'

Dalia (Asian female, Speedwell) explained that she had not applied for university this year because she was upset by her teachers' predictions in sociology. In this example, she describes how she feels her teachers perceived her and how this related to her predicted grades:

> *I was always quite opinionated and got involved in things but I never was the star pupil. I didn't hand in my homework all the time, on time and things, but I think it just shocked them . . . I wasn't the hardest working one there and I still got an A [at AS Level] as well . . . I think they might have resented that a bit, the fact that I did do well.* (Dalia, Speedwell)

Dalia felt she had changed her university subject choice from Law to Management and then to English partly due to her uncertainty about grades and as a result she was faced with rewriting her personal statement for the Universities Central Admissions System (UCAS) form. In the end she found the process very stressful and decide to focus on achieving the best grades she could in her examinations and postponing a university application until later. Dalia explained,

> *. . . it's just really draining. I just thought 'oh I really don't have a clue what I'm gonna do here,' and there isn't really anyone I thought I could speak to either about it because, I mean each student has their own, you know, their own problems with it so you can't really share it.* (Dalia, Speedwell)

Dalia's commentary offers insights into the way other people's perceptions of an individual's ability may influence their choices with respect to higher education participation. In the following example, Sarah (white female, Goldsmiths) explains that the reason she did not achieve the grades her teachers had predicted at AS level was because of her lack of ability in performing well in examinations. She went on to explain that she was no longer planning to apply to HE because she was not confident of securing the necessary grades. Sarah explained:

> *I was estimated to get an A, for example, in my AS Sociology I was supposed to get an A but I got a C in the end because I'm just not very good at exams and writing essays and stuff like that. . . . .* (Sarah, white female, Goldsmiths)

Predicted grades, determined by teachers, were mentioned frequently by young people as factors influencing their choices. The predicted grades also had an influence on young people's academic self-concepts and learner identity.

Social/Cultural register of meaning and action

Reay et al. (2005) have drawn attention to the way individuals socially classify themselves. They identify a 'sociocultural' register of meaning and action that relates to 'social classifications of self and institutions' (ibid., 19). The sociocultural register is linked to individuals asking the question, *'how will I fit in?'* The findings from the S2 study presented here support and extend this view by Reay and her colleagues. It is argued that individual classifications are important and that these are linked to individuals' perceptions of how they have been classified by others. S2 data indicated students had a tendency to consider their suitability to current and prospective educational institutions in terms of their perceived chances of fitting in. The study findings suggested that individuals develop their identities based on both their own self-perceptions and the perceptions of significant others such as family, friends and teachers. This finding is supported by both the sociology and psychology literature, with foundations, for example, in work by Cooley (1902) on the looking-glass self and by Mead on the 'I' and the 'me' (Mead, 1934). Young people's perceptions of whether a place was for people like themselves seemed very much based on sociocultural norms and expectations. This reflects recent work by Reay, Crozier and Clayton (2010). The interviews showed evidence of young people seeking to reconstruct events and biographies in ways which gave their lives consistency and meaning. There were numerous examples where young interviewees described how significant others had tried to persuade them to apply to higher education. For example, Eddie's parents felt he should apply for university and both Robyn and Katie were strongly encouraged to apply by staff at school, who suggested they would be wasting their potential if they did not go to university.

The S2 survey findings indicated several significant group differences regarding feelings and attitudes towards HE between male and female participants. Males were significantly more likely than females to think that 'university life would be easier than getting a job'. Females were significantly more likely to feel that university is for everyone no matter what their background and they were also more likely to think they would enjoy studying at university.

In the S2 survey sample as a whole, 77% of young people felt they would make friends easily at university although this was statistically significantly more likely to be the case for Westside students. A similar proportion of young people (77%) felt they would 'fit in easily to university life' although this was significantly less likely to be the case for EMA recipients compared to their counterparts from higher income families. Eighteen per cent of survey participants did not feel that university was for 'people like me'. Young people from Eastside institutions were more likely to feel this way as were EMA recipients compared to their respective counterparts. However, the findings also indicated some important variations within institutions and within social groups.

The S2 survey data indicated that those students who intended to apply for higher education were significantly more likely to think they would make friends easily at university. Non-university applicants were significantly more likely to feel that university was not for people like them and they were also significantly less likely to feel that they would fit in easily to university life. There were significant ethnic group differences in individuals feeling that they would 'fit in easily to university life'. White students were most likely to feel that they would fit in compared to all other ethnic groups. The findings indicate that alongside socio-economic background, ethnicity and gender may also play a role in whether an individual feels they will fit in at university. These findings highlight difficulties of making generalizations about inequalities based on group characteristics. In this example, Adam (white, male, Goldsmiths) explains that he may not easily fit in because he feels he does not share the same interests as his peers:

> *Well if you take my childhood I did ballet for 7 years which didn't help me fitting in and then I've . . . I dunno, it's just I'm not interested in this whole culture . . . which is based on . . . going out drinking and it's not that I don't drink, I just don't see it as a defining factor of my lifestyle, which quite a lot of people, certainly of my age, seem to.* (Adam, white male, Goldsmiths)

Emotional register

The third register of meaning and action is linked to individual emotions in relation to their decision-making processes. Based on the S2 study findings, it is argued that individuals frequently use emotive language in their discourses around higher education choices, suggesting that their pathways are influenced by emotional as well as pragmatic choices. This third emotional register is linked to the question, '*how will I feel?*' Several of the young interviewees spoke about their feelings and emotions in relation to higher education and the influence this had on their decision-making processes.

Drawing on the S2 group interviews, a number of survey items were designed to explore emotional aspects of young people's decisions in relation to higher education. This included comparing how confident young people were about applying for an HE place as well as questions about coping with the workload at university, fitting in, feeling stressed and enjoying themselves. The emotional register of meaning and action is used to describe the emotions that young people expressed and implied were influential in their decision-making processes around plans for applying for higher education. Overall, three out of four individuals in the S2 survey felt they would enjoy university (76%). The figures indicated a general trend of young people from lower socio-economic groups being less likely to feel they would make friends easily at university and this is echoed in the wider literature (Archer et al., 2003; Brennan and Osborne, 2008; Reay et al., 2010; Vignoles and Powdthavee, 2010). Half of the survey sample (50%) thought that university life would be very stressful although 85% thought it would be fun. Just over a third of survey participants thought university would be both stressful and fun (36%, n_2=211). Six out of ten young people were 'confident about applying for a place at university' but a similar number (58%) were worried about the costs of going to university with around a third of the sample of young people experiencing both sets of emotions (35%, n_2=208).

Overall, those students applying for a university place were less likely to be negatively influenced by these emotional factors in their decision-making and perceptions of HE. Students who were applying for higher education were both significantly less likely to feel university would be stressful and significantly more likely to think it would be fun. They were also significantly more likely to feel very confident about applying for a place at university compared to their counterparts and to believe they would enjoy undergraduate study. White students were most likely to be worried about getting into debt if they went to university, and Asian students were least likely to be worried, compared to other ethnic groups. In terms of gender, females were more likely than males to feel worried about getting into debt if they went to university.

Compared to the rest of the survey sample students from lower socio-economic backgrounds (as indicated by their EMA eligibility status) were significantly more likely to feel university would be a stressful experience and they were also less likely to think that university would be 'fun' although this latter difference was not statistically significant. Students from lower-income families were significantly more likely to be worried about getting into debt if they went onto higher education.

These findings suggested that individuals held contrasting emotions in tension and perhaps some individuals are better equipped to deal with such tensions. Elster describes how individuals may adapt their preferences as a way of reducing tension that is difficult to handle (Elster, 1983). In deciding to apply for university some young people accepted that it would push their comfort zone in some ways. However, others, like Dalia and Rowan end up not applying for higher education at least in part due to the emotional strains they experience. It seemed that images of universities, student life and studying were used as relational concepts in individuals' own self-concepts and these issues are considered in relation to the examples that follow. In the following example, Helen talked about some of her anxieties in relation to higher education saying,

> But I'm _quite scared_ though because I don't know, it sounds silly, I don't mean
> to put myself down a lot, but I come from that road, and it's not the sparkliest
> of areas. I don't know how they'll feel about me and my accent and how I
> talk. . . . Because I'm not really well pronounced and things like that. And
> _I worry_ if they might be quite hostile to me . . . I'm not gonna ever pretend to
> be anybody else so that I fit into a certain . . . although, _I get nervous_ about
> what people think of me . . . But, you know, you learn to deal with stuff like
> that as you get older, don't you? 'If people can't hear me they'll have to say
> wont they? Like "eh", no-one says "eh", what if they don't understand and it's
> stuff like that _that worries me_ about people from University'. (Helen, white
> female, Sherwood)

The language referring to Helen's emotions is underlined to highlight her concerns. Helen expanded by saying that she used the term 'they' to refer to other students. She says she has heard university students around Sheffield talking and thought they mostly had 'London accents'. Helen is worried especially because of her accent and explained how she thought people will think, 'well she must be from somewhere that she hasn't had much education, what's she doing in university?' In this example, Helen is using an emotional register of meaning and action to make sense of her potential position in the field of education. She imagines what the other students may be like although Helen had not actually visited a university at the time of the interview.

In this interview, Helen constructs herself as working class in contrast to, 'more privileged people'. There is a sense that these people have some kind of ownership of the social space, culture and customs of university life. However, Helen attempts to assert her right to share this space and is adamant that it will not change her. Helen described earlier in the interview that she felt working class and here she constructs her identity as fixed with her 'working classness' as a point of reference. While other young people may slip into the dominant culture of university life without feeling the essence of their identity is under threat, Helen illustrates how her identity is at risk. Later in the extract she alludes to a latent anxiety that others may see her as, 'a right common tramp'. Helen seems to perceive a social risk in being a 'working-class' person in a middle-class milieu.

Archer et al. (2003: 93–4) write about the varying experiences of students in relation to HE based on factors relating to social class. For example, they argue that, '. . . working class students may perceive higher education as a threat to their class identity'. These seemingly dominant issues of social class are compounded by more subtle factors that influence an individual's well-being freedom in relation to their decisions around higher education. In shaping an individual's well-being freedom, Chapter 5 has illustrated, for example, the role of relationships with significant others and the freedom an individual has to aspire.

In a second example, Amy engages the emotional register of meaning and action in explaining her concerns about going to university. Amy described being, 'absolutely terrified' of the prospect of having to make new friends at university. She explained that she had been bullied by her peers both at primary and secondary school and lacked confidence as a result. There were other examples where young people seemed to set boundaries on the kind of higher education they felt would be suited to them and for several individuals this related to studying locally and continuing to live at home. Amy explained that this aspect of university life also scared her,

I'm absolutely terrified because, I mean, I'm staying at home as well . . . so that means that I'm gonna be even less involved in the union things . . . and that's my main concern, that I'm not gonna be able to make friends because I've never been in the, like the sort of place where I've been completely alone before. (Amy, white female, Goldsmiths)

The third example illustrates that the emotional register is used by both males and females. Tom (white male, Goldsmiths) also reported that he had been bullied when he was younger. He explained that he had been, 'beat up by just about everybody . . . because I was smarter at the time than everyone else and I didn't like football'. Tom would be the first in his family to go onto higher education and explained how he felt:

a bit excited because I'm the first to do something at long last. A bit nervous because there's part of me that thinks that I'm going to university and my brothers will start taking the mick, 'oh you're a swot now' and 'you're a student' and yeah when my cousin comes over they always point and go 'student, student' and take the mick out of him so I think they'd probably do the same to me which is annoying. (Tom, white male, Goldsmiths)

Although Tom uses the emotional register of meaning and action it is possible that there may be different trends in the range of the register used by different groups relating, for example, to gender. This could not be ascertained from the S2 study but warrants further investigation. These examples illustrate that some young people, at least, bring an emotional dimension to their vision of what university might be like. In contrast to the examples of Sarah and Dalia, in the cases of Helen, Amy and Tom they are able to overcome their anxieties and intended to apply for university despite their concerns.

In this example, James (white male, Goldsmiths, non-EMA) described being pressurized by his parents to apply to certain universities and to follow in the footsteps of his elder brother who had succeeded in gaining a place at Cambridge University:

> ... *my parents were really, really bugging me about it at the time to pick good Universities and I like, yeah, well like my dad was trying to get me to apply to Cambridge even though my grades weren't big enough. He was like 'oh just apply for the hell of it' and I was thinking, 'no because they'll just reject me straight away' and my mum wanted me to go to Aston. She kept on going 'oh apply to Aston, apply to Aston' and yeah and so I just, I dunno, I think I just picked them all quickly just to get it over with I guess. I dunno. Maybe I should have spent more time on it.* (James, white male, Goldsmiths)

James rushed into applying to institutions he is not familiar with in places he has never visited. This example illustrates that the emotional register is not bounded by socio-economic group or by academic ability. In a similar way, Eddie, who feels literally forced into applying for university, deliberately applies to institutions on the south coast of England as far away as possible from his parents. While Archer and her colleagues (2003) comment that the middle-class habitus experiences less friction and disjuncture when it comes into contact with the educational field, in contrast, Power et al. (2003: 81), 'question the homogeneity of middle classness and the consequently assumed ease of progression [in higher education]'. These examples help to illustrate the insight the capability approach offers when evaluating the issue of participation in HE. Government analyses have tended to focus on participation and non-participation in HE noting that young people from lower social classes are under-represented in higher education (DfES, 2003; HEFCE, 2005, 2010). The examples of James and Eddie highlight the different kinds of concerns young people may have in relation to higher education coming from higher social-class backgrounds and with family experience of higher education. From a capability perspective their well-being freedom has been constrained by their experiences, albeit in different ways from their lower SEG counterparts.

The higher education application process

The UCAS application form is comprised of a number of sections relating to previous educational experience and attainment, a ranked choice of HE courses and institutions and a personal statement written by students. This statement is aimed at supporting the application by justifying course choices, drawing attention to extra-curricular achievements, additional responsibilities and other relevant experience. The application is supported by a written reference from a senior member of staff at school or college. Applications are usually made online and, in England, most offers or rejection letters are sent without students being interviewed. At the time of the S2 study students were required to submit their completed form around late October of their final school or college year and this was the case in all institutions involved in this case study. The UCAS process was not intended to be a major focus of this study but issues related to university applications cropped up repeatedly in the group and individual interviews and some important concerns were raised.[3]

The process of applying to higher education via UCAS emerged as a significant factor in whether or not some young people had the capability to realize their aspirations in relation to higher education. Young people's choices in relation to higher education also appeared to be linked to their abilities to negotiate the processes of application to higher education from practical, emotional and social standpoints. However it was found that the negotiation process helps to determine not only where an individual chooses to apply for a higher education place but whether they apply at all. For some, the process of applying for a higher education place appeared to be linked to an individual's sense of entitlement in relation to their perceived eligibility for higher education opportunities and their chances of success. However, it was also linked to confidence, identity, learning dispositions and broader aspirations.

It has been acknowledged for some time that, 'for some students who have no family background in higher education, the process of admissions may be extremely stressful' (HEFCE, 2001: 16). Concerns about the admissions process led to the Schwartz report which set out principles for fair access to HE institutions (Schwartz, 2004). However, three years on it was found that, 'Amongst the majority of institutions practice had not changed as a result of the Schwartz Report' (Department for Innovation, Universities and Skills (DIUS), 2008: 7). It was also reported that, 'very few institutions attach weighting to contextual data (for example, first-generation applicant)' and very few applicants are interviewed in person (DIUS, 2008). The UCAS application process is related to the genesis of capabilities shown as point '9' in Figure 7.1 (p. 140).

Among those students who did want to go onto higher education the UCAS process was found to be a barrier to some young people. Particular issues related to completing the personal statement, identifying appropriate courses and being put off applying to HE where their teachers predicted grades for them did not match the grades specified in course prospectuses. Some students received substantial support from teachers, careers advisors and parents in completing their UCAS forms and others experienced markedly poorer support. For example, Dalia explained how she was thinking of contacting the universities she was interested in to get advice about what type of employment would be valuable although she admitted she was unsure of how to go about doing this:

> *I don't understand how you do it, who you speak to, you know. I can just imagine it's, obviously I'm gonna have to do it, but I can imagine it's gonna be a bit of a faffing about, trying to get hold of the right person, and I almost feel like I'll be disrupting people by ringing, because they probably get thousands of calls all the time and things, and I don't know ... I just thought, oh I don't have a clue what this is all about.* (Dalia, Speedwell)

Dalia was not aware of anyone she could go to at school that might be able to help her with this process. In another example, Rowan (white female) wanted to study English at university and then go on to train as an English teacher. Her parents had no experience of higher education and she felt they were not able to support her in developing her aspiration. Rowan felt overwhelmed by the variety of English courses on offer and was worried about making the 'wrong' choice or appearing 'daft' if she contacted a university for advice. There appeared to be limited opportunities for young people to visit and look around the universities they were considering applying to. In the end Rowan did not make a university application.

There was little evidence that many young people had made personal contact with higher education institutions other than to attend open days and occasional interviews. Among those who did attend a range of open days the experiences reported varied dramatically in quality, depth and opportunities to find out about specific subject areas. The experiences seemed to depend on individual initiative and luck. An individual could potentially engage in a two-way interaction with the HE field by telephone contact or written communication although there was little evidence in the S2 study that young people were inclined to make contact in this way. The examples of Dalia and Rowan above illustrate the kinds of student perceptions that may detract from contacting HEIs in this way.

A visit by a young person to a university can be seen as a deliberate act of them entering the field of HE, albeit on a 'visiting' basis. Other ways of engaging with the HE field are explored in this section and the example raised here will be returned to later in this section. It is important to note that the boundaries of a field are invisible, porous and overlap with other fields of action. Although many young people had attended at least one general university event this was not necessarily timely in relation to the development of their aspirations. Furthermore the universities visited were often not those that individuals planned to apply to and institution-organized opportunities to see specific departments related to individual course choices were sparse. Hence, the visits allowed very limited scope for young people to find out about the courses and departments that were relevant to them and often the day consisted of more general information being given along with a tour of accommodation, sport facilities, lecture theatres and so on to show what a university is like rather than to choose a specific course. It was rare for students to be interviewed by universities they had applied to and so again the opportunities to find out more about the course curriculum, pedagogy, organization and assessment were limited.

In the S2 interviews a number of young people acknowledged that winning a higher education place was subject to them 'playing a game' whereby they felt pressure to exaggerate or distort their abilities, identities and achievements in order to succeed. This seemed to present more issues for students who were less confident and perhaps feared being 'found out' (Reay, 2001). Dalia said that she felt that many students lied in their university application forms but she would not have the confidence to do that in case she was then caught out in a university interview. She explained,

> I'd rather just say what I have done, what I haven't done but it just seems unfair that it isn't as simple as that any more. I mean people that do lie about those things can end up you know with good opportunities and things. (Dalia, Speedwell)

Some 'risk-taking' applicants may feel more confident to exaggerate their abilities and achievements because they have a greater pool of cultural capital upon which to draw. They may be more likely to risk writing something in their UCAS application which is not exactly true because they feel they will be able to get away with it if later questioned in an admissions interview at an HEI. The risk-takers may feel a greater sense of entitlement to a higher education based on family experience, social background and cultural resources, and therefore feel that the application process is just a paper exercise. Those with significant others interacting in the HE field whether, for example, as a student or as a member of academic staff have a different way of learning about the HE field through the eyes of others. On the other hand, students without a family pedigree in higher education may place much greater weight and gravity on the UCAS application process. They and their families may already question whether they are 'special enough' to be worthy of a higher education place. Being found out as a liar on their application would be doubly damaging to them and hence the risks are far greater than for their middle-class counterparts. The outcome of this is that some students potentially suffer a double disadvantage in competing for a higher education place. First, they may suffer from a lack of social or cultural capital and, secondly, they are less prepared to risk presenting an airbrushed or inflated image of themselves. The act of using a written statement to convey the individual's HE potential to the university admissions tutor could be viewed as a way of engaging with the HE field 'by proxy'. In this case the individual does enter into a configuration of relations in the HE field through the use of a composed personal statement sent as a virtual representation of themselves. Here, the confident risk-taking students, with a 'feel for the game', can appear larger-than-life elevating their potential status in the field whereas the less-confident, risk-averse individuals present less of themselves, thus reducing their agency in the HE field. While some individuals may thrive on this gamesmanship others may fear being found not to live up to the expectations set by the statement they make about themselves. A further significant factor which has emerged from the study findings related to an individual's willingness to reflect upon, and their capacity to reconstitute, their habitus, consciously or unconsciously, in the light of their experiences of the HE field. The data suggest that for some young people this is one of the purposes for participating in HE. Others, like Helen, actively resisted the possibility of change. She commented, 'I talk like I talk and that's all there is to it because that's how I were brought up. I'm not gonna ever pretend to be anybody else so I fit in'.

It seems that an individual's attitude towards stability and change of habitus may ultimately contribute to their well-being freedom and achievement in the HE field as well as in continued interactions in other fields such as family and social groups of which an individual is a member. Mills has argued that habitus is, 'constituted by reproductive and transformative traits' and argues that there are possibilities for, 'the restructuring of students' *habitus*' (Mills, 2008: 79).

However, this may be contingent on the individual's disposition towards change and adaptation in relation to immersion in an unfamiliar field.

Examples of six choice pathways and their origins

In this section the discussion of young people's decision-making processes is continued by looking at a variety of pathways pursued by young people in the S2 interview sample. This allows the analysis of young people's well-being freedom and achievement to go below the surface of evaluations based only on the pathways individuals take. The means by which these pathways are determined becomes a crucial part of the informational focus.

Aspiration to apply to higher education

The flowchart in Figure 7.1 (p. 140) leads to six different outcomes in relation to young people's higher education choices (labelled a–f). The list of outcomes aims to highlight the diversity of pathways young people may follow rather than being exhaustive. Examples are used to offer insights into the variation in well-being freedom individuals may experience in relation to their choices. Hence it is argued, that the overall binary statistical outcomes in terms of application or non-application to university, do not adequately represent the advantages or disadvantages individuals experience. It is argued that the perspective of the capability approach, and in particular the notion of well-being freedom helps to address this weakness and has particular value in relation to understanding complex decision-making processes.

These relate to individual's decisions either to apply or not to apply for a university place on leaving school or college. Findings are drawn from the S2 individual interviews.

HE applicants

Many individuals in the S2 study expressed the aspiration to go onto higher education and many were able to do so. Rosa (white female, Speedwell) is a good example of a student who has achieved excellent examinations grades and has been supported in various ways by her family and school. In addition she has shown diligence, commitment and initiative in seeking out extra support. For example, Rosa sought a quiet place to work at school when not in lessons. She had a part-time job and was saving towards the cost of university. Rosa also described being highly motivated and had a rigorous revision method which she described in detail.

Adam is another good example of a student who has successfully applied for the university course of his choice. His father works in higher education and Adam has been able to draw on his father's knowledge and experience of being an actor in the HE field. In particular, Adam's father has helped his son to draft his personal UCAS statement giving Adam confidence that it was of the 'right' standard.

In contrast, Aisha, applied for a university place hoping to fulfil her ambition to become a midwife. Aisha (Eastside, Asian female) explained in her interview that following some hospital work experience she had considered working as a support worker and then applying later to study midwifery at university. She thought she may be more likely to gain a place with some work experience. However, Aisha's UCAS application to study midwifery at university was unsuccessful in leading to an offer of a university place. Aisha's impression was that midwifery was a very competitive course to get on. She commented,

> . . . they just want . . . probably want outstanding, you know people that have like a . . . probably got straight distinction in their course, go for the top, you know and I'm just in the middle I think. . . . Yeah. I'm not nothing special. I think they go for the ones that are special. (Aisha, Asian female, Sherwood)

As a result of her experience Aisha has remodelled her biography from someone who she felt has the potential to be a successful midwife and graduate to someone who is 'nothing special'. For Aisha, the university application process became a negative experience and it appears to have influenced how she values herself. In the literature there are numerous examples of students recounting negative experiences of schooling and higher education, particularly relating to class but also other aspects of individual identity (Burke, 2002; Archer et al., 2003; Power et al., 2003; Unterhalter, 2003; Reay et al., 2005). The S2 study findings relate to work by Reay claiming that while some students 'find themselves' through a HE experience there are many others who risk 'losing themselves' (Reay, 2001: 337).

HE non-applicants

Examples of students who failed to realize their aspirations to apply for university at the time of the S2 interviews included Sarah, who was put off applying due to lower than expected predicted grades from her teachers (linked to the performative and cognitive register) and Rowan, who struggled to gain support in choosing a suitable course (related to support from college, Connexions and family).

Dalia, is an example of an individual who aspired to apply for a university place but who has not been able to fulfil this aspiration. In her interview, Dalia explained her decision not to apply with several different, yet overlapping, reasons. Dalia was disappointed with her teachers' predicted grades. She also described how this affected her motivation. In the following extract from Dalia's interview she explains how she found the process of completing a university application a barrier in itself. This related particularly to the section of the form where students are required to write a personal statement about themselves. She explained,

> *I just didn't know what to do with it and I thought well where do I start? What do I say, because I felt like if I didn't add certain things then I'd be wasting, you know, my opportunity really . . . and I just thought what do I need to add in, what don't I? . . . . And I just thought 'oh God why am I writing this?' and I just thought this is such a mess . . . that was actually part of why I decided not to apply, as well, because I just thought I really don't know what I'm gonna put . . .*
> (Dalia, Asian, Speedwell)

Dalia's experience contrasted with other students who had greater help with the application process. This did not only relate to whether parents had academic capital but it depended on the family relationships too and opportunities for discussion. Dalia's parents had separated and she alternated staying with each parent. This may have made it more difficult for Dalia to access the support she needed.

Ambiguous about applying to higher education

Some of the young people in S2 were unsure about whether they wanted to go on to HE either in the immediate future or in the longer term. Among this uncertain group, some applied for a university place anyway, either as an 'insurance' against not having an alternative plan and/or under pressure from significant others including family members and staff at school or college.

HE applicant

Martha was unsure about whether she wanted to go to university at the time that her college was going through the UCAS process with students. She explained,

> *Well I did apply to University but I just thought I don't want to go. I just one day just decided. I'd been like I thought I best apply in case I do really want to go but I've never been 100% wanting to go but now I'm fed up of being learning*

in like a traditional classroom. I'd rather be more hands-on like I want to do like an apprenticeship type thing. I couldn't bear going to University for like 4 years. I'd just get so bored and I know I'd quit and it'd be like a waste of money really so . . . (Martha, white female, Sherwood)

In this extract Martha shows her ambivalence towards going on to university. She constructs the HE field as being like college in terms of the expected mode of, 'learning in a traditional classroom' and learning over a period of years. Martha anticipates the lack of opportunity to undertake a 'hands-on' course at university. Martha also refers to lacking motivation in a classroom setting as well as being conscious of the financial implications of going to university. Hence multiple overlapping factors influence Martha's decision not to go onto HE. Martha does not differentiate the diversity of possibilities within HE and hence her well-being freedom to pursue a course that may suit her needs is limited. Martha explains that she applied to university because, 'I didn't know what I could do, but now I've looked into it I've realised it's not the only option in life'.

Martha has been able to draw on the cultural capital within her family in considering alternative avenues other than HE. Her father and brother are both in the police and Martha thinks she would like to join the police force in the future although she explained new recruits are not usually accepted under 21 years of age. Martha's mother works in a school and this is how Martha initially gained information about Modern Apprenticeships. Again, Martha did her own follow-up research on the internet. Martha explains that she has applied independently from college to take up a modern apprenticeship and commented,

College didn't really help me but I thought apprenticeships were just like mechanics, electrical kind of things, like man jobs but they're not at all but I never realised that until I found out for myself. I think that's what the college need to encourage because University isn't like for everyone. (Martha, white female, Sherwood)

Martha is able to access knowledge about the possibility of an apprenticeship via her mother and her own initiative. In Martha's case the college emphasis on university application constrained her well-being freedom but fortunately due to the family capital she was able to access, together with her own research, she was able to find out about alternatives to HE which suit her aspirations. Martha explained that she had not ruled out the possibility of university but it was not something she would consider until later in life. She is very interested in the idea of applying to join the police when she is older and is aware that a degree is not an essential requirement. Martha explained,

> *My dad's a policeman, my brother's a policeman and it just seems like such a fascinating job, like I've been into work with my dad a few times and it's always different; there's never the same job twice.* (Martha)

Martha stood out from all of the interviewees because she was able to articulate a clear understanding of at least three different future pathways which she had reason to value. From a capability perspective Martha has a real opportunity of choosing a future she has reason to value from a range of valued alternatives, despite the fact that this was not facilitated by school. Martha highlighted that there is an enormous pressure on young people to go into HE immediately on leaving school or college, and while HE may expand some capabilities it may also limit individual freedom in other ways.

HE non-applicant

Rita (white female, Riverdale) explained that she was not ready to apply for university on leaving college. She wanted to enjoy life and travel around the country. She said it was important for her to have time to 'play' but that she may consider going to university at a future point in time. Rita's comments struck a poignant chord as she emphasized the relative lack of 'play' in many young people's lives. This point of transition between school and college and between youth and adulthood is constructed around decision-making and an expectation of knowing about the future. Play is not seriously considered within English education policy for post-school transitions and, for example, enjoying a university social life is incidental to the government's role for education in their socio-economic agenda. On the other hand, enjoyment and socializing are integral to the way many young people think about their futures. This reinforces the relevance of the aims put forward by Summerhill School, discussed in Chapter 1. Indeed, Nussbaum identifies 'play' as one of the ten Central Human Capabilities defining it as, 'Being able to laugh, to play, to enjoy recreational activities' (Nussbaum, 2005b: 44). Rita's comments served as an important reminder of the many different ways of being and doing that are of value to members of society of all ages.

Not wanting to apply for HE

Applicants

Eddie explained that his parents had been keen for him to pursue a medical career. Eddie described how his parents had aspirations for him to apply to HE but he did not want to at this stage. Eddie's parents only realized he had not applied for HE when they attended a parents' evening at college. When his parents became aware of the situation they were very annoyed because they wanted him to go to university. Eddie explained that after his parents had spoken to college staff he was sent by the college principal to see the college careers advisor and 'forced to apply' for a university place. He explained, 'I didn't want to do it, I didn't want to do it, so basically I got forced to apply for university. . . . At some point I was even praying not to get any offers'. In retaliation Eddie applied for courses as far away from Sheffield as possible. He had not visited any of them and when I asked Eddie if he knew how to reach the HEIs he had applied to he commented,

> No to be honest I don't know how to get down there. . . . Don't know how to get down to any of them. I know the course of London and I know you've got to get to London first and then probably catch another train or something to different places . . . (Eddie, black male, Sherwood)

This evidence suggests that close examination of the nature of children and young people's participation in education is required in order to evaluate development in terms of social justice. Education participation cannot be assumed to constitute valued ways of being and doing for a given individual. Nor can it be assumed to be indicative of relative freedom between individuals.

Katie (white female, Goldsmiths) was clear that she did not want to apply for a university place. She wanted to get a job and to continue competing as a British Team kick-boxer. Katie was pressurized by school to apply for HE as she was an able student with A grade predictions in all of the subjects she was studying at A2. Katie applied for a nursing degree and said she found writing her personal statement easy, explaining it was,

> . . . fairly easy . . . you just write about yourself don't you? It's not really that difficult . . . I just said that I'd been interested in it for a long time, just all the stuff you're supposed to say, do you know what I mean like everybody's written a personal statement and lied about it, do you know what I mean like that's what you're basically told to do isn't it? You make yourself sound over-interested don't you? (Katie, white female, Goldsmiths)

At the time of the interview Katie did not know whether her teachers were aware that she was not going to university and explained that she had applied to keep them happy. Her story gave the impression that Katie's teachers did not really know what her real aspirations and interests were and she had not gained any support from school in pursuing her passion to be a successful sportswoman.

Katie had managed to secure sponsorship from private companies of her own volition and had travelled abroad representing Great Britain in several international kick-boxing competitions. This example underlines the limitations of evaluating the government's widening participation strategy by looking at numbers of applications to university.

It is evident from the S2 study findings that not all students relied on the cognitive and performative register to guide their decision-making in the same way. For example, some of the young people in the study explained that while they did not want to apply to HE they had ended up applying anyway due to institutional and/or parental pressure. In these instances, individuals had varying reasons for their choices of institutions not only related to their academic performance. For example, Eddie, said he felt forced into applying for university and therefore chose south coast institutions to be as far away from his parents as possible.

Non-applicants

Robyn is an example of a young person who did not want to apply to university and who actually did not apply. However, she experienced continual pressure from pastoral staff at Goldsmiths to apply and was told that if she did not she would be 'wasting her talent'. Unfortunately Robyn did not receive the help she needed to look into how to achieve her own aspiration to work abroad in Tenerife once she left school. During the follow-up telephone interview with Robyn the year after the S2 survey Robyn reported that she had failed to achieve her aspiration to work abroad. Robyn said that she had been unable to get sufficient information and guidance regarding work visas and seeking employment abroad. Thus she had abandoned her initial plans and applied for a university place in Sheffield for the following year.

Knowledge of HE

The S1 interview findings showed that although many students did have aspirations to go to university there was also little evidence of their knowledge regarding what going to university would be like, types of courses, institutions, financial issues and subject prerequisites. Plans often appeared not to be well thought through and crucial information seemed lacking. Significant numbers of young people said they would like to feel better informed about different kinds of future opportunities beyond school and college. This reflects the concern highlighted by Elster's concept of pre-commitment. Where knowledge is limited and manipulated by others this may influence an individual's capability to aspire to different kinds of futures. While there is clearly a strong emphasis on promoting higher education in line with current government policy it may be that this is at the expense of assisting young people in fully exploring a balanced range of future opportunities.

In S2 it was found that opportunities to talk with Connexions Advisors seemed limited. In S2 just over four out of ten (44%, N_2=580) had met with their Connexions Advisor during the year preceding the survey. Less than half the general sample (45%) reported that they had enough opportunity to talk about their aspirations with Connexions Advisors. The quality of interactions with the Connexions Advisors seemed to vary significantly.

Only 16% (93) individuals had seen a Connexions Advisor more than once in the last year. The S2 study findings indicate a mixed experience for young people in terms of accessibility and usefulness of advice from Connexions. Several of the interviewees talked about the importance of being known by those adults from whom they were expected to seek advice and guidance about their future. One of the main concerns young people had about the Connexions Advisors they encountered was that they did not have an ongoing relationship with them and this had led to problems of credibility and trust in the advice given. The following quotations from the S2 individual interviews illustrate the problems young people faced in accessing appropriate guidance:

> . . . *I just felt we were on completely different wavelengths about what I wanted to do.* (Amy, white female, Goldsmiths School)

> *I thought well she doesn't have a clue who I am or anything about me . . . I just thought 'oh God I'm lost here' and I thought I need someone that knows me, that knows my skills and my qualities, what they think I'd be good at . . .* (Dalia, Asian female, Goldsmiths School)

> *She was the worst Connexions lady ever . . . you told her what you wanted to do and then she sort of advised you on to what she thought you were good at without actually knowing you . . .* (Helen, white female, Sherwood)

The government aims to offer prospective HE applicants 'better' information about HE so that they can make 'better choices' and has outlined proposals for achieving this in the Students at the Heart of the System White Paper (2011). While well-intentioned, the choice of data to be made available to prospective HE applicants is at best biased, skewed and ambiguous if not misleading. This is discussed further in Chapter 8. UCAS applicants are provided with 'key' information from the HEIs they investigate on the UCAS and Unistats websites. This includes data on entry grades required, employment destinations six months after graduation and the percentage of course graduates in graduate jobs. Data is also due to be provided by HEIs on average salaries achieved by their graduates although at present this information is scant. The UCAS portal provides access to data from the National Student Survey (National Student Survey (NSS), 2012) which is comprised of current undergraduate views on their university experience.

The NSS survey participants are asked to comment on assessment, academic support, organization, learning resources and personal development. However, the statements to which students are asked to respond in the NSS are highly ambiguous and will undoubtedly lead to subjective responses that are impossible to compare. For example, the NSS survey asks students to rate the extent to which they agree with the statements, 'overall I am satisfied with the quality of the course' and, 'I have received sufficient advice and support with my studies' (NSS, 2012). However, such highly subjective non-comparable data is limited in informing potential HE applicants to a course as what will 'satisfy' one individual will not satisfy another. Overall the Unistats data are hard to interpret and an individual is unable to ascertain from the data the likelihood of themselves falling into a more or less desirable future career. For example, factors such as gender, regional accent, social class and ethnicity may play an important part in influencing outcomes of individuals. But in addition, each individual is unique and aggregated analyses of the benefits of certain pathways are limited in what they say about individuals. Expectations may well be linked to stocks of cultural capital, knowledge of the field of HE, ability and may be shaped by adapted preferences.

The provision of information under the premise that this will enable all potential HE learners to stand on an equal footing overlooks the social context of choice-making. Skeggs (2004: 39) points out that middle-class choice forms around a sense of entitlement as well as access to resources. In this sense, information and knowledge gained about the nature of HE is assimilated into a socially contextualized habitus and way of looking at the world.

The information is presented as if it is value-free and impartial but this is far from the case. Students are increasingly being encouraged to value their education on the basis of the instrumental economic value that might be reaped in the job market. Little or no attention is devoted to the ways in which the experience of learning might constitute human development and flourishing and in itself be an activity the individual has reason to value.

Perceptions of the HE field

The decision to apply for a HE place is an iterative process and it is framed to a significant degree by individual's perceptions of the HE field. Helen (white female, Sherwood) describes her perception of the HE field as an opportunity to recreate her identity from someone that 'nobody would take notice of' to becoming 'a university student'. In this sense Helen perceived the possibility of entering the HE field in the role of 'university student' as an opportunity to elevate her status. Thus the field of HE is constructed as an opportunity for social advancement.

Important features regarding young people's positioning in relation *to* and *in* the HE field were identified. Reay et al. have described how an individual's habitus is developed in and through interactions in different fields (Reay et al., 2005). The first feature refers to the way young people anticipated positioning themselves in relation *to* the field. Some individuals decided not to enter the field at all while others wanted to enter the HE field but remain living at home or living separate from home but nearby. Some individuals wanted to move away from their family home and/or town to go to university and many wanted to live in student accommodation. The second aspect of the way individuals related to the HE field concerned the way they anticipated relating to other social actors *in* the field which was in turn related to the way they perceived the role of being a student.

Gibbons and Vignoles (2009) found that, the geographical proximity of HEIs did not make a significant difference to individual's decisions to participate in HE. However geographical factors were found to have important bearings on differences in HE choices for different income and ethnic groups (Gibbons and Vignoles, 2009: 35). They argue that the quality of education an individual may be able to access is influenced by whether participants are prepared to move away from home. The physical proximity to educational provision is not necessarily linked to higher rates of participation and complex reasons for non-participation have been identified (Berges, 2007). A third of the S2 sample (34%) reported that if they applied for university they would only consider local universities. There were significant group differences for this variable based on EMA eligibility. EMA recipients were more likely than non-recipients to want to study locally if they went onto HE. Forty-one per cent said they would prefer to remain living at home if they were to go on to higher education. Helen explains her position commenting,

> *I don't know how they'll feel about me and my accent and how I talk. Because I'm not really well pronounced and things like that.* (Helen, white female, Sherwood)

Helen had applied for a place at Sheffield Hallam University and planned to stay living locally. Even then, she was unsure whether other people in the university environment would be able to make sense of her localized accent reflecting her upbringing in the Brightside area of Sheffield. She also explained that it made sense to stay in Sheffield because she knew the bus routes and how to get to the Sheffield Hallam campus. Although this may reflect practical reasoning it also resonates with Reay et al.'s research which noted that while remaining at home allows these young people to, 'retain the comforts of the familiar', it comes, 'at the cost of developing as confident academic learners' (Reay et al., 2010: 111).

Reay et al. observe that, 'when *habitus* encounters a *field* with which it is not familiar, the resulting disjunctures can generate not only change and transformation, but also disquiet, ambivalence, insecurity and uncertainty' (Reay, Crozier and Clayton, 2009: 1105). They found this particularly to be the case when working-class students entered elite higher education institutions. In fact, the S2 findings suggest that even before an individual enters the higher education field, the habitus is affected by an imagined immersion in that field. If this is the case then the individual's perception of the field they are considering entering, in this case higher education, is of critical importance.

Fields within fields

The S2 findings indicated that at times young people use their experience of the broader field of education to develop understanding of the sub-field of HE. There was evidence of individuals considering how they felt HE might be similar to, or different from, their experiences in school or college. Drawing on the research findings it is argued that an individuals' capability to participate in the field of HE seems to partly depend on the way in which perceptions and understandings of the field are formed. Individuals seem to anticipate the field of HE based on interactions with actors in the social networks in which they participate. These social networks may, for example, include actors from an individual's family, school or college, workplace or friendship groups. In addition, an individual's capability to participate in HE seems to be linked to the value of their capital portfolio in the HE field. This portfolio is developed through an individual's sociocultural background, interaction in different fields and through their social networks. Furthermore the choices young people make in terms of the range and form of their participation in the HE field are diverse, for example, relating to involvement in university residence and social life. Ultimately, the individual develops a perception of the anticipated location of their habitus in the HE field in academic, social and emotional terms as well as relating to power differentials between peers and university staff.

Images of the HE field were related to young people's perceptions of modes of teaching, learning, support and assessment in HE and individuals' perceptions of whether it would suit them. This was linked to young people's perceptions of the opportunities available to study a subject in-depth and if they felt they would be up to the required standards. The perceived contrasts in pastoral care provided in HE compared to schools and colleges were mentioned in relation to notions of coping with work and meeting deadlines. Some young people in the interviews felt that at university students were expected to be self-motivated and responsible for meeting deadlines without interventions from staff. Some perceptions of HE related to the relationship of the field of HE to other areas of life. For example the perceived financial benefits of job-seeking as a graduate compared to non-graduate were mentioned and around half of the S2 sample (49%) felt entering HE would be easier than getting a job. The financial implications of undertaking a HE were frequently mentioned both in terms of the initial cost of fees and living expenses.

Individuals' anticipated relationships regarding the HE field

Young people may come into contact with various discourses of HE through significant others as well as lesser known individuals and strangers in different fields. Individuals have a range of possibilities differentially available to them to assist them in developing a conception of the field of HE. Table 7.1 overleaf summarizes six key ways in which young people in the S2 study gathered insights into HE. The list is not necessarily exhaustive but helps to highlight how young people may be differentially empowered to develop a comprehensive view of the HE field. This has repercussions in terms of their capabilities to determine their futures in relation to this field.

This conception may influence, first, whether or not an individual intends to participate in HE and, secondly, their preparation for entering and inhabiting the new field. The information gleaned may vary in quality, accuracy and value-bias. It is argued that the development of a holistic concept of the field of HE is an important factor in developing an individual's capability for participation in the field of HE. Reay et al. (2010: 120) note that for those students experiencing dissonance between their habitus and the area of the HE field they encounter, they will have more 'identity work' to do as well as experiencing higher levels of anxiety and stress.

Hence, entry to the field of HE does not tell us about the degree of well-being freedom an individual experiences within this new field. Even within the

Table 7.1 Summary of how young people in the S2 study developed understandings of the HE field

---

1. Individual has no experience of HE field and no member of their social networks has experience either. No input has been received from an actor in the HE field.
2. Members of an individual's social networks have experience of the HE field, for example, a parent who has been to university in the past, or a friend who has been on a university visit.
3. Individual knows someone who currently inhabits the HE field, for example a sibling who is a student or a parent who is an academic.
4. Individual has experience of the HE field, for example, by participating in a university visit or an HE summer school.
5. Individual gains insights from a previously unknown actor in HE field. This may occur in different ways, for example,
    i) by the individual going into an HE environment, with which they are unfamiliar.
    ii) by an actor coming to visit an individual in a field in which the young person is familiar (e.g. a school or college environment).
    iii) the individual retrieving information from the HE field without entering it or coming into direct contact with actors in the HE field. The latter may involve processes such as telephone calls, emails or internet searches.
6. Knowledge of the field mediated by a 'broker' actor, body or website (for example www.direct.gov.uk/Unistats/UCAS) which is associated with the HE field but not part of an HEI. A proxy for direct knowledge of the field but risks misrepresentation.

---

field of HE itself there are many variations, for example, in relation to different institutional and disciplinary cultures. Marginson (2007: 3) suggests there may be a polarization occurring within the HE field with gravitation towards an 'elite sub-field' and a 'mass-sub-field' connected by a range of 'intermediate' institutions.[4] These internal variations will further differentiate an individual's well-being and agency freedoms.

Conclusion

The young people's explanations of how they went about making plans for the future were fragmented, messy and even contradictory at times. Thus it was difficult to tease out a hierarchical set of factors that influenced an individual's choices. Indeed, many of the young people who participated in the interviews commented that they had not previously had the opportunity of talking in depth about their aspirations and choices. This seemed to be reflected in many of the interviews where somewhat chaotic accounts were given of the multiple factors young people associated with their HE choices. The relative weight and impact of individual factors appeared not only unclear to me but also to the young people themselves. In a sense what seemed important was not the individual factors but the overall impact on an individual of a constellation of conversion factors which may be linked to fields related to family, educational institutions, work and social networks as well as individuals' own perceived personal abilities and traits. There was a sense that many of the individuals who had given up, put off or adapted their aspirations did this in response to the overall impact of constraints rather than necessarily as a consequence of any one factor.

The HEFCE (2010) quantitative outcome-based indicators of participation rates for HE in the United Kingdom may suggest positive progress has been made in making HE more accessible and inclusive yet the qualitative data presented here show that the situation is much more complex. The findings showed that although many students aspired to HE there were others who did not. Furthermore there were a number of students who felt compelled to apply for HE while their alternative aspirations were ignored. The processes by which students were encouraged to apply for HE revealed tensions in terms of the narrowing of choice and the reduction of individual agency experienced by some students. The importance of the nature of individual participation in decision-making and engagement regarding HE emerged as a significant factor in the provision of a socially just education strategy. This underlines the intrinsic value of an individual having the real *freedom* to choose a future they have reason to value as argued by Sen (1992).

Ball et al. observe, 'In the late modern period, the self is constantly engaged in a process of self-construction and reconstruction as part of a contingently reflective lifetime biographical project which responds to new risks and new opportunities' (Ball et al., 2000: 2). Improved understandings of how young people construct their identities in relation to HE may contribute towards improving institutional practices which allow individuals to fulfil their aspirations without threatening their identity. Understanding the complexities of identity construction and reconstruction is a vital part of furthering knowledge of how policy works in practice and in recent years there has been some valuable work undertaken in this area (Archer et al., 2003; Reay et al., 2005; Sen, 2006a). The importance of educational institutions in contributing to all young people's well-being freedom emerges as a crucial element.

The findings show a more nuanced interpretation of young people's positions as applicants or non-applicants to HE. The S2 data indicated that young people do not all have the same *range* of capability in relation to the freedom to participate in HE. For example, students' choices may be limited based on ability, perceived ability, course speciality or length and hours of courses. Some, like Amy, are limited by university living costs and feel they can only choose from local institutions. Others, such as Helen, are 'scared to leave the city'. The findings draw attention to a potential problem with a policy focus on achieving a 'threshold' in terms of *absolute* participation in HE as it does not say anything about the variation in *relative* capability to participate in HE that different young people face. The government focus on a 'threshold' in terms of raising HE participation rates to a target level is unhelpful in understanding the variation in capability to participate in HE that young people experience. This underlines Sen's argument that rather than drawing up a generic list of capabilities to be pursued in multiple contexts, in fact it is more justified to develop context-specific goals in relation to developing individual well-being freedom (Sen, 2005a).

While it has been claimed by Furlong and Cartmel that, 'class and gender divisions remain central to an understanding of life experiences' they also argue that individuals tend to explain negative outcomes based on their own failings (2007). It is possible that biographical interpretations may underplay the significance of structural constraints. Ball, Maguire and Macrae observe that, 'young people now see their decision-making as individual "choice"' rather than the product of structural constraint' (Ball et al., 2000). In this context, while structural inequalities relating to traditional stratifications according to class, gender and ethnicity may have broad-reaching ramifications, these are not necessarily recognized by individuals in their biographies and self-concepts. Furlong and Cartmel remark that, 'although social structures, such as class, continue to shape life chances, these structures tend to become increasingly obscure as collectivist traditions weaken and individualist values intensify. As a consequence of these changes, people come to regard the social world as unpredictable and filled with risks which can only be negotiated on an individual level, even though chains of interdependence remain intact' (Furlong and Cartmel, 2007: 2–3). Since the individual's self-concept helps to shape their habitus this leads to a symbiotic relationship between the individual and the fields in which they interact.

Not all young people are choosing a higher education pathway from the full complement of HE experiences available. The narrowing of choice may be linked to institution, course, full or part-time study and staying at home or living away. Those young school and college leavers not planning a higher education have an even more limited range of options. In the light of the variable experiences of the young people in the S1 and S2 studies, a critical evaluation of the 'promises' made about the value and role of higher education is undertaken in Chapter 8.

The Promise of Higher Education

Introduction

In general, the term higher education (HE) is used to encapsulate higher learning taking place in a range of settings including (but not limited to) universities, colleges of higher education and further education colleges. Institutions of HE have traditionally been described in relation to the balance of activities undertaken such as teaching, learning, research, consultancy and outreach work. The structure of HE in England has evolved significantly during the course of the last century, and in the early twenty-first century, and can be seen as a changing and dynamic entity.

HE is not monolithic and Marginson (2007) and Brabazon (2007) have both disputed the position that there is a single criterion of what counts as a university and both point to differences between institutions. Current WP discourse legitimizes meritocracy discourse and tends to promote a monolithic view of universities. There is little differentiation between courses at different institutions and little consideration of the variance in future employment opportunities particularly for young people with different social characteristics and living in different areas (Joseph Rowntree, 2005). This chapter explores some of the promises made to prospective HE applicants, in the light of the S1 and S2 study findings, and highlights some ethical concerns associated with current HE policy in England.

The forms, functions and meanings of HE are constantly being deconstructed and reconstructed within different discourses over time and what emerges is a greater uncertainty about commonality and shared understanding between different ideas of HE among both providers and participants. While there are arguably many similarities among HE providers in England there are also many different opportunities on offer both within and between institutions (Brennan and Osborne, 2008). Even where location, course and resources are equal, Sen observes, 'differences in age, gender, special talents, disability, proneness to illness, and so on can make two different persons have quite divergent opportunities of quality of life *even when* they share exactly the same commodity bundle' (Sen, 1999b: 69).

Given the dynamics of the complex physical and virtual nature of the field of HE it is clear that one person's experience may differ substantially from the experience of another. The variation in experiences of participation in HE is largely opaque to many of the individuals targeted by WP policy in schools and colleges. The level and form of participation an individual is able to experience will emerge from a combination of factors such as personal background and social and cultural *capital*, institutional *habitus* as well as structural features. Indeed, there is a diverse range of higher education institutions in the United Kingdom, and elsewhere, and this is coupled with great diversity of student intake in different places. Institutions achieve varying degrees of socio-economic and ethnic diversity. Within institutions themselves there is a vast range of courses, sites, teaching methods and facilities. Brennan and Osborne observe that, 'it remains the case, of course, that at institutional level there are large differences in the proportions of students from different social and educational backgrounds' (Brennan et al., 2008: 180). They also note how the diversity of students interacts with the diversity of institutions to, 'generate differences in student experience of higher education' (ibid., 180). In this sense, the diversity of student intake in itself cannot be said to be indicative of equality of experience or advantage among the HE student population.

Archer (2007: 639) has noted in relation to this point that, '"WP students" are being offered access only to a "lesser" or "diluted" version of higher education'. Crozier et al. (2008: 167) conclude from their recent study that, 'there is a polarisation of recruitment between different types of universities' which is related to 'students' own sociocultural locations; namely class, gender, age and ethnicity'. Ultimately, the diversity of opportunity to participate in the social milieu of a given higher education institution both creates and reinforces inequalities. Individuals are not only excluded at the point of entry to higher education but within the realms of higher education institutions themselves.

The promise of choice

There is a policy rhetoric of choice for students in HE. The SHS White Paper (2011) emphasizes choices at the point of entry to HE in terms of the plethora of courses available at a wide variety of institutions. It is assumed that 'powerful, comprehensive, authoritative data' available via the government-sponsored 'Unistats' website (www.unistats.direct.gov.uk) will enable young people to make the 'right' choices about what and where to study (UCAS, 2012). HEIs, under government directives, have a responsibility to provide a standardized set of data to prospective applicants via the Unistats website. Users of the site are able to compare institutions and courses on, for example, entry grades, graduate employment rates, average salary and student feedback on the course experience.

Information is provided online by Unistats showing the top ten 'professions' for graduates, from specific courses, with a job six months after finishing their degree course. The categories are very misleading as they do not indicate 'professions' as such but rather broad areas of employment such as, 'sale assistants and retail cashiers'. No data are given on drop-out and non-completion rates, which are significant in many institutions, to provide a fuller picture for potential candidates. The average salaries given for different institutions fail to take account of variation across social class, gender, ethnicity, regional accent or other social factors. Similarly, there is an emphasis on the choices graduates have on course completion in terms of the availability of a wide range of employment in graduate posts. However, there will be different employment prospects for individuals with different grades and from different institutions and in relation to gender, with females, for example, more likely to take career breaks, or work part-time, during their working lives. In the S2 study, Helen (white female, Sherwood) commented, 'if you've got a degree, you can do anything'. Her comment was typical of many students' voices on the image of HE that has been promoted to them, by the government, by HEIs and by schools and colleges. All are complicit in generating this illusion. The reality of choice is very different. Not everyone has the capability to choose from a wide range of HEIs. Not everyone successfully completes their course. Not everyone secures long-term graduate employment. The world is not everyone's oyster, so to speak. Thus, many individuals are being asked to compete, at their own expense, in a competition where only a few can 'win' on the advertised terms, that is to say, narrow economic returns. Perhaps the greatest concern about the key information now provided to prospective

HE applicants is the highly economic instrumentalized perspective that it gives about the nature and role of HE. Alternative ideas of the role of the university are being subsequently eroded as young learners are introduced to HE as a means to an instrumental end that is by no means guaranteed.

The moulding of choice

Stephen Ball draws attention to the tendency in policy discourse to shift the responsibility for learning in ways which make the individual more accountable for their learning. 'Learners are to take responsibility for themselves, but within a framework where certain sorts of choices and decisions are effectively prescribed by policy' (Ball, 2004: 3). Ball highlights a contradiction in the policy discourse where although it is suggested that young people are being encouraged to fulfil their potential, this is a potential moulded by policy to suit the broader economic needs of society. Essentially Ball argues that while, on the one hand, young people are being encouraged to have a greater sense of self, on the other government policy is manipulating what kind of self that should be. The policy discourse of *low* aspirations becomes synonymous with aspirations that do not fit the learner identity envisaged by government. Individuals are held to account and deemed to have an aspiration deficit. In this way attention is diverted from challenges to the adequacy of the education system itself in meeting diverse individual needs and towards a rhetoric of choice promoting the interests of the state.

The potential risks and losses an individual may endure through their higher education (e.g. anxiety, large debts, cultural isolation) are often skated over by teacher and careers advisors keen to boost WP targets. In a similar vein, the benefits of non-university options are often downplayed or ignored altogether leading to what Elster termed, 'pre-commitment' (Elster, 1983). In other words individuals are likely to end up pursuing the HE options marketed by government because they have no other attractive viable opportunities available.

The illusion of widening participation

The Higher Education Statistics Agency (HESA, 2012) reported that only 481,855 out of 639,860 applicants were accepted for full-time undergraduate study in 2009/10. In other words, not everyone gets in. The limited number of HE places in England is under-emphasized to young applicants and, due to Coalition reforms of the funding structure for HE, it is likely that places will be constrained further, especially in the subjects and institutions where non-traditional students (those without a family history of HE) are most likely to apply.

Thus the government strategy to widen participation in HE is not so much about increasing numbers in HE but about attaining more even socio-economic representation of those gaining entry to the field. This relates to underlying government motives to 'unleash' individual potential for societal benefit (DfE, 2009). If HE remains a zero-sum game in this respect, then while some students may be able to realize the aspiration of going onto HE, others will be unsuccessful. Although present and past governments have pursued a policy ostensibly aimed at increasing numbers in HE, in fact, the present system has a limited capacity and is unable to meet the aspirations of all current applicants, let alone any future rises in applications.

Creating a defendable policy of widening participation is arguably one where there is transparency and realism about the 'game plan'. It is clear, under the present policy directives, that not all those who wish to enter higher education are able to do so, not only depending on the strength of their application, but due to the limited capacity of the present HE sector. And yet the Coalition government is strongly in favour of continuing to, 'raise aspirations' to increase HE participation. In fact, unless capacity is increased substantially, HEIs will become more selective and this is in tension with the stated aim of widening participation.

From widening participation to differentiated participation

A greater focus on the nature of participation in formal educational settings would help towards developing individuals' well-being freedoms and expanding capabilities among young people. The capability approach can inform policies and practices that enhance the ability of young people to determine, pursue and achieve their aspirations. This could facilitate a closer examination of young people's participation in decision-making about their life trajectories and the experiences and consequences of educational processes in which individuals engage. Government policy to expand participation in HE in England narrowly constructs the meaning of experience and participation in HE. By contrast, Roger Hart's model of young people's participation, related to citizenship and decision-making (based on earlier work by Arnstein), using a ladder to signify different levels of participation and non-participation (Hart, 1992), is far more comprehensive. Each ascending rung corresponds to an increasing level of participation beginning with 'manipulation'. Those who are manipulated are seen simply as being used to support the causes of others and moving up the ladder Hart identifies five hierarchical ways in which young people can participate more meaningfully in decisions affecting them. At the top level eight, children initiate shared decisions with adults allowing them maximum involvement in decisions affecting their lives. Although the model was developed with reference to children's citizenship it can be applied to understanding the variation in student participatory experiences in (higher) education. The model illustrates that there are many different levels at which young people might participate in their education too and simply looking at numbers enrolled in different stages of education may give a false impression of progress towards democratic ideals. In order to maximize the potential of formal education processes to expand young people's capabilities it is vital that attention is focused on developing more meaningful participation of young people.

The promise of value for money

There is a growing sense of the marketization of HE where credentials are now being sold as essential commodities (Thomas, 2001; Levidow, 2002). This has been highlighted by numerous writers (Pugsley, 1998; Maguire, Ball and Macrae, 1999; Moogan and Baron, 2003). Stamp considers the rise of brand differentiation within the HE sector and comments, 'the scramble for an effective market position is ever more dependent on the management of external perceptions of the organisation through brand value' (Warner and Palfreyman, 2001: 160). Now in recent years, with the raising of tuition fees, students have come to be viewed more openly as consumers of education who are to be persuaded of the 'value for money' they will achieve by successfully completing a HE course. The *graduate premium* is the term used to describe the valued-added by having a degree and in this respect potential university applicants are encouraged to view HE in instrumental economic terms, as a means to an end.

The cost of HE

Since the Aimhigher widening participation initiative was first launched, in 2001, under New Labour, the cost to students of a HE has increased dramatically. Proposals to lift the cap on tuition fees to £9,000 per year from October 2012 led to widespread public protests. The children whose aspirations were being 'raised' in the direction of HE several years ago have experienced 'moving goalposts' in terms of the cost of HE facing them on leaving school or college under the new fee regime (Browne, 2010; BIS, 2011a). Some of these young people have pursued the pathway of HE in the absence of any other commensurate valued choice of post-school or college pathway. If the fees increased ten-fold it is difficult to say what other option they would choose. The government has insisted that the cost of HE does not differentially affect whether people from different socio-economic backgrounds will apply for university and that therefore the system is fair. However, this overlooks the point that actually most young people contemplating applying for HE lack another viable alternative. In this sense they could be seen as backed into a corner where, whatever the costs, university will still seem like the most appropriate choice. A capability perspective helps to highlight the lack of agency of young people facing these circumstances. The travesty is that many young people enter HE assuming that they will recoup their investment in the marketplace at a later date. The employment data, from Unistats, as well as elsewhere, shows that this is not the case (Joseph Rowntree, 2005; Sutton Trust, 2009). There may be other intrinsic and non-economic benefits of university for the individual and wider society from their participation HE but these are neither promoted to young people nor the main grounds upon which many individuals choose to study for a degree.

There is no assurance from the Coalition government that university tuition fees, or repayment terms, will remain stable in the future. Indeed, even prior to the new Coalition fee regime coming into practice in Autumn 2012, the think-tank, Demos, had already produced a report recommending that the repayment terms of student loans should be made less generous, that higher interest rates be charged on student loans and fees should not be waived after 30 years (as originally proposed). Demos argued that this way the state could afford to loosen restrictions on student numbers, introducing more competition into the sector. These changes would in turn, allegedly, drive down tuition fees while also aiding social mobility by allowing more people to enter higher education (Grist, 2012). In 2012, the Coalition undertook a public relations (PR) exercise on fee rises, concentrating on emphasizing the lower monthly payments students would make in repaying loans compared to the previous fee plans under labour. The government focus on comparing changes in monthly repayments under the new fees arrangements diverts attention away from the more than tripling of the overall total fee loans to be paid back compared to previous years. The discourse of lower monthly payments suggests that the Coalition fees package is a cheaper option when clearly it is not. The average graduate, at 2012 levels will be expected to pay back up to £27,000 in fee loans plus maintenance loans. The lack of an up-front tuition fee payment was also highlighted by government 'ambassadors' in schools, along with a raise on the salary level an individual needed to reach before any fees were repaid at all. However, the PR exercise failed to highlight that individuals will pay a far higher fee overall plus a higher rate of interest. At the time of writing, no legal protection was in place to prevent further fee and interest rises. In order to secure greater agency for individuals contemplating HE, the government would need to address these issues of ethics and offer greater transparency at point of sale (that is when 'selling' HE to children as young as 10 or less) and in terms of after-sales policies. In other words, clarity about whether, once a loan is taken out, the repayment terms may be altered. A further question to contemplate, for a government concerned with parity, is whether non-university entrants should be entitled to borrow similar levels of capital, on similar terms, to pursue alternatives to HE.

The graduate premium

The Browne Review which recommended increasing tuition fees to HE reported that, 'the return to graduates for studying will be on average around 400%' (Browne, 2010: 3). However, there is a serious lack of transparency over future earnings of graduates with great variation and a minority securing long-term well-paid jobs on graduation.

While it is reported that a graduate's lifetime earnings are, on average, £100,000 higher than non-graduate earnings net of tax (House of Commons, 2009) this figure hides widespread variation across course, institution and individuals themselves (Brown and Smetherham, 2005). Indeed, Ian Watmore, former Permanent Secretary of the former Department for Innovation, Universities and Skills (DIUS), stated, 'The statistic [relating to £100,000 higher graduate earnings] is clearly an average and it matters massively what jobs people do subsequently' (House of Commons, October, 2008: 9). Interestingly, Hinchcliffe and Jolly (2009) found that many of the attributes employers look for in graduate employees were not specifically linked to HE and could potentially be developed in other ways, for example, communication and interpersonal skills. In addition it has been observed that, 'as any particular level of qualification becomes more widely held across the workforce, the less information it offers employers about those who possess it' (Panel for Fair Access to the Professions (PFAP), 2009: 32).

Indeed, the UK government has introduced measures to provide additional support for graduates who have been unemployed for six months or longer since graduating and this is a scenario few young people would have contemplated when embarking on their chosen higher education course three or four years ago (Hankinson, 2010).

Although a university degree may increase the chances of an individual securing a 'graduate' job on course completion, there is great variation in the terms of posts available. Many posts are temporary, junior posts with limited opportunity to advance. Securing a post may often require moving home, or long and expensive time-consuming commutes. Becker (1975) has considered the rate of return on investment in human capital through education and training specifically by looking at increases in earnings. However, what is unclear is the impact of habitus and the kinds of capital Marjoribanks writes about such as social and academic capital and the question of difference in economic returns for individuals from diverse social backgrounds. In relation to this point, the government commissioned enquiry by the Panel of Fair Access to the Professions (PFAP) reported that the targets to fill the growing number of professional positions will only come about by recruiting from a more diverse socio-economic base than has traditionally been the case (PFAP, 2009). Alan Milburn led the enquiry by PFAP and he concluded, 'Britain remains too much a closed shop society' (Milburn, 2009: 6). The PFAP report entitled, Unleashing Aspirations, echoes findings reported by the Sutton Trust which provided evidence that lawyers, judges, journalists, medics and politicians are overwhelmingly recruited from the higher social classes (Sutton Trust, 2009). PFAP concluded that, 'there is evidence that selection and entry procedures – underpinned by cultural and attitudinal barriers – reinforce the social make-up of the professions' (PFAP, 2009: 21). The Panel also found that 'the UK's professions have become more, not less, socially exclusive over time' and they also found evidence of 'qualification inflation' where professions now called for qualifications not previously necessary (PFAP, 2009: 20). The PFAP Panel further reported that, 'although only 7% of the population attend independent schools, well over half the members of many professions, for example, 75% of judges, have done so' (Milburn, 2009: 18). Milburn points out, 'it is not just that such elitism is unjust socially. It can no longer work economically' (Milburn, 2009: 7). These figures and biases in recruitment to the professions are not reported to young HE applicants and thus the illusion of parity is suggested.

Social mobility

Coalition Education Policy, particularly as expressed in the SHS White Paper, assumes that HE is a 'magic bullet' for social mobility yet this is not the case (BIS, 2011a). The assumption that educational reform can effectively address issues of structural inequalities in society has been disputed in numerous ways by many theorists over time (Gambetta, 1987, Hodkinson and Sparkes, 1996; Ball, Macguire and Macrae, 2000; Gillborn and Youdell, 2000; Slack, 2003). HEIs vary enormously, for example, in their access to resources, staffing ratios and drop-out rates. Students from lower socio-economic backgrounds, without a family history of HE, are more likely to go to less prestigious institutions. Thus, there is a 'sorting' process that goes on at entry to HEIs in relation to different places of study, subject areas, types and level of qualification. Rather than increasing social mobility current CEP may be reinforcing class and social hierarchies in the working population of graduates. This creates two sets of tiered social hierarchies, one for all social classes without a degree and one for all with one. In addition, students with the same level of qualification, from the same course at the same institution, may have different prospects in the job market. As Bourdieu argued,

> There has been a devaluation as a simple effect of inflation, and also as a result of the change in the 'social quality' of the qualification holders. The effects of educational inflation are more complicated than people generally imply because a qualification is always worth what its holders are worth, a qualification that becomes more widespread is ipso facto devalued because it becomes accessible to people without social value. (Bourdieu, 1993: 97–8 in Reay et al., 2005: 163)

Hence, social mobility is about more than simply increasing participation in HE among lower socio-economic groups as implied by the SHS White Paper (BIS, 2011a).

Conclusion

Government education policy in England, is predominantly focused on a narrow economic instrumental view of the role of HE and alternative discourses of HE are silenced in public arenas by an overemphasis in this direction. However, within the academy itself there is a long tradition of powerful and competing discourses regarding the role of HE in addressing economic, social, intellectual, moral and political concerns within society. These discourses have created a plurivocal conception of HE within which there is both unity and disunity (Foucault, 1972). However, the vocabulary and ideas, expressed through the rhetoric of political policies, act to constrain the possibilities for individuals to interact with HE. The promotion of HE based on the promise of financial rewards for graduates serves to privilege economic discourse at the expense of wider intellectual and moral ideals for HE. Furthermore, by placing HE on a pedestal because of its perceived potential to overcome macro-social and economic problems, the impetus to explore alternative means of addressing societal concerns is subdued. These concerns have been echoed elsewhere (Ball, 1997). Hence it is argued that there are potential challenges on several fronts: to HE itself, to individuals engaged in HE as well as to those who are not. Brennan and Naidoo have argued that, 'the internal processes of HE . . . have implications for the shape and cohesion of society and for the quality of life of individuals' (Brennan and Naidoo, 2008: 288). They raise the moral question of the responsibility of HEIs to make knowledge available to society irrespective of issues of increasing learner participation within the institutions involved. In other words Brennan and Naidoo present a flipside to the access argument in the sense that they perceive universities as having a role in letting knowledge out as well as getting learners in. However, the processes of selection and de-selection of knowledge to be pursued by universities become more pressing in times of austerity. For example, courses that are not economically viable will be cut while academics may be encouraged to apply for government research grants which predetermine the realms of knowledge to be pursued (Crace, 2009; Hodges, 2009: 5).

Governments and international bodies need to be able to defend the discourses they deploy. Introducing the key concepts of the capability approach into current discourses may, in Foucault's terms, be able to 'rupture' the dominant discourses of HE (Foucault, 1972). The capability approach offers a new and powerful vocabulary for rethinking dominant discourses of HE that could lead to a significant paradigm shift both for policy and practice. This may make way for a rethinking of new constructions of HE in the interests of human flourishing. Round argues that, in the context of HE, 'established discourses can affect not only how people talk about university, but also how they understand it' (Round, 2005: 1). Discourses can be powerful in shaping young people's constructions of HE and by their nature have the potential to either enhance or limit individuals' well-being freedoms. This has significant repercussions for the morality of government promises regarding the promotion of higher education to young people. Thus, there is an ethical and moral onus on policymakers and practitioners to examine the discourses, policies and practices used to describe and promote HE to young people.

The New Pursuit of Justice

Introduction

Aspirations are not hierarchical, linear or constant. They are more complicated than previously thought, driving ethical policy back to the drawing board in terms of the pursuit of both social justice and human flourishing. Over the last eight chapters, the complex and dynamic nature of young people's aspirations, in relation to government strategies to widen participation in higher education in England, has been examined. Key concepts from Amartya Sen's capability approach were synthesized with Pierre Bourdieu's sociology to create the Sen-Bourdieu analytical framework (SBAF). This framework facilitated new insights into the way young people's aspirations may be transformed into capabilities. Rethinking the relationship between aspirations and capabilities led to the positioning of the capability to aspire as a meta-capability. Conceptual advances in understanding the nature of aspirations were reported and, drawing on concepts from social choice theory, this culminated in the development of a new typology of revealed, concealed, adapted and apparent aspirations. The processes of support and hindrance experienced by young people as they strive to realize their aspirations were identified. These processes were theorized using the notion of 'conversion factors' leading to re-examination of the way in which disadvantage is constructed within widening participation discourses. New understandings of young people's relationships to higher education and their decision-making pathways in this area have also been explored. In particular, a new emotional register of meaning and action was identified to help understand the different ways in which young people construct the possibility of their participation in higher education.

Developing policy using a CA calls for a focus on introducing new language into the hegemonic discourse around aspirations and strategies to widen participation in HE. Changes may be related to shifts from 'raising aspirations' to 'nurturing aspirations' and from 'widening participation' to 'widening capability'. Further thought and discussion need to take place to consider ways in which the language and concepts of the capability approach can be introduced and developed in relation to dominant educational policy discourses. For example, the notions of well-being freedom, adaptation and capability are all new ideas that would theoretically underpin CA policy strategies and therefore new language and understanding need to be generated. The changing discourse in itself offers a promising mechanism for instituting positive change in policies to encourage young people to consider HE.

There is scope for developing education policy to take greater account of the three dimensions of participation identified in this book relating to young people's decision-making, their experiences in education and the outcomes related to that education. Specific barriers have been highlighted drawing on the S1 and S2 research evidence. These relate predominantly to institutional, family and work-related factors. The findings offer direction for self-evaluation at the institutional level regarding these barriers, for example, around opportunities for guidance, out-of-hours study facilities and so on. The research methodology presented in Chapter 4 offers a template for the exploration of other factors which are perceived by young people to assist and impede the development and realization of their aspirations. An extended model of the evaluative space within the capability approach has been presented that takes account of the context-specific meta-capability of aspiration.

In the following sections, first two overarching issues are raised in relation to applying Sen's CA to educational matters. These are the concepts of 'process freedom' and 'democratic deliberation'. Applying these concepts to the fields of education helps to orientate approaches to policy and practise development. Following these considerations the discussion turns to focus on finding a way forward for ethical policy and practice. Recommendations are made specifically with regard to institutional practices and staff development. The final section makes some concluding remarks about the role of aspirations and education in the pursuit of social justice.

Evaluation of widening participation

From a capability perspective there are elements of the widening participation agenda that are in keeping with the goals of expanding capabilities. However, broadening access to HE would need to be one of several options for expanding an individual's capabilities and only then if a given individual had reason to value HE in the first place. The findings from the S2 study highlight that division and labelling may enhance the capability sets of some individuals while compromising the capabilities of others. The research findings showed evidence of newly marginalized groups resulting from the way WP policy is being implemented and that the impact of the policy has been as much about new forms of exclusion as about inclusion. A new kind of sub-segregation may be occurring, particularly in schools and colleges dominated by students from lower-class socio-economic backgrounds without a history of higher education. There is cause for concern where aspirations are silenced due to negative reasons such as fear of ridicule, anxiety about not fitting in with institutional norms and the prejudice of others. An open institutional commitment to accepting the value of alternative futures to HE, even for the most able students, would enhance the agency of young people to openly discuss and develop their aspirations.

Young people will benefit from wider support in the crucial transition phase from post-16 education to the wider world. The efforts should not begin and end in sixth form education but need to be part of a lifelong endeavour. Ethical policy would support young people in developing critical awareness of the advantages and disadvantages of the different future pathways they consider. One recommendation regarding HE trajectories is that young people are able to become aware of the diversity of HE providers, courses and the differential value of qualifications based not only on the institutions but, on social interactions and the young people themselves. Injustices do exist, but ethical practice which makes the system more transparent at least prepares young people for the situations they may encounter. Not all individuals can succeed in gaining graduate jobs, and hence there is an onus on governments, in England and elsewhere, to develop more holistic policies providing for both graduate and non-graduate human development. Support for youth development is needed in the long term as well as in the short term.

One of the risks associated with HE widening participation policy is giving the message that going to university constitutes a 'higher aspiration' than leaving school to do something else. This may result in negative stereotypes being created of people, including parents, who have not been to university. This raises ethical questions about how schools guide individuals in terms of their identity construction and the development of aspirations. The emphasis placed on religious and family-oriented aspirations in the S1 sample highlighted the possibility that current widening participation policy in England may not take adequate account of cultural differences in aspirations. A holistic approach would recognize the diversity of individuals. Widening participation policy aims to promote social harmony but this should not necessitate a move towards homogenization in terms of values and identity.

The narrow WP policy focus on raising educational aspirations does not acknowledge the comprehensive range of aspirations that constitute an individual's full *aspiration set*. The functioning of aspiring to HE is seen as a success indicator in evaluating WP policy impact in schools and colleges. However, as illustrated in Chapter 5, expressed aspirations only indicate an individual's 'revealed' aspirations, and some times not even that. Some expressed aspirations are merely, 'apparent' aspirations, adopted and/or expressed in response to expectations or pressure from significant others. Therefore, the focus on expressed aspirations at best indicates an individual's 'revealed' aspirations, but not necessarily the whole picture of the range of aspirations held by an individual. In seeking to learn more about students' well-being freedom it is pertinent to create opportunities for students to share a range of aspirations, whether with adults or peers. Individuals may or may not choose to take advantage of those opportunities.

Process freedom

The argument for compulsory education is supported in various ways. For example, many hold the view that children are not able to reason sufficiently about what is in their best interests and so adults and the state must protect their interests until they reach a state of maturity where they are able to reason for themselves. Indeed, one of the roles of education may be to develop this critical ability to reason. Other arguments for compulsory education relate to the human rights agenda while others relate to the broader social and economic agendas of society as a whole. The latter may be in tension with both the rights and capabilities of the individual.

Sen argues that, 'capabilities and the opportunity aspect of freedom, important as they are, have to be supplemented by considerations of fair processes and the lack of violation of people's right to invoke and utilise them' (Sen, 2005a: 157). Sen's understanding of the process aspect of freedom can be applied to the notion of compulsory education. In a sense, compulsory schooling goes against Sen's conceptualization of process freedom which he separates from opportunity freedom. It is evident that where an individual values the freedom to participate in education, but is nonetheless compelled to participate in education, then the process aspect of their freedom is violated, 'since an action is being forced on him/her (even though it is an action they would have freely chosen)' (Sen, 2005a: 153). This point is especially pertinent in the context of the government's recent proposal to raise the participation age (RPA). Under Coalition proposals, by 2015, young people will be required to be in education or training until the age of 18. There is a concern that, in order for schools, colleges and local authorities to meet the new targets, young people will be pressurized into enrolling in education and training against their own volition. Evidence was presented earlier, in Chapter 6, from the S2 study, that showed young people were being cajoled into HE even when substantial fees are involved. Chadderton et al. (2010) provide a disturbing account of the experiences of careers advisors working for the former Connexions service. She reported that careers advisors were under pressure from managers to prevent young people from becoming NEETs (not in employment, education or training) and that in order to meet funding targets managers had encouraged statistics to be fabricated. Advisors had faced ethical dilemmas over placing students on courses that were not suitable for them simply in order to fulfil the government requirements to keep unemployed young people in education or training (Chadderton et al., 2010). It is salutary to begin from this understanding since it would be easy to overestimate the extent and nature of freedom afforded to individuals by virtue of the establishment of an organized, and potentially state-funded, system of schooling. In compelling young people to participate in education the process aspect of their freedoms is being violated and so there needs to be a strong reason for doing so. Matters become much worse, if the individual would not have freely chosen to undertake the activities asked of them in the compulsory educational setting. From Sen's CA, in this case both the individual's process and opportunity freedom would be violated.

An additional consideration is the danger that, in seeking to articulate education for well-being, individuals' process freedoms may inadvertently be violated. Not only in relation to making education compulsory but also by becoming overly prescriptive about pedagogical techniques and curriculum requirements. The individual's freedom to determine the capabilities they wish to develop may thus be suppressed. Despite a Coalition government mantra of more choice and competition, Secretary of State for Education, Michael Gove, has expressed explicit support for a return to teaching classical literature and learning poetry by heart. These prescriptions for the content of school curricula may have merit but they need to be subject to a fair process of reasoned and participatory deliberation including the relevant stakeholders. Not least in these deliberations should be the voice of students.

Martha Nussbaum also makes a case for supporting a compulsory liberal arts programme. At higher education level, Nussbaum argues for including at least two semesters of philosophy, technical economics, factually accurate historical information, religious education, learning a foreign language and gaining an understanding of global interdependency and global human values (2010: 90). However, Nussbaum's proposal that all undergraduates should be required to study particular subjects violates Sen's notion of process freedom (Sen, 1999b: 291). Ultimately, there are divergent positions on developing lists of capabilities for specific contexts. In taking forward on one hand, the calls of Nussbaum (and others) for lists of context-specific capabilities and on the other hand, Sen's desire for democratic deliberation, a focus on developing the agency of children and young people to participate meaningfully in such debates is crucial.

Democratic deliberative processes

Sen argues that relevant capabilities are best determined through public deliberation in specific contexts (Sen, 2005a). Sen emphasizes the crucial role of public debate in ranking and weighting the importance of different capabilities in contrasting contexts (Sen, 2005a, 2009). However, Cameron and Ojha (2007) have identified an 'idealistic risk' in Sen's emphasis on deliberative democratic processes in determining capabilities in a specific context (Cameron and Ojha, 2007: 66). Clark agrees with this view that Sen is over-optimistic about possibilities for public deliberation, commenting, 'it is not so much the method itself that is fraught but its potential for abuse' (Clark, 2005: 7). This line of criticism follows work by Deneulin and Stewart (2002) who argue that democratic processes may not be enough to bring about the changes needed in policy or practice (Deneulin and Stewart, 2002: 69–70).

The concerns expressed about Sen's support of a democratic deliberative process of determining context-specific capabilities centre around the effectiveness of public debate and also the extent to which such processes may be corrupt. In addition, the critique of over-reliance on public deliberation rests on what Cameron et al. argue is Sen's idealistic assumption that different parties will enjoy equal rights and power relations in such processes. Drawing on Bourdieu's concept of doxa they draw attention to the more common reality of unequal involvement in decision-making. In Bourdieurian terms, individuals participating in public deliberation are in effect playing a game where individual habitus combines with predetermined rules to create a, 'practical anticipation' of the future in terms of what is 'sensible' in relation to the game being played (Bourdieu, 2009: 68). For example, a group of doctors and patients discussing patient care will be imbued with 'collective belief[s]' about the hierarchies and power relations that govern which ideas are taken forward and put into practice (ibid., 2009: 66). There is a tacit acceptance of the rules by both the privileged and non-privileged. The concerns raised by Cameron and Ojha (2007) are warranted if public deliberative processes, in determining which capabilities should be of value, are subject to power differentials such as those highlighted here. Cameron and Ojha (2007: 83) conclude, 'we do see conscious agency improving [my emphasis] deliberative processes and associated procedural ethics'. In this case it seems that public deliberation on the issues that concern Sen may be an important, although imperfect, exercise.

However, there may be cause for some optimism about the possibility for achieving arenas where reflective, democratic debate over the capabilities and functionings which may be supported through education of various kinds. In Chapter 1 references were made to A. S. Neill's Summerhill school and his alternative views on the role of education. In 2011, I visited Summerhill School, located on the outskirts of the village of Leiston, near the Suffolk coast in England. It is an unusual school in that a special 'meeting' is regularly held where any member of the Summerhill School community can propose topics for debate. The Summerhill community took a vote on whether to admit visitors to the 'meeting' and I was thus granted entry to the proceedings. Around 70 children and adults sat quietly as the 'meeting' proceeded, taking it in turns to speak and listen and vote when invited to do so by their student chair, facilitated by a student ombudsman and secretary.

School rules can be both proposed and revoked by any member of Summerhill, the curriculum can be made and unmade, individuals can be 'brought up' for misdemeanors with full discussion and voting on how each issue should be addressed. Students at the school take turns to chair the meeting with each member of the Summerhill community, adults and children alike, entitled to a single vote on any matters raised. For years, Summerhill has been seen as a very unconventional, perhaps even anarchic institution. Children only go to lessons if they choose to and when they do go to lessons they may find themselves making paper aeroplanes or meditating in the open air. However, in 2011, Summerhill received an Ofsted school inspection report, recognizing several areas of outstanding achievement (the highest possible grade for the report). I did not find the school to be chaotic or disrespectful. The children were polite, friendly and generally self-assured. They each had a voice and they used it. There is merit in looking more closely at the practices of a school like Summerhill where the power dynamic between adults and children and the field of education is radically different from more traditional education establishments.

Finding a way forward

In this section, consideration is given to some specific institutional practices that may facilitate the development of young people's aspirations and capabilities in and through educational processes.

Staff development

Specifying a list of capabilities that all young people should develop during their schooling would not meet Sen's criteria of protecting individuals' process freedoms. Therefore, an alternative way forward may be to consider the kinds of skills and approaches that might help teachers and other educational practitioners to work with young people to develop their aspirations and capabilities.

For example, staff development focused on examining and developing understanding of the concepts of aspiration and capability could be a starting point. This may facilitate the development of an institutionally based self-evaluation that could look at the ways the school or college supports the development of students' aspiration formation and their transformation into capabilities. Acknowledging the existence of concealed aspirations and developing practices that accommodate aspiration change may be fruitful. Alertness to the positive as well as negative reasons for adaptation of preference may also help practitioners to discuss these issues with students (should they so wish). Overall, developing a 'capability ethos' in schools and colleges, is about developing a more holistic view of young people's lives and an openness about how they can feel they can flourish.

Students need to be given the opportunity to revisit the exploration of aspirations over time in a holistic way in recognition of the changes which take place. Students may benefit from discussing their changing aspirations and being encouraged to think in more depth about the change processes regarding their aspirations (e.g. whether changes are due to conflict issues, motivation and so forth). Developing a capability-based framework for evaluating and reviewing change may be helpful with respect to this matter.

Policy development underpinned by new conceptualizations of the processes influencing aspiration change could reduce the level of change due to 'negative' constraints such as 'lack of knowledge' or 'lack of support from school or college' as reported in Chapter 6.

Relationships

The study has shown that developing the capability to realize aspirations is a crucial middle stage between aspiration formation and achievement of those aspirations. Building meaningful relationships between students and staff over a period of time was important to S1 and S2 students. Individuals wanted credible, reliable and timely access to information and guidance on a range of options including but not limited to HE. Many students identified the need to feel encouraged and supported in their endeavours. The support included parents and teachers and related to both emotional and financial issues. The greater awareness adults have of what individual students are trying to achieve, the more ways they may identify which can help to support them. Pedagogical practice which seeks to promote stronger partnerships between the home and school may support this process.

Time to talk

Students also highlighted the need to talk about their aspirations and many reported not having enough time at school to do so. This may be achieved most readily through one-to-one work with a key member of staff who has an ongoing relationship with individual students and is experienced in pastoral work. One possibility would be to build up a profile of individual students' aspirations, the factors that can help them and the barriers they face. These profiles could be reviewed with a key member of staff at regular intervals to allow opportunity to reflect, discuss changing aspirations and broader circumstances and plan how best to help students achieve their aspirations. Pastoral staff may be best placed to undertake these activities although in the interviews some students supported the idea of having someone such as a youth worker they could talk to about their different aspirations and needs. Some of the problems identified with careers interviews were their sporadic and untimely nature, lack of familiarity with staff and lack of connections between career and other aspirations. Young interview participants highlighted the importance of continuity of staff. Opportunities to talk with peers in a structured group setting is another way of giving students more time to explore their aspirations and needs. Research participants in both S1 and S2 gave spontaneous positive feedback on the opportunities they had through the research process to talk about their aspirations in the individual and group interviews. In addition, listening to students' voices in an effort to understand better how they construct their identities can inform improvements in institutional support to help young people to realize their aspirations without undermining their sense of identity.

Educational institutions can contribute to the well-being freedom of their students by considering how they can best support the *real* lives that young people are living. For example, the S2 findings indicated the growing normality of students undertaking paid work in the labour market alongside studying 'full-time'. Acknowledging the extensive engagement in paid work and domestic labour of many young learners may lead to more flexible arrangements in the design and provision of learning opportunities. Education can take place in the community, family, informal learning environments, outdoor centres, religious institutions and increasingly via digital media technologies. Developments in digital media technology may facilitate innovative course design and modes of assessment. Thinking innovatively about timetabling, credit for work-based learning and development of transferable skills such business skills could contribute to recognizing a broader range of young people's tangible achievements. Many institutions already demonstrate good practices in this respect and there is the potential to build on their success.

Decision-making

The research evidence, from studies S1 and S2, offers new insights into decision-making processes, particularly in relation to HE application through the UCAS process. Hence this pathway was used as an example to show how policy strategy may be able to improve support in decision-making by young people during the crucial transition stage from post-16 education to the wider world. In Chapter 7, it was reported from the study S2 that young people were not always able to follow their chosen pathway in terms of applying, or not applying, for a university place. Self-perceptions and the perceptions of others were sometimes influential and the UCAS process itself was difficult for many to negotiate. The combined influence of sociocultural, emotional, performative and cognitive factors, together with images of higher education and the expectations of others led to young people both succeeding and failing to realize their aspirations. Two policy implications follow on from these findings.

First, there is case for reviewing the UCAS process to consider ways of making the system easier to negotiate with greater support. Secondly, there is an implication that if the UCAS process has the unintended outcome of failure to realize aspirations (FTR) then the same may well be happening with respect to non-HE aspirations where the system of application is much less well-defined. Alan Milburn (Leader of the 2009 Panel for Fair Access to the Professions) has suggested that, 'in a globally competitive economy, the key to success depends on unlocking the talents of all our people' (Milburn, 2009: 27). This belief chimes well with the social desire to develop human flourishing by encouraging the 'capability to aspire' and by assisting young people in converting their aspirations into capabilities. However, an attitude shift is needed to overcome the government bias towards focusing on certain kinds of talents that are judged to be more worthwhile than others. Addressing this prejudice is at the heart of change for social justice and ethical policy and practice in education.

The majority of school and college-leavers aged 18–19 years old do not go onto higher education and this is an enduring trend (HEFCE, 2010). Emphasizing HE as the best possible option beyond school or college risks alienating the majority of young people in England.[1] The Sen-Bourdieu analytical framework, developed in Chapter 3, offers foundations for a more holistic policy. Policies which acknowledge the potential disjuncture between family (and institutional) *capital* and the individual young person may be better able to promote human flourishing than those policies that imply an unproblematic relationship in the transmission and utilization of different forms of capital. This is in the interests of developing all young people to have a positive role in society which will bring multiple economic benefits too. The policy sub-strand related to HE needs to be developed alongside other equally strong strands of education policy that endeavour to support a diverse range of young people's aspirations not limited to HE. This offers the opportunity to encourage well-being freedom and agency freedom, facilitating the development of human flourishing.

The development of modern apprenticeships (BIS, 2011d) and work-based training opportunities offers some optimism but the persistence of a 'closed-shop' mentality to internship opportunities and many professions means there is still a great deal of work to be done (PFAP, 2009). As discussed earlier, Chadderton et al. (2010) have already warned of the pressures facing careers advisors to enrol students on courses once they leave school to avoid raising the NEET statistics.

In future the Coalition plans to raise the participation age (RPA) to 18[2] by 2015 may exacerbate these pressures.

Developing critical agency

The degrees of agency of different individuals to effect change, whether for their personal goals or for the well-being of others, vary dramatically. The political, social and economic context of a society has a key role in combination with the power dynamics between individuals.

According to Sen, 'what is needed is not merely freedom and power to act, but also freedom and power to question prevailing norms and values. The pivotal issue is critical agency' (Sen, 2002: 258). Sen discusses this idea of critical agency in relation to the role of women, however, the analysis is also pertinent to considering young people's agency. He comments,

> ... the agency of women is effective in promoting those goals which women tend to value. When those values are distorted by centuries of inequality, for example yielding the perception that boys are to be welcomed more than girls, then the empowerment of women can go hand in hand with persistent inequality and discrimination in some fields ... Indeed, the agency of women can never be adequately free if traditionally discriminatory values remain unexamined and unscrutinised. While values may be culturally influenced (we have provided some evidence corroborating this presumption), it is possible to overcome the barriers of inequality imposed by tradition through greater freedom to question, doubt, and – if convinced – reject. An adequate realisation of women's agency relates not only to the freedom to act but also to the freedom to question and reassess. Critical agency is a great ally of development. (Sen, 2002: 274)

Applying the concept of critical agency to WP, may lead to questioning the traditional value of a higher education over alternative trajectories. It may lead to greater curiosity about why people from all social classes and backgrounds currently subscribe to the enduring value of HE. Once the dominant paradigm is questioned through the development of critical agency the door opens to other ways of being and doing individuals may have (more) reason to value.

Policy success indicators

Although school practitioners may aim to implement policies in ways that meet the needs of students, the extent to which this might be achieved depends to some extent on institutional needs and the mode of management of a given school (Foskett et al., 2004). As long as school performance is based on indicators such as number of pupils going on to higher education it will be difficult to transform practices away from targeting outcomes. Therefore a paradigm shift to a greater focus on the development of aspirations, capabilities and well-being would demand a re-examination of appropriate measures of success. These may be process driven as well as outcome driven.

The assessment criteria have focused on general population outcomes and are therefore quite limited. Indicators such as staying on rates after Year 11,[3] examination results, numbers participating in activities and ultimately the number of students going on to higher education are limited. A successful outcome for one individual will not necessarily be the same as for someone else, because their aspirations and needs differ such as one student wanting to join the army and another wanting to work at the local mosque to further religious aspirations. However, students can share the common goals of, first, exploring and identifying their personal aspirations and needs and, secondly, working towards developing the capabilities they have self-determined. Complementing the broader scale statistics-based performance indicators with assessment of student progress towards individual goals through engagement with an ongoing process of reflection and exploration may help to assess capability as well as achievement. In the future, developing individuals' skills which enable them to take ownership of such a process will allow them to continue identifying and addressing their evolving needs, better enabling them to achieve their changing aspirations in the future. It is possible that this might include aspirations to go to university for those who did not choose this route straight from school.

The CTA contributes significantly to the development of an individual's capability set. Nurturing the capability to aspire requires a paradigm-shift in policy strategy to recognize the importance of a range of aspirations and not only aspirations to go onto higher education. The recognition of the freedom to decide what is worth aspiring to is fundamentally important in terms of individual agency and social justice. The implication is that policy may benefit from reflecting the importance of developing the capability to aspire to a range of valued futures. Policy strategies may be able to influence practice by highlighting the importance of nurturing the capability to aspire. Context-specific strategies will need to be devised for achieving this goal. Ideally this needs to involve students as well as other stakeholders in a meaningful deliberative open process. Although revealed aspirations (the functioning of aspiring) may seem apt as a proxy variable for the CTA there are limitations to this means of appraisal. A focus on the capability to aspire and the autonomy of young people's aspirations may offer benefits for more holistic and just approaches to human development.

The CA has been criticized by Walby (2012) with regard to the difficulty of measuring capabilities. The model of aspirations presented in Chapter 5 and the relationship of aspirations to capabilities, examined in Chapter 6, provide a way forward. There is significant scope to compare in more detail an individual's capability set with their aspiration set. This will begin to provide information about the agency and freedom of a given individual over and above looking at functionings, such as HE particpation. Policy strategy which provides opportunities to explore both the development and change of aspirations may facilitate greater success in young people being able to realize their aspirations.

Conclusion

Griffiths (2009) argues that 'social justice' is a verb that is only made possible through action. In this sense, a point is never reached when we can say we have achieved social justice in education, it must be an active and ongoing endeavour.

We need to humanize a dehumanized policy framework for education and social justice. Presently the emphasis is on rational decision-making based on ostensibly objective information. However, the policy lacks empathy for the deep emotional labour that all young people experience as they grow up and transit multiple fields of social interaction. Bringing emotion into policy and practice would generate a more authentic empathetic approach to education for and with young people.

Injustices associated with social class, gender and ethnicity are deeply embedded in the culture and histories of British society. This is not a justification for their enduring nature but recognizes that reducing inequalities with respect to these variables is a long-term project involving multifaceted changes across society, not only in education, but in all areas of social life. However, injustice arising from the unequal treatment of young people in formal education on the basis of their aspirations is unnecessary and difficult to justify from a moral viewpoint. In many cases this bias towards HE aspirations compounds existing inequalities based on enduring sociocultural factors including social class, ethnicity and gender as well as ability. In other cases young people who may be regarded in hegemonic discourse as 'advantaged', based on the factors identified, may be disadvantaged by their school and college experience. This may occur where their aspirations do not coincide with government aspirations implicit in education policy. This new form of discrimination is insidious because it is cultivated by government policy which ironically aims to reduce social inequalities. The WP agenda is commendable in many ways as it seeks to overcome certain kinds of inequalities in relation to elitism in HE. However, the way the WP policy is being implemented is unintentionally creating new forms of inequalities in other areas as well as reinforcing some of the inequalities it seeks to overthrow. If the government is to succeed in addressing the multifaceted issues of inequality in education then the WP agenda must become one strand of a holistic multi-strand policy, that does not only seek to promote HE.

The capability approach shows how a more holistic approach to education policy can embrace a plurality of conceptions of the good and respect for the ways of living an individual, and not only the state, has reason to value. Sen offers us a range of conceptual tools within the CA which can be used to review and create policy. The choice of tool(s) will determine the trajectory of both evaluation and development in any given area. Tools must be chosen by policymakers, practitioners and others according to the specific situation. Perhaps instead of policies to 'Widen Participation' we should consider 'Expanding Capability'?

Nieto argues, '... all our students deserve to dream and ... teachers and schools are in the best position for "creating a chance" to do so ...' (Nieto, 1994: 422). It is not for policymakers or careers advisors, with little knowledge of the young people concerned, to determine whether an individual's aspiration is feasible or not. Aspirations may have a finite timescale. Possible ways of being and doing may become less possible in future circumstances, for example, linked to health, availability of time, resources or the timing of events. However, the overall question of feasibility is a lifelong question and not something that should be decided by a Connexions Advisor in one spurious meeting at a point in time. Neither should it be determined by the predicted (nor even actual) grades of young people considering whether or not to apply to university. Because circumstances change. We change as individuals. Our social relations, networks, field of action, physical and mental abilities and environment change.

If the organizers of public programmes, parents, teachers, careers offices or other representatives are left to judge the feasibility of aspirations then some individuals may be 'written off' in terms of their abilities to achieve particular aspirations. The judgements of others may be skewed by stereotypes, assumptions and stakeholder influence. Thus the capability to aspire needs to co-exist with other capabilities. This may include the capability to critically reflect on one's aspirations, to refine, revise or defer them. Mental or physical recording of aspirations may be helpful so that they are not forgotten or written off. An aspiration that seems out of reach to a 10-year-old may become more achievable as a teenager or young adult as circumstances, skills and values develop. I remember being very inspired by hearing Sheffield-born Helen Sharman speak about her experience as the first British astronaut. The talk was publicized with Helen as a child, dressed in a homemade spacesuit. Who would have thought then that Helen would realize her aspiration to travel into space, let alone become a pioneer for her nation? Nussbaum criticizes Elster for being, 'suspicious of any desire that is formed through adjustment to reality' (2005: 137). She comments that, 'we get used to having the bodies we do have, and even if, as children, we wanted to fly like birds, we simply drop that after a while, and are probably the better for it' (2005: 137). In Nussbaum's note on this point she says it is not necessarily bad to give up such a desire. However, this is different from saying we are probably better for it as we will never know. Had Helen Sharman given up the idea of flying in space she would not have become Britain's first astronaut. Nussbaum goes on to comment, '. . . someone as a child may want to be the best opera singer in the world (as I did), or the best basketball player – but most people adjust their aspirations to what they can actually achieve' (ibid., 2005a). However, not everyone does. Jessica Ennis did not give up on her aspiration to be the best in the world in her field of sport. Jessica was the public face of the 2012 Olympic Games. She was a Sheffield schoolgirl, much like many other young people in the S2 study. Who would have thought that Jessica would become a world-class athlete, representing her country at the Olympic Games?

Developing the capability to aspire is a valuable lifelong skill in a context where individuals live in dynamic and changing times. My daughter's primary school teacher tells her that often people learn more by getting things wrong than by getting them right. The same might be said of aspirations to some extent. The first formulation of an aspiration may be rough cut, unfinished, not clearly defined. However, careful handling, polishing and time for maturity to develop may yield a far more polished valued goal for the individual that they can begin to pursue, perhaps with support from others. The point about the feasibility of aspirations is that the question of feasibility does not necessarily need an immediate response. The danger of writing off an aspiration prematurely is that it can then be lost. Once a line is drawn in the sand and something is regarded as impossible, it is unlikely that the aspiration will be revisited. By contrast, allowing feasibility to remain open to question allows for revisiting, refining and reframing aspirations so that they may become achievable in the future.

My mother used to say, 'all living things must be watered'. I think she meant that everything that lives, including people, needs nurturing. She definitely extended that to the way she brought up her children. Education policymakers, practitioners and parents are the gardeners of the future, and reflection is called for on how all living things, and especially children, can be nurtured to enable them to flourish. Aspirations can be thought of like theories, possible, or 'true', until proven otherwise. Together, human beings have succeeded in performing heart transplants and putting a man on the moon, alongside a multitude of other extraordinary feats. Yet these achievements were not accomplished overnight. Some aspirations may end up 'on ice' waiting for the right constellation of circumstances such as a change of government, law, attitudes, age of maturity, resources and perhaps even an element of chance. Individuals may feel more or less empowered to effect change over these circumstances and thus developing agency is critical in the development of capabilities based on individual aspirations. If education policy and practice can evolve to support all young people, in developing both their aspirations and their capabilities, then who know what may become possible?

Appendix I

Example of Group Stimulus Material

Your Aspirations for the Future

When I think about what I <u>would like to do</u> in the future I think of . . .

When I think about the person I <u>would like to be</u> in the future I think of . . . . . .

The things that would make it <u>easier for me</u> to achieve my aspirations and ambitions are. . . . . .

The things that make <u>it harder for me</u> to achieve my aspirations and ambitions are. . . . . .

Example of a Higher Education Mind Map

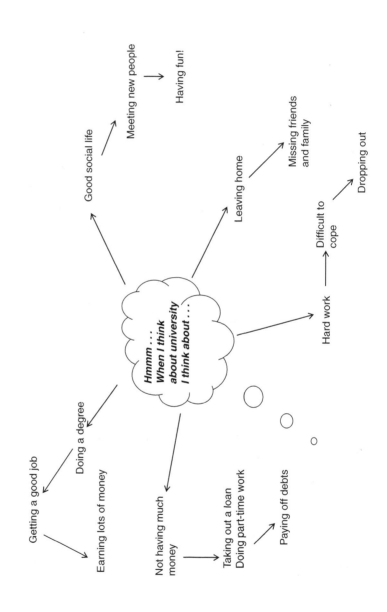

Appendix III

Four Sequential Stages of Quantitative Data Analysis Used in Study S2

Stage of analysis	Non-parametric tests
Univariate	Frequencies and sample distribution of one variable at a time
Bivariate	Spearman's correlation Cross-tabulations Chi-squared analysis (2 nominal variables) Mann-Whitney (2 independent samples) Wilcoxon signed-ranks (paired samples) Kruskall-Wallis (more than two samples)
Multivariate	Layered Chi-squared analysis (3 or more variables). Treated as categorical data.
Special sub-group studies	For example based on intention to go onto HE; Experience of conflict with significant others regarding aspirations; involvement in paid work in addition to studies.

Sources: Oppenheim, 1996: Hinton, Brownlow, McMurray and Cozens, 2008.

Appendix IV

Summary of S2 Individual Interviewee Backgrounds

Participant (institution)	A*-C GCSEs (total GCSEs)	Post-16 studies	Planning to go onto HE (home or away)	EMA	Work
Rosa Speedwell	12	A2 Chemistry, Further Maths, Physics, English and General Studies	Yes (away)	Y	3–4 hours a week in bookshop
Lisa Speedwell	10 (10)	A2 Dance, Theatre Studies and Psychology	No	N	11–15 hours a week
Adam Speedwell	11 (12)	A2 Sociology, Spanish, English AS Mathematics	Yes (away)	N	No
Dalia Speedwell	9 (11)	A2 Sociology, Psychology and English	No	Y	<10 hours a week
John Speedwell	11 (12)	A2 Sports Studies and Health and Social Care (double)	No	Y	Electrical shop @ 20 hours a week
Michael Speedwell	8 (12)	AVCE Health and Social Care	No	Y	<10 hours
Sarah Goldsmiths	11 (11)	A2 Music, Maths and Sociology	Yes	N	11–15 hours a week
Tom Goldsmiths	10	A2 (did History, Economics, Business and IT at AS)	Yes	N	Over 20 hours a week

Name / School		Subjects	University		Work
Amy Goldsmiths	10	A2 Theatre Studies, Biology, Chemistry and Physics	Yes (home)	N	Boots, 7.5 hours a week, has saved £1,000 for university
Robyn Goldsmiths	11 (12)	A2 English, Psychology and Geography	No	Y	11–15 hours a week
Katie Goldsmiths	N/A	A2 Sociology, Psychology, Sports Studies AS English	Applied but not going	Y	11–15 hours a week
James Goldsmiths	12 (12)	A2 Psychology, History and Theatre Studies	Yes	N	11–15 hours a week
Stephen Riverdale	11 (13)	AVCE IT, A2 Geography and Accounts	Yes	Y	No
Israh Riverdale	9 (12)	A2 Law and Psychology, AS Critical Thinking and Accounts	Yes	Y	ad hoc in brother's phone shop, £30 per day
Rowan Riverdale	9 (10)	A2 English Literature and Language, Psychology and AS Critical Thinking	No	Y	Less than 10 hours a week
Rita Riverdale	6 (7)	A2 Sociology, Art and Psychology	Yes (maybe later)	Y	No
Jack Sherwood	8 (10)	A2 Mathematics, Further Maths, Psychology and AS Computing (dropped English after AS gaining a B)	Yes	N	@ 15 hours, Tescos
Eddie Sherwood	8 (9)	Achieved 2 AS science passes at previous school sixth. Now doing A2 Economics, Mathematics and Law	Coerced into applying	N	@ 20 hours a week, pizza restaurant. Pays some bills
Salma Sherwood	6 (10)	A2 English and Sociology, AS Business Studies, GCSE Mathematics	Yes (home)	N*	Retail <10 hours a week, paid <£4.50 per hour

Continued

Participant (institution)	A*-C GCSEs (total GCSEs)	Post-16 studies	Planning to go onto HE (home or away)	E M A	Work
Aisha Sherwood	7 (10)	BTEC Health Studies (equivalent to 3 A2s). GCSE Mathematics	Yes	Y	@20 hours retail, pays £30 for satellite television
Helen Sherwood	9 in total	Advanced BTEC Diploma in Art and Design (equivalent to 3 A Levels)	Yes	Y	12 hours retail @ £200 pm
Nadeem Sherwood	9 (12)	A2 Biology, Chemistry and Psychology	Yes (home)	Y	No
Martha Sherwood	9 (10)	A2 Geography and Psychology, AS History. Has taken AS Business Studies and retook GCSE Mathematics	No	N	@ 16 hours a week, supermarket, @£420 per mth. Saving £50–100 pm for car

Notes

Acknowledgements

1 See www.capabilityapproach.com for further information.
2 See websites for these organizations in the references section of the book for further details.
3 TARDIS stands for a Time and Relative Dimensions in Space machine and refers to the spacecraft used in the fictional English series of Dr Who. The 'TARDIS' is able to transport occupants to different points in time and space (for more information see www.bbc.co.uk/doctorwho/characters/tardis).

Introduction

1 Ofsted stands for the Office for Standards in Education, a government body responsible for inspecting school standards in England.

Chapter 1

1 Sixth form is a term used in England to denote 16–19 educational provision.
2 A* is the highest grade that is awarded at A level and at GCSE level in England.
3 The UK Coalition have proposed that from 2013 students stay on in education/training until 17 and from 2015 they stay on until reaching 18 years of age. There will be legal duties on school, college, employers and local authorities introduced gradually over the first two years.
4 Trow (1972) describes a participation rate of 40% or above as universal participation and his analysis may provide some insight into the decision to aim for this otherwise arbitrary target.
5 'The Higher Education Initial Participation Rate (HEIPR) is defined as the sum of the initial participation rates by ages 17–30' (DIUS, 2008). For the year 2006/7 the former Department of Innovation, Universities and Skills estimated the initial participation rates at 18 and 19 as 20% and 9% respectively while the overall HEIPR was 39.8%. The gender difference is substantial with the overall male HEIPR at 34.8% compared to 44.9% for females aged 17–30 (accessed www.dcsf.gov.uk February 2008).

6 These figures do not include students who dropped out before 1 December of their first academic year or those students who changed courses. It was stated in the Public Accounts Committee enquiry into WP that the actual figure for non-completion of HE courses is closer to 22% (House of Commons, 2008).

Chapter 2

1 Sen's terms, *agency freedom* and *well-being freedom* are explained later in this chapter.

2 See, for example, Jeremy Bentham (1907) *An Introduction to the Principles of Morals and Legislation* (Oxford, Clarendon Press). Library of Economics and Liberty [Online] available from www.econlib.org/library/Bentham/bnthPML1.html. Herein Bentham describes the principle of utility as, 'that principle which approves or disapproves of every action whatsoever, according to the tendency it appears to have to augment or diminish the happiness of the party whose interest is in question: or, what is the same thing in other words, to promote or to oppose that happiness. I say of every action whatsoever, and therefore not only of every action of a private individual, but of every measure of government' (Bentham, 1907; paragraph 1.3).

3 See John Rawls 'principles of fairness', in *A Theory of Justice* (1971).

4 In addition, Nussbaum has a different interpretation of the notion of 'capability' from Sen, and endorses a list of ten 'Central Human Capabilities' which she regards as fundamental entitlements (Nussbaum, 2005b: 335).

5 For a fuller discussion of well-being and agency freedoms and achievements see, for example, Sen, 1985, 1992 and 1999b.

6 See for example, *Journal of Human Development and Capabilities* (2011). Special issue on Human Rights and Capabilities, 12(1).

7 See for example, Sugden, 1993; Qizilbash, 1996, 2008; Pettit, 2001; Sen, 2001, 2005a, 2009; Clark, 2005; Kuklys, 2005; Terzi, 2005; Robeyns, 2005a; Venkatapuram, 2011.

8 See also Gasper and Staveren, 2003; Nussbaum, 2005a; Terzi, 2007.

9 See for example, Bridges, 2006; Robeyns, 2006; Walker, 2006a and 2006b; Watts and Bridges, 2006b; Unterhalter, 2003; Walker and Unterhalter, 2007. There have also been two recent special journal issues on the application of the CA in the field of education: *Prospero* (2007) *A Journal in New Thinking in Philosophy for Education*, Volume 13; *Studies in Philosophy and Education* (2009), Volume 28.

10 See also the *Cambridge Journal of Education* (2012) Special Issue on the Capability Approach and Education, 42(3).

11 GCSE stands for General Certificate of Secondary Education. GCSEs are the standards schools examinations taken by students at the end of Year 11 in secondary schools in England, generally at the age of 16.

Chapter 3

1 See for example, P. Bourdieu, and J. Passeron (2000) *Reproduction in Education, Society & Culture* (London, Sage); P. Bourdieu (2009*) The Logic of Practice* (Cambridge, Polity Press); M. Grenfell (Ed.) (2008) *Pierre Bourdieu – Key Concepts* (Stocksfield, Acumen). Also special journal issues have been dedicated to Bourdieu's sociology of education, for example, the *British Journal of Sociology of Education*, 25(4), 2004 and the *Journal of Education Policy*, 20(6), 2005.

2 Harker quotes Bernd Schwibs (1985) German publication, *Gespräch mit Pierre Bourdieu. Neue Sammlung 3* (Stuttgart, Klett-Cotta). Although this is not a primary source, the quote is included because the metaphor is apt for describing the circumstances of an individual entering the field of HE without the cultural *capital* that might otherwise secure their position and comfort in the *field*.

Chapter 4

1 See Comim et al. (2008) Part II for further discussions relating to operationalizing the CA.

2 For contrasting views on the idea of autonomy see, M. Hand (2006) Against Autonomy as an Educational Aim, *Oxford Review of Education*, 32(4), pp. 535–50.

3 See Alkire (2005) and Part III in Volume I of Basu and Kanbur (2009) for further discussion of interpersonal comparisons.

4 See J. Elster (1983) and D. Bridges (2006) on adapted preferences.

5 AVCE stands for, 'Advanced Vocational Certificate of Education' and A/S stands for 'Advanced Subsidiary Qualification'.

6 At the time of the study FSM was a means-tested benefit available to children whose parental income fell below £15,000 pa. At the time of the study EMA was a means-tested benefit of £10–£30 per week available to young people in full-time post-16 education where their parental earnings fell below £30,000pa.

7 The YPR refers to those young people entering HE either at age 18 or 19.

8 Year 11 pupils were aged 15–16 years and in their last year of school prior to reaching the legal leaving age of 16, at the time of the study.

9 The Connexions service was a public service for young people aged 13–19 in England. It is also available to young people up to the age of 25 if they have learning difficulties or disabilities. Connexions Advisors offered information, advice and guidance to young people to help with decisions relating to careers and learning. They offered advice on other matters, for example, related to work, health and relationships.

10 See the 'question bank' at www.qb.soc.surrey.ac.uk/surveys.

11 N_1 refers to the S1 sample and N_2 refers to the S2 sample.

Chapter 5

1   'True' is used here to denote actual aspirations held by an individual. This contrasts with 'apparent' aspirations which reflect the perceived or actual aspirations and expectations of others, cultural norms and values but not the 'true' aspirations of the individual.

2   Connexions Advisors were assigned by the former Labour government to provide advice, information and guidance to young people on education, employment and training. The role of the Connexions services was superseded by the establishment of the National Careers Service in April 2012 under the Coalition government.

3   Cell counts were too small to undertake a chi-square test using the variable of ethnicity.

4   CH refers to the author in the role of interviewer.

5   Apparent aspirations are not included in this formula as they do not form part of the true aspiration set. If an individual later adopts an apparent aspiration this may be expressed through the existing aspiration terms.

6   A Mann-Whitney test was conducted to look at group differences of the ranking of parental involvement in decision-making using the grouping variable of perceived parental conflict with aspirations.

7   Guidance lessons were provided at Goldsmiths School in order to facilitate students' university applications in Year 13 (aged 17–18). Ostensibly they were also to provide opportunity to discuss options other than HE but there was no evidence that any activities took place that were not oriented specifically to HE during the research period.

Chapter 6

1   Sen makes a similar point in relation to the association between rights and capabilities (Sen, 2005b).

2   *Doxa* refers to the assumptions, norms and rules governing a '*field*' of action which Bourdieu likened to the rules governing a game. Individuals act in the *field* based on 'presuppositions' or unspoken rules. Bourdieu defines *doxa* as, 'the relationship of immediate adherence that is established in practice between a *habitus* and the *field* to which it is attuned, the pre-verbal taking-for-granted of the world that flows from practical sense' (Bourdieu, 2009: 66–8).

3   'Gifted and talented' describes children and young people with an ability to develop to a level significantly ahead of their year group (or with the potential to develop those abilities):

> 'gifted' learners are those who have abilities in one or more academic subjects, like maths and English
>
> 'talented' learners are those who have practical skills in areas like sport, music, design or creative and performing arts Skills like leadership, decision-making

and organisation are also taken into account when identifying and providing for gifted and talented children. (www.direct.gov.uk, 2012).

Chapter 7

1 In theory it is possible that some students living in Eastside may have attended a Westside school prior to starting post-16 studies although this would have involved a significant daily commute with additional time and financial costs. No such students were identified in this study.
2 Figure 7.1 does not reflect all permutations of young people's choices as, for example, some choose to defer entry to higher education or apply at a later stage. Similarly, some young people apply for a place but do not then either accept or take up places. Among those individuals who do take up a university place many change course and/or institution or fail to complete their initial course.
3 Consultations are in progress regarding changing the universities and colleges admissions procedure due to ongoing concerns particularly with regard to the efficacy of predicted grades as a way of assessing university potential.
4 Marginson draws on Bourdieu's concept of *field* in his analysis to help describe the power relations at play between the elite and mass sub-fields.

Chapter 9

1 Young people are defined in different ways by policy documents, legislation and over time with the upper age limit being generally at or below 25 years of age. The 2004 Children's Act established the role of the Children's Commissioner and The 11 Million Strategy (www.11million.org.uk). Under this strategy, children and young people were defined as up to 18 years of age and up to 21 years of age for those who are in care or have mental health illnesses. It is estimated that around 11 million children and young people in the United Kingdom fall within these boundaries. In this chapter 'young people' is the term used to define individuals up to 25 years of age when discussing general policy issues and up to 19 years of age when referring to the young people who participated in the S1 and S2 research.
2 As outlined in the 2010 schools White Paper, The Importance of Teaching (DfE, 2010).
3 At the time of writing the legal school-leaving age was 16, usually reached during Year 11 of schooling.

References

Action on Access (2003) *The Aimhigher Partnership: Progress Report on the Effective Integration of Excellence Challenge and the Aimhigher: Partnerships for Progression* (Bradford, University of Bradford).

Agarwal, B., Humphries, J. and Robeyns, I. (Eds) (2005) *Amartya Sen's Work and Ideas – A Gender Perspective* (London, Routledge).

Alkire, S. (2005) *Valuing Freedoms – Sen's Capability Approach and Poverty Reduction* (Oxford, Oxford University Press).

— (2008) Using the Capability Approach: Prospective and Evaluative Analyses. In F. Comim, M. Qizilbash and S. Alkire (Eds) *The Capability Approach. Concepts, Measures and Applications* (Cambridge, Cambridge University Press).

Appadurai, A. (2004) The Capacity to Aspire: Culture and the Terms of Recognition. In V. Rao and M. Walton (Eds) *Culture and Public Action* (Stanford, Stanford University Press).

Archer, L., Hutchings, M. and Ross, A. (2003) *Higher Education and Social Class. Issues of Exclusion and Inclusion* (London, Routledge Falmer).

Arrow, K. J., Sen, A. and Suzumura, K. (1997) *Social Choice Re-examined Volume I.* Proceedings of the IEA conference held at Schloss Hernstein, Berndorf, Austria.

Ball, S. J. (1990) *Politics and Policy Making in Education* (London, Routledge).

— (1994) *Education Reform – A Critical Post-Structural Approach* (Buckingham, Open University Press).

— (1997) *Education Reform – A Critical and Post-structural Approach* (Buckingham, Open University Press).

— (2004) Participation and Progression in Education and Training 14–19: Continuity, Futurity and Life in the 'Real' Economy – 'That's About it Really', *Nuffield Review of 14–19 Education and Training Working Paper 24* (London, Institute of Education).

Ball, S. J., Maguire, M. and Macrae, S. (2000) *Choice, Pathways and Transitions Post-16. New Economies in the Global City* (London, Routledge Falmer).

Becker, G. S. (1975) *Human Capital: A Theoretical and Empirical Analysis* (Chicago, University of Chicago Press).

Becker, H. S. (1974) Labelling Theory Reconsidered. In P. Rock and M. McIntosh (Eds) *Deviance and Social Control* (London, Tavistock).

Bentham, J. (1907) *An Introduction to the Principles of Morals and Legislation* (Oxford, Clarendon Press). Library of Economics and Liberty [Online] available from www.econlib.org/library/Bentham/bnthPML1.html.

Berges, S. (2007) Why the Capability Approach is Justified, *Journal of Applied Philosophy*, 24(1), pp. 16–25.

Berlin, I. (1969) *Four Essays on Liberty* (Oxford, Oxford University Press).

— (1979) *Four Essays on Liberty* [reprint of original paperback published 1969] (Oxford, Oxford University Press).

Biggeri, M. (2007) Children's Valued Capabilities. In M. Walker and E. Unterhalter (Eds) *Amartya Sen's Capability Approach and Social Justice in Education* (Basingstoke, Palgrave Macmillan).

Biggeri, M., Ballet, J. and Comim, F. (2011) *Children and the Capability Approach* (Basingstoke, Palgrave Macmillan).

Bogdan, R. G. and Biklen, S. K. (1992) *Qualitative Research for Education*. Second Edition (Boston, Allyn & Bacon).

Bourdieu, P. (1986) The Forms of Capital. In J. Richardson (Ed.) *Handbook of Theory and Research for the Sociology of Education* (New York, Greenwood).

— (2009) *The Logic of Practice*. Fifth reprint (Cambridge, Polity Press).

— (2010) *Distinction* (London, Routledge).

Bourdieu, P. and Passeron, J.-C. (2000) *Reproduction in Education, Society & Culture*. Second Edition (London, Sage).

Bourdieu, P. and Wacquant, L. (1992) *Invitation to Reflexive Sociology* (Cambridge, Polity).

Bowe, R., Ball, S. and Gold, A. (1992) *Reforming Education and Changing Schools* (London, Routledge).

Brabazon, T. (2007) *The University of Google. Education in The (post) Information Age* (Aldershot, Ashgate).

Bradshaw, J. and Mayhew, E. (Eds) (2005) *The Well-being of Children in the UK*. Second Edition (London, Save the Children).

Brennan, J. and Naidoo, R. (2008) Higher Education and the Achievement (and/or) Prevention of Equity and Social Justice, *Higher Education*, 56(3), pp. 287–302.

Brennan, J. and Osborne, M. (2008) Higher Education's Many Diversities: Of Students, Institutions and Experiences; and Outcomes? *Research Papers in Education*, 23(2), pp. 179–90.

Bridges, D. (2006) Adaptive Preference, Justice and Identity in the Context of Widening Participation in Higher Education, *Ethics and Education,* 1(1), pp. 15–28.

Browne, J. (2010) Securing a sustainable future for higher education. An independent review of higher education funding and student finance, October.

Burchardt, T. (2009) Agency Goals, Adaptation and Capability Sets, *Journal of Human Development and Capabilities*, 10(1), pp. 3–19.

Burke, P. J. (2002) *Accessing Education. Effectively Widening Participation* (Stoke-on-Trent, Trentham Books).

Callender, C. (2008) The Impact of Term-time Employment on Higher Education Students' Academic Attainment and Achievement, *Journal of Education Policy*, 23(4), pp. 359–77.

Cambridge Journal of Education (2012) *Special Issue on Education and the Capability Approach*, 42(3).

Cameron, J. and Ojha, H. (2007) A Deliberative Ethic for Development. A Nepalese Journey from Bourdieu Through Kant to Dewey and Habermas, *International Journal of Social Economics*, 34(1/2), pp. 66–87.

Carles, P. (Director) (2001) *La Sociologie Est un Sport de Combat*, (France, C P Productions).

Caviglioli, O. and Harris, I. (2001) *Mapwise. Accelerated Learning Through Visible Thinking* (Stafford, Network Educational Press).

Chaddeton, C. and Colley, H. (2010) *Career Guidance Unbound: A Case of Strategic Resistance?* Paper presented at BERA annual conference, University of Warwick, 1–3 September.

Chitty, C. (2009) *Education Policy in Britain* (Basingstoke, Palgrave Macmillan).

Clark, D. A. (2005) *The Capability Approach: Its Developments, Critiques and Recent Advances,* Global Poverty Research Group. Accessed at www.gprg.org.

Cohen, G. A. (2006) Equality of What? On Welfare, Goods, and Capabilities. In M. C. Nussbaum and A. Sen (Eds) *The Quality of Life* (Oxford, Oxford University Press).

Cohen, L., Manion, L. and Morrison, K. (2003) *Research Methods in Education*. Fifth Edition (London, Routledge Falmer).

Comim, F. (2008) *Measuring Capabilities*. In F. Comim, M. Qizilbashand and S. Alkire (Eds) *The Capability Approach. Concepts, Measures and Applications* (Cambridge, Cambridge University Press).

Comim, F., Qizilbash, M. and Alkire, S. (Eds) (2008) *The Capability Approach. Concepts, Measures and Applications* (Cambridge, Cambridge University Press).

Cooke, R., Barkham, M., Audin, K., Bradley, M. and Davy, J. (2004) How Social Class Differences Affect Students' Experience of University, *Journal of Further and Higher Education*, 28(4), pp. 407–21.

Cooley, C. H. (1902) *Human Nature and the Social Order* (New York, Scribner's).

Crace, J. (2009) Parallel University, *Guardian*, 20 October, 2009, p. 1.

Crozier, G., Reay, D., Clayton, J., Colliander, L. and Grinstead, J. (2008) Different Strokes for Different Folks: Diverse Students in Diverse Institutions – Experiences of Higher Education, *Research Papers in Education*, 23(2), pp. 167–77.

Curry, D. (2008) House of Commons Public Accounts Committee (20 October 2008) *Widening Participation in Higher Education*. HC 725. Oral Evidence (London, The Stationary Office Limited).

David, M., Parry, G., Vignoles, A., Hayward, G., Williams, J., Crozier, G., Hockings, C. and Fuller, A. (2008) *Widening Participation in Higher Education. A Commentary by the Teaching and Learning Research Programme* (London, Institute of Education).

Dearing, R. (1996) *Review of Qualifications for 16–19 Year Olds* (London, SCAA).

Deneulin, S. and Stewart, F. (2002). Amartya Sen's Contribution to Development Thinking, *Studies in Comparative International Development*, 37(2), pp. 61–70.

Deneulin, S., Nebel, M. and Sagovsky, N. (Eds) (2006) *Transforming Unjust Structures – The Capability Approach* (Dordrecht, Springer).

Department for Business, Innovation and Skills (2010) *Letter to the Higher Education Funding Council from the Department for Business, Innovation and Skills* (London, BIS).

— (2011a) *Higher Education. Students at the Heart of the System*, June (London, BIS).

— (2011b) *New Challenges, New Chances. Further Education and Skills System Reform Plan: Building a World Class Skills System*, December (London, BIS).

Department for Education (2010) *The Importance of Teaching White Paper* (London).

Department for Education and Skills (2003) *White Paper: The Future of Higher Education* (London, DfES).

— (2006) *Widening Participation in Higher Education* (Nottingham, DfES).

Department for Innovation, Universities and Skills (2008) *Fair Admissions to Higher Education – A Review of the Implementation of the Schwartz Report Principles Three Years On: Report 1 – Executive Summary and Conclusions.*

Department for International Development (2006) *Millennium Development Goals. Education Factsheet. Policy Division Info Series. PD Info 048. (DfID).*

Department for Education (2011) *The Importance of Teaching White Paper* (London).

Department for Education (2003) *The Future of Higher Education: What it Means to Students and Parents* (London).

Department for International Development (2006) *Millennium Development Goals. Education Factsheet. Policy Division Info Series. PD Info 048* (DfID).

Dworkin, R. (1981) *Taking Rights Seriously.* New Impression with a Reply to Critics. Third Impression (London, Duckworth).

Elster, J. (1983) *Sour Grapes: Studies in the Subversion of Rationality* (Cambridge, Cambridge University Press).

— (2000) *Ulysses Unbound: Studies in Rationality, Precommitment and Constraints* (Cambridge, Cambridge University Press).

Equal Opportunities Commission (2006) Facts About Men and Women in Great Britain 2006. Accessed 18 August 2006 at www.eoc.org.uk.

Erickson, B. H. (1996) Culture, Class and Connections, *The American Journal of Sociology*, 102, pp. 217–51.

Farmer, C. (2003) *Home Office Citizenship Survey: Top-Level Findings from the Children's and Young People's Survey* (London, DfES).

Fevre, R. (1997) *Some Sociological Alternatives to Human Capital Theory and Their Implications for Research on Post-Compulsory Education and Training. Patterns of Participation in Adult Education and Training.* Working Paper 3 (Cardiff, University of Wales).

Fitz, J., Halpin, D. and Power, S. (1994) Implementation Research and Education Policy: Practice and Prospects, *British Journal of Educational Studies*, XXXXII (1), pp. 53–69.

Flores-Crespo, P. (2007) Situating Education in the Human Capabilities Approach. In M. Walker and E. Unterhalter (Eds) *Amartya Sen's Capability Approach and Social Justice in Education* (Basingstoke, Palgrave).

Foskett, N., Dyke, M. and Maringe, F. (2004) *The Influence of the School in the Decision to Participate in Learning Post-16* (Southampton, University of Southampton).

Foucault, M. (1972) *The Archaeology of Knowledge*. Translated by A. M. Sheridan (London, Tavistock).

Freire, P. (1972) *Pedagogy of the Oppressed* (London, Penguin).

Furlong, A. and Cartmel, F. (2007) *Young People and Social Change. New Perspectives*. Second Edition (Maidenhead, Oxford University Press).

Gambetta, D. (1987) *Were They Pushed or Did They Jump?* (Cambridge, Cambridge University Press).

Gasper, D. (2002) Is Sen's Capability Approach an Adequate Basis for a Theory of Human Development? *Review of Political Economy*, 14(4), pp. 435–61.

Gasper, D. and Staveren, I. (2003) Development as Freedom – And as What Else? *Feminist Economics*, 9(2–3), pp. 137–61.

Gewirtz, S., Ball, S. J. and Bowe, R. (1995) *Markets, Choice and Equity in Education* (Buckingham, Open University Press).

Gibbons, S. and Vignoles, A. (2009) *Access, Choice and Participation* (London, CEE) Accessed 4 March 2009 at www.lse.ac.uk.

Gillborn, D. and Youdell, D. (2000) *Rationing Education. Policy, Practice, Reform and Equity* (Buckingham, Open University Press).

Gove, M. (2008) *A Failed Generation: Educational Inequality under Labour* (London, The Bow Group).

— (2011a) *Speech Delivered at the University of Cambridge*, 24 November.

— (2011b) *Restore Elitism to Our Schools*, Article in the *Daily Mail*, 28 September.

— (2012) *Education Select Committee*, Oral Evidence Session, 31 January, London, Westminster.

Grenfell, M. and James, D. (2004) Change *in* the Field – Chang*ing* the Field: Bourdieu and the Methodological Practice of Educational Research, *British Journal of Sociology of Education*, 25(4), pp. 507–23.

Griffiths, M. (2009) *Justice, Joy and Educational Delights*, professorial inaugural lecture, University of Edinburgh, 24 March.

— (2010) *Social Justice and Educational Delights*, paper presented at the Philosophy of Education Society of Great Britain Annual Conference, Oxford.

Griffiths, M., Berry, J., Holt, A., Naylor, J. and Weekes, P. (2006) Learning to be in Public Spaces: In from the Margins with Dancers, Sculptors, Painters and Musicians, *British Journal of Educational Studies*, 54(3).

Grist, M. (2012) *Future Universities. Towards a Genuinely Sustainable System* (London, Demos).

Hand, M. (2006) Against Autonomy as an Educational Aim, *Oxford Review of Education*, 32(4), pp. 535–50.

Hankinson, A. (2010) The Lost Generation, *Observer Magazine*, 31 January 2010, pp. 33–7.

Harker, R. (2000) Bourdieu – Education and Reproduction in S. Ball (Ed.) *Sociology of Education, Major Themes*, Volume II, pp. 831–54 (London, Routledge).

Hart, C. S. (2004) *A Study of Students' Aspirations and Needs in Relation to Aimhigher Widening Participation Policy*. MPhil Thesis (Cambridge, University of Cambridge).

— (2007) The Capability Approach as an Evaluative and Developmental Framework for Education Policy: The Example of Widening Participation in Higher Education in England, *Prospero*, (13), pp. 34–50. [Special Issue on the Capability Approach].

— (2009) Quo Vadis? The Capability Space and New Directions for the Philosophy of Educational Research, *Studies in Philosophy & Education*, 28(5), pp. 391–402. [Special Issue on the Capability Approach].

Hart, R. A. (1992) *Children's Participation. From Tokenism to Citizenship*. Innocenti Essay No. 4 (Florence, UNICEF).

HEFCE (2001) *Strategies for Widening Participation in Higher Education. A Guide to Good Practice*, 01/36 (HEFCE). Accessed 20 January 2006 at www.hefce.ac.uk.

— (2003) *HEFCE Strategic Plan 2003–08* (London, HEFCE).

— (2005) *Young Participation in Higher Education* (London, HEFCE).

— (2010) *Trends in Young Participation in Higher Education: Core Results for England* (London, HEFCE).

— (2012a) *Statement on the End of Aimhigher*. Accessed at www.hefce.ac.uk, January 2012.

— (2012b) *Statement on Widening Participation*. Accessed at www.hefce.ac.uk, January 2012.

Higher Education Statistics Agency (2009) *Percentage of Young Entrants to Full-Time First Degree Courses in 2005/06 Who Are No Longer in HE in 2006/07*. Accessed 5 March 2009 at www.hesa.ac.uk/dox/performanceindicators/0607.

— (2011) *Table T3a – Non-continuation Following Year of Entry: Full-time First Degree Entrants 2008/09*. Accessed online at www.hesa.ac.uk.

Hinchliffe, G. and Jolly, A. (2009) *Exploring Graduate Identity*, Paper Presented at the Capability Approach Education Network, 8 February, University of Cambridge.

Hinton, P. R., Brownlow, C., McMurray, I. and Cozens, B. (2008) *SPSS Explained* (London, Routledge).

HM Treasury (2010) *Spending Review* (London, TSO).

Hodges, L. (2009) If You Want to Get Ahead Go to Coventry, *Independent*, 6 August, p. 5.

Hodkinson, P. and Sparkes, A. (1996) *Triumphs and Tears: Young People, Markets and the Transition from School to Work* (London, David Fulton Publishers).

Hodkinson, P. (1996) Monograph. *A New Theory of Career Decision-Making* (Manchester Metropolitan University, unpublished).

House of Commons Public Accounts Committee (20 October 2008) *Widening Participation in Higher Education*. HC 725. Oral Evidence (London, The Stationary Office Limited).

— (February 2009) *Widening Participation in Higher Education. Fourth Report of Session 2008–09*. Report, together with formal minutes, oral and written evidence (London, House of Commons).

Joseph Rowntree Foundation (2005) *Findings: Informing Change. Early Labour Market Experiences of Graduates from Disadvantaged Families* (York, Joseph Rowntree Foundation).

Kay, H. and Walker, A. (2006) *Young Participation in Higher Education in the Parliamentary Constituencies of Nottingham North, Bristol South, Sheffield Brightside and Hodge Hill – Brightside Strand* (Sheffield Hallam University, unpublished).

Kelly, A. (2007) *School Choice and Student Well-Being. Opportunity and Capability in Education* (Basingstoke, Palgrave).

Kuklys, W. (2005) *Amartya Sen's Capability Approach: Theoretical Insights and Empirical Applications*. PhD Thesis. University of Cambridge.

Kysel, F. (1992) *Leaving School: Attitudes, Aspirations and Destinations of Fifth-year Leavers in Tower Hamlets, Educational Research*, 34(2), pp. 87–105.

Laureau, A. and Horvat, E. M. (1999) Moments of Social Inclusion and Exclusion, Race, Class and Cultural Capital in Family School Relationships, *Sociology of Education*, 72, pp. 37–53.

Lemert, E. M. *Human Deviance, Social Problems and Social Control*. Second Edition (Englewood Cliffs, Prentice Hall).

Lessmann, O., Otto, H. and Zielger, H. (Eds) (2011) *Closing the Capabilities Gap. Renegotiating Social Justice for the Young* (Opladen, Barbara Budrich) [Germany].

Levidow, L. (2002) Marketizing Higher Education: Neoliberal Strategies and Counter Strategies. In K. Robins and F. Webster (Eds) *The Virtual University? Knowledge, Markets and Management* (Oxford, Oxford University Press).

Liberal Democrat Party (2012) Liberal Democrat website. *Statement on University Fees*. Accessed at www.libdems.org.uk, January 2012.

Lingard, B., Taylor, S. and Rawolle, R. (2005) Bourdieu and the Study of Educational Policy: Introduction, *Journal of Education Policy*, 20(6), pp. 663–9.

Litoselliti, L. (2003) *Using Focus Groups in Research* (London, Continuum).

Lukes, S. (1974) *Power: A Radical View* (London, Macmillan).

Maguire, M., Ball, S. and Macrae, S. (1999) Promotion, Persuasion and Class Taste: Marketing (in) the UK Post-Compulsory Sector, *British Journal of Sociology of Education*, 20(3), pp. 291–308.

Marginson, S. (2007) *Global Flows and Global Field: A Theoretical Framing of Worldwide Relations of Power in HE*. Paper Presented at the International Forum, 32nd Annual Conference of the Association for the Study of Higher Education, 7–10 November, Louisville, Kentucky.

Marjoribanks, K. (1998) Family Background, Social and Academic Capital and Adolescents' Aspirations: A Mediational Analysis, *Social Psychology of Education*, 2, pp. 177–97.

— (2002) *Family and School Capital: Towards a Context Theory of Students' School Outcomes* (Dordrecht, Kluwer).

Mead, G. H. (1934) *Mind, Self and Society*. In C. Morris (Ed.) (Chicago, University of Chicago Press).

Medchild (2006) *Tools for Measuring the Well-being of Children*. Proceedings of the Seminar held in Rome, 20 March 2006. MedChild Paper 4 (Genoa, MedChild Institute).

Metcalf, H. (2003) Increasing Inequality in Higher Education: The Role of Term-time Working, *Oxford Review of Education*, 29(3), pp. 315–29.

Milburn, A. (2009) The Panel on Fair Access to the Professions (2009) *Unleashing Aspirations: The Final Report of the Panel on Fair Access to the Professions* (London, Cabinet Office).

Mills, C. (2008) Reproduction and Transformation of Inequalities in Schooling: The Transformative Potential of the Theoretical Constructs of Bourdieu, British *Journal of Sociology of Education*, 29(1), pp. 79–89.

Moogan, Y. J. and Baron, S. (2003) An Analysis of Student Characteristics within the Student Decision-Making Process, *Journal of Further and Higher Education*, 27(3), pp. 271–87.

Naidoo, R. (2004) Fields and Institutional Strategy: Bourdieu on the Relationship Between Higher Education, Inequality and Society, *British Journal of Sociology of Education*, 25(4), pp. 457–71.

National Census (2001). Accessed at www.data.gov.uk/dataset/census_2001_national_ report_for_england_and_wales.

National Centre for Social Research (2002) *Survey of Smoking, Drinking and Drug Use Among School Children in England 2002*. Accessed 18 August 2006 at www.qb.soc. surrey.ac.uk/surveys.

— (2003) *British Social Attitudes Self-Completion Questionnaire 2003*. Accessed 18 August 2006 at www.qb.soc.surrey.ac.uk/surveys.

National Student Survey (2011) *National Student Survey Results Overview*. Accessed at www.unistats.direct.gov.uk

Nieto, S. (1994) Lessons from Students on Creating a Chance to Dream, *Harvard Educational Review*, 64(4), pp. 392–426.

Nuffield Review of 14–19 Education and Training (2005) *Annual Report 2004–05* (Oxford, University of Oxford).

Nussbaum, M. C. (2003) Capabilities as Fundamental Entitlements: Sen and Social Justice, *Feminist Economics*, 9(2–3), pp. 33–59.

— (2005a) *Women and Human Development*. 8th Printing (New York, Cambridge University Press).

— (2005b) Capabilities as Fundamental Entitlements: Sen and Social Justice. In B. Agarwal, J. Humphries and I. Robeyns (Eds) *Amartya Sen's Work and Ideas – A Gender Perspective* (London, Routledge).

— (2006a) *Frontiers of Justice: Disability, Nationality, Species Membership* (London, Belknap).

— (2010) *Not for Profit* (Princeton, Princeton University Press).

OECD (2008) *Economic Policy Reforms. Going for Growth* (OECD, OECD Publishing).

Ofsted (2011) *Summerhill School Independent School Inspection Report*, October.

Oppenheim, A. N. (1996) *Questionnaire Design, Interviewing and Attitude Measurement*. New Edition (London, Pinter Publishers).

Oyserman, D. and Markus, H. R. (1990) Possible Selves and Delinquency. *Journal of Personality and Social Psychology*, 59(1), pp. 112–25.

Padron, M. H. and Ballet, J. (2011) in M. Biggeri, J. Ballet and F. Comim(Eds) *Children and the Capability Approach* (Basingstoke, Palgrave Macmillan).

Panel on Fair Access to the Professions (2009) *Unleashing Aspirations: The Final Report of the Panel on Fair Access to the Professions* (London, Cabinet Office).

Pettit, P. (2001) Symposium on Amartya Sen's Philosophy: 1. Capability and Freedom: A Defence of Sen, *Economics and Philosophy*, 17, pp. 1–20.

Pogge, T. (2002) Can the Capability Approach be Justified? *Philosophical Topics*, 30(2), pp. 167–228.

Pollard, A. and James, M. (2011) *The Framework for the National Curriculum in England – Report on a Page*. Accessed at www.tlrp.org/sh/ncrpage.html

Power, S., Edwards, T., Whitty, G. and Wigfall, V. (2003) *Education and the Middle Class* (Buckingham, Open University Press).

Pugsley, L. (1998) Throwing Your Brains at it: Higher Education, Markets and Choice, *International Studies in Sociology of Education*, 8(1), pp. 71–90.

Qizilbash, M. (1996) Capabilities, Well-Being and Human Development: A Survey, *Journal of Development Studies*, 33(2), pp. 143–62.

— (2008) Amartya Sen's Capability View: Insightful Sketch or Distorted Picture? In F. Comim, M. Qizilbash and S. Alkire (Eds) *The Capability Approach. Concepts, Measures and Applications* (Cambridge, Cambridge University Press).

Rawls, J. (1971) *A Theory of Justice* (Cambridge, MA, Harvard University Press).

Rawolle, S. and Lingard, B. (2008) The Sociology of Pierre Bourdieu and Researching Education Policy, *Journal of Education Policy*, 23(6), pp. 729–41.

Reay, D. (1998) 'Always Knowing' and 'Never Being Sure': Familial and Institutional Habituses and Higher Education Choice, *Journal of Education Policy*, 13(4), pp. 519–29.

— (2001) Finding or Losing Yourself: Working Class Relationships to Education, *Journal of Education Policy*, 16(4), pp. 333–46.

— (2004) Gendering Bourdieu's Concepts of Capitals? Emotional Capital, Women and Social Class, special issue, *Sociological Review Monograph Series: Feminism after Bourdieu*, 52, supplement 2, pp. 57–74.

Reay, D., Crozier, G. and Clayton, J. (2009) 'Strangers in Paradise?' Working-Class Students in Elite Universities, *Sociology*, 43(6), pp. 1103–21.

— (2010) 'Fitting In' or 'Standing Out': Working-Class Students in UK Higher Education, *British Education Research Journal*, 36(1), pp. 107–24.

Reay, D., David, M. and Ball, S. (2005) *Degrees of Choice: Class, Race, Gender and Higher Education* (Stoke on Trent, Trentham).

Reed-Danahay, D. (2005) *Locating Bourdieu* (Bloomington, Indiana University Press).

Robeyns, I. (2002) *Gender Inequality: A Capability Perspective*. Unpublished PhD thesis (Cambridge, University of Cambridge).

— (2003) *The Capability Approach: An Interdisciplinary Introduction.* Presented at the training course for the Third International Conference on the Capability Approach, Pavia, Italy, September 2003.

— (2005a), The Capability Approach: A Theoretical Survey, *Journal of Human Development*, 6(1), pp. 93–114.

— (2005b) Sen's Capability Approach and Gender Inequality. In B. Agarwal, J. Humphries and I. Robeyns (Eds) *Amartya Sen's Work and Ideas – A Gender Perspective* (London, Routledge).

— (2006) Three Models of Education: Rights, Capabilities and Human Capital, *Theory and Research in Education*, 4(1), pp. 69–84.

Round, A. (2005) *An Academic Point: Analysing the Discourse of Higher Education*, Paper presented at the SRHE Annual Conference, Edinburgh.

Saito, M. (2003) Amartya Sen's Capability Approach to Education: A Critical Exploration, *Journal of Philosophy of Education*, 37(1), pp. 17–31.

Schwartz, S. (2004) *Fair Admissions to Higher Education: Recommendations for Good Practice. Admissions to Higher Education Review* (London, DfES).

Scott, P. (1995) *The Meanings of Mass Higher Education* (Buckingham, SRHE and OUP).

Seginer, R. (1988) Adolescents' Orientation Toward the Future: Sex Role Differentiation in a Sociocultural Context, *Sex Roles. A Journal of Research*, 18(11–12), pp. 739–57.

Sen, A. (1982) *Choice, Welfare and Measurement* (Oxford, Blackwell).

— (1985) Well-being, Agency and Freedom. The Dewey Lectures, 1984. *Journal of Philosophy,* 82(4), pp. 169–221.

— (1992) *Inequality Re-Examined* (Oxford, Clarendon Press).

— (1995) Rationality and Social Choice, *The American Economic Review*, 85(10), pp. 1–24.

— (1999a) *Commodities and Capabilities* (Oxford, Oxford University Press). Original publication (1985) Amsterdam, North-Holland.

— (1999b) *Development as Freedom* (Oxford, Oxford University Press).

— (2001) Symposium on Amartya Sen's Philosophy: 4. Reply, *Economics and Philosophy*, 17 (pp. 51–6).

— (2002) *India: Development and Participation* (Oxford, Oxford University Press).

— (2002a) *Rationality and Freedom* (Cambridge, USA, Harvard University Press).

— (2005a) Capabilities, Lists and Public Reason: Continuing the Conversation. In B. Agarwal, J. Humphries and I. Robeyns (Eds) *Amartya Sen's Work and Ideas – A Gender Perspective* (London, Routledge).

— (2005b) Human Rights and Capabilities, *Journal of Human Development*, 6(2), pp. 151–66.

— (2006a) *Identity and Violence. The Illusion of Destiny* (London, Penguin).

— (2006b) Capability and Well-being. In M. C. Nussbaum and A. Sen (Eds) *The Quality of Life* (Oxford, Oxford University Press).

— (2009) *The Idea of Justice* (London, Penguin).

Serrokh, B. (2011) in M. Biggeri, J. Ballet and F. Comim (Eds) *Children and the Capability Approach* (Basingstoke, Palgrave Macmillan).

Skeggs, B. (2004) Exchange, Value and Effect: Bourdieu and the Self, special issue, *Sociological Review Monograph Series: Feminism after Bourdieu*, 52, supplement 2, pp. 75–95.

Slack, K. (2003) Whose Aspirations Are They Anyway? *The International Journal of Inclusive Education*, 7(4), pp. 325–35.

Sugden, R. (1993) Welfare, Resources and Capabilities: A Review of Inequality Re-Examined by Amartya Sen, *Journal of Economic Literature*, 31(1947–62).

Sutton Trust (2004) *Entry to Leading Universities* (London, Sutton Trust).

— (March 2009) *The Educational Backgrounds of Leading Lawyers, Journalists, Vice Chancellors, Politicians, Medics and Chief Executives*. The Sutton Trust submission to the Milburn Commission on access to the professions.

Tagore, R. (1999) *The English Writings of Rabindranath Tagore*. In S. K. Das (Ed.) (New Delhi, Sagar). Part III, Essay on My School, pp. 399–419.

Terzi, L. (2005) *Equality, Capability and Social Justice in Education: Re-examining Disability and Special Educational Needs*. Unpublished PhD thesis. London, University of London.

Thomas, L. (2001) *Widening Participation in Post-Compulsory Education* (London, Continuum).

Thompson, P. (2008) *Field*. In M. Grenfell (Ed.) *Pierre Bourdieu. Key Concepts* (Stocksfield, Acumen).

Times Higher Education Supplement (2009) *Global Revolution*, 26 November, pp. 33–6.

Trow, M. (1972) The Expansion and Transformation of Higher Education, *International Review of Education*, 18(1), pp. 61–84.

UCAS (2012) website accessed at www.ucas.ac.uk, January 2012.

Unicef (2005) *Childhood Under Threat. The State of the World's Children* (Unicef).

— (2007) *Child Poverty in Perspective: An Overview of Child Well-Being in Rich Countries*. Report Card 7 (Florence, UNICEF Innocenti Research Centre).

United Nations (1990) *United Nations Convention on the Rights of the Child* (Unicef).

Unterhalter, E. (2003) The Capability Approach and Gendered Education: An Examination of South African Complexities, *Theory and Research in Education*, 1(1), 7–22.

Vasagar, J. (2012) School Leavers Still Keen on University Life but Soaring Tuition Fees Hit Mature Students Hard. *Guardian*, Tuesday 31 January, p. 4.

Vaughan, R. (2007) Measuring Capabilities: An Example from Girls' Schooling. In M. Walkerand and E. Unterhalter (Eds) *Amartya Sen's Capability Approach and Social Justice in Education* (Basingstoke, Palgrave Macmillan).

Venkatapuram, S. (2011) *Health Justice. An Argument from the Capabilities Approach* (Cambridge, Polity Press).

Vignoles, A. and Powdthavee, N. (2010) Diversity of Experiences in Higher Education. In M. David (Ed.) *Improving Learning by Widening Participation in Higher Education* (London, Routledge).

Walby, S. (2012) Sen and the Measurement of Justice and Capabilities: A Problem in Theory and Practice, *Theory, Culture and Society*, 29(1), 99–118.

Walker, M. (2006b) Towards a Capability-Based Theory of Social Justice for Education Policy-Making, *Journal of Education Policy*, pp. 163–85.

— (2007) Selecting Capabilities for Gender Equality in Education. In M. Walker and E. Unterhalter (Eds) *Amartya Sen's Capability Approach and Social Justice in Education* (Basingstoke, Palgrave Macmillan).

Walker, M. and Unterhalter, E. (Eds) (2007) *Amartya Sen's Capability Approach and Social Justice in Education* (Basingstoke, Palgrave Macmillan).

Warner, D. and Palfreyman, D. (2001) (Eds) *The State of UK Higher Education. Managing Change and Diversity* (Buckingham, SRHE and OU).

Watts, M. (2006) Disproportionate Sacrifices: Ricoeur's Theories of Justice and the Widening Participation Agenda for Higher Education in the UK, *Journal of Philosophy of Education*, 40(3), pp. 301–12.

Watts, M. and Bridges, D. (2004) *Whose Aspirations? What Achievement? An Investigation of the Life and Lifestyle Aspirations of 16–19 Year Olds Outside the Formal Education System* (Cambridge, Centre for Educational Research and Development, Von Hugel Institute).

Weatherley, R. and Lipsky, M. (1977) Street-Level Bureaucrats and Institutional Innovation: Implementing Special-Education Reform, *Harvard Educational Review*, 47(2), pp. 171–97.

Wegerif, R., Mercer, N., Littleton, K., Rowe, D. and Dawes, L. (2004) *Talking for Success: Widening Access to Educational Opportunities through Teaching Children How to Reason Together* (RG01–22). Final Report to the Esmee Foundation, March 2004.

White, J. (2007) Well-being and Education: Issues of Culture and Authority, *Journal of Philosophy of Education*, 41(1), pp. 17–28.

Williams, A. (2002) Dworkin on Capability, *Ethics*, 113(1), pp. 23–39.

Williams, B. (1987) The Standard of Living: Interests and Capabilities. In G. Hawthorn (Ed.) *The Standard of Living* (Cambridge, Cambridge University Press).

Willis, P. E. (1977) *Learning to Labour: How Working Class Kids Get Working Class Jobs* (Farnborough, Saxon House).

Yeshanew, T., Rutt, S. and Morris, M. (2005) NFER Quantitative Methodology Looking at the Relationship between School and Pupil Level Factors and Student Aspirations to Further and Higher Education, *Paper presented at BERA Annual Conference*, University of Glamorgan, September 2005.

Websites

www.11million.org.uk
www.bbc.co.uk
www.capabilityapproach.com
www.connexionsdirect.com
www.dcsf.gov.uk
www.dfes.gov.uk
www.direct.gov/unistats/ucas
www.outwardbound.org.uk
www.qb.soc.surrey.ac.uk/surveys
www.raleighinternational.org
www.tallships.org
www.ucas.ac.uk
www.unistats.direct.gov.uk
www.yses.org.uk

Subject Index

Page numbers in **bold** denote figures/tables.

Author Index